Readings in Vedic Literature

The Tradition Speaks for Itself

Satsvarūpa dāsa Goswami

THE BHAKTIVEDANTA BOOK TRUST
Los Angeles · London · Paris · Bombay · Sydney · Hong Kong

Printed in the United States of America

First Printing: 10,000 copies
Second Printing: 20,000 copies
Third Printing: 5,000 copies
The Bhaktivedanta Book Trust
3764 Watseka Avenue
Los Angeles, California 90034

Library of Congress Cataloging in Publication Data

Goswami, Satsvarūpa dāsa, 1939-
Readings in Vedic literature.

Bibliography: p.
Includes indexes.
1. Vedic literature—Addresses, essays, lectures.
2. Hinduism—Addresses, essays, lectures. I. Title.
BL1107.G67 294'.1 76-24941
ISBN 0-912776-88-9

evaṁ paramparā-prāptam . . .

This supreme science
was thus received
through the chain
of disciplic succession . . .
—*Bhagavad-gītā* 4.2

Dedicated
to my spiritual master
His Divine Grace
A. C. Bhaktivedanta
Swami
Prabhupāda

Contents

READINGS

APPENDIXES

Foreword

It is only just, in a karmic sense, that an academic scholar be asked to write the foreword for a book that rejects the views of most academic scholars on the historical development of the *Vedas*. To protect my own academic status (and perhaps incur further bad *karma*), I should say at the outset that I do not as a scholar accept Satsvarūpa dāsa Goswami's views on the origin of the *Vedas*, and I question his use of evidence from the epics and *Purāṇas*, which I consider non-Vedic, to prove that these same sources have Vedic authority. At the same time, I recognize that such objections are mere pedantry from the standpoint of the living tradition. Much academic scholarship is like the proverbial medical example: the operation is successful, but the patient dies. Traditions that are healthy never take scholarly diagnoses too seriously, and they stay alive by staying off the operating table.

There is much more than rejection of academic or "empirical" scholarship involved here, however: there is a point of view that has its own validity and, within its set of assumptions, its own high standards of scholarly study. Having indicated my own academic reservations, I must add that I am nonetheless impressed by Satsvarūpa dāsa Goswami's presentation. His initial chapter is one of the best statements available on the importance of the *guru* in transmitting spiritual knowledge, his chapters on "Essential Elements of Vedic Thought," "Vedic Literature—*Siddhānta* and History," "The Teachings of the *Ācāryas,*" and "Impersonalism Versus Theism" are excellent summaries of devotional theology as found within the Indian religious tradition, and his chapter on "The Vedic Social Philosophy" gives a compelling vision of "the God-centered society."

The point of view that runs throughout the work is one best represented textually in the *Bhagavad-gītā* and *Bhāgavata Purāṇa*. The viewpoint is graphically portrayed in a late addition to the *Bhāgavata Purāṇa,* the *Bhāgavata Mahātmya,* where Bhakti (Devotion) is depicted as a young woman with two sons—Jñāna (Knowledge) and Vairāgya (Freedom-from-desire)—who, incongruously, have grown old and weak and must be nursed back to health by their still young and vigorous mother. Knowledge and Detachment on their own, it is explained, will wither away in this debased age; Devotion alone has the power to restore them to youth and vitality. Transferred to a theory of Vedic knowledge, this position leads directly to the thesis set forth by Satsvarūpa dāsa Goswami: that the truth and impulse to spiritual discipline of the *Vedas* are maintained only where they are transformed by the vital power of devotion to the Personal Lord.

There is an inherent problem of communicating this viewpoint in the unfamiliar idiom of Sanskrit theological language, but the position is not unfamiliar in the West; indeed, one can argue that the vitality of Western religious traditions has depended no less on a continuing renewal of ancient authority on the basis of new spiritual insights. All Christian churches accept continuing revelation in one form or another, and saints, reformers, popes, theologians, evangelicals and charismatic healers all claim new understanding of the unchanging truth of the Scriptures through the power of the Holy Spirit. Talmudic commentaries, rabbinical interpretations, reform movements and Hassidic mysticism have similarly given new life and meaning to ancient Torah.

A religious tradition without saints and mystics, without new revelations, without the experience of the Holy that gives new meaning to ancient teachings—such a tradition, no matter where in the world it may be, is spiritually dead. Satsvarūpa dāsa Goswami shows us in this book that the Vedic tradition, as transmitted in its dynamic devotional aspect, is in no such danger.

DR. THOMAS J. HOPKINS
Department of Religious Studies
Franklin and Marshall College

Preface

My plan to write this book grew out of encouragement from professors in whose classes I taught while touring as a lecturer for the Los Angeles Center for Vedic Studies. In November, 1973, Dr. Alton Becker invited me to speak before the faculty and students of the Center for South and Southeastern Studies, at the University of Michigan. My paper proposed a fresh attitude toward Vedic studies: an attempt to appreciate the Vedic knowledge on its own merits, as it exists apart from the interpretations of empirical Western scholarship. Dr. Becker found the viewpoint enlivening and advised me to develop it further. From conversations with college students who knew only the current Vedic textbooks, I became convinced that students of Vedic literature would be more enthusiastic if they could believe that the literature they were studying was not merely a hodgepodge of myths, but could actually give them a new and coherent view of life. My travels led me to meet with Vedic scholars such as Dr. Edward Dimock (University of Chicago), Dr. Thomas Hopkins (Franklin and Marshall College), and Dr. Joseph O'Connell (University of Toronto). All of these gentlemen saw my outline, and they confirmed that this book would be useful as a foundation for Vedic studies.

My own interest in the Vedic tradition began in 1966. In that year I met His Divine Grace A.C. Bhaktivedanta Swami Prabhupāda, who in the previous year had arrived in the United States to teach Vedic culture. I had received a B.A. in English literature from Brooklyn College, and I was doing graduate work toward a career as a writer. But I decided instead to devote my life to studying the *Vedas,* and in September, 1966, Śrīla Prabhupāda accepted me as his *śiṣya* (disciple). I have been a personal secretary to Śrīla Prabhupāda since 1970, and in 1972 I received the *sannyāsa* order of life (awarded for scholarship and renunciation). Overall, for the last ten years I have been studying the Vedic literature, writing articles about it, and lecturing in United States colleges on behalf of the Center for Vedic Studies.

The attempt herein is to present a Vedic textbook and anthology for undergraduates that allows them to hear a great tradition speak for itself.

Śrī Śaṅkara

Śrī Rāmānuja

Śrī Madhva

Śrī Kṛṣṇa Caitanya

Guide to Sanskrit Pronunciation

Throughout the centuries, the Sanskrit language has been written in a variety of alphabets. The mode of writing most widely used throughout India, however, is called *devanāgarī,* which literally means "the city writing of the *devas,* or gods." The *devanāgarī* alphabet consists of forty-eight characters, including thirteen vowels and thirty-five consonants. The ancient Sanskrit grammarians arranged the alphabet according to concise linguistic principles, and this arrangement has been accepted by all Western scholars. The system of transliteration used in this book conforms to a system that scholars in the last fifty years have almost universally accepted to indicate the pronunciation of each Sanskrit sound.

The short vowel **a** is pronounced like the **u** in b**u**t; long **ā** like the **a** in f**a**r; and short **i** like the **i** in p**i**n. Long **ī** is pronounced as in p**i**que, short **u** as in p**u**ll, and long **ū** as in r**u**le. The vowel **ṛ** is pronounced like the **ri** in **ri**m. The vowel **e** is pronounced as in th**ey**; **ai** as in **ai**sle; **o** as in g**o**; and **au** as in h**ow.** The *anusvara* (**ṁ**), which is a pure nasal, is pronounced like the **n** in the French word *bo***n,** and *visarga* (**ḥ**), which is a strong aspirate, is pronounced as a final **h** sound. Thus **aḥ** is pronounced like **aha,** and **iḥ** like **ihi.**

The guttural consonants—**k, kh, g, gh,** and **ṅ**—are pronounced from the throat in much the same manner as in English. **K** is pronounced as in **k**ite, **kh** as in Ec**kh**art, **g** as in **g**ive, **gh** as in di**g h**ard, and **ṅ** as in si**ng.** The palatal consonants—**c, ch, j, jh,** and **ñ**—are pronounced from the palate with the middle of the tongue. **C** is pronounced as in **ch**air, **ch** as in staun**ch h**eart, **j** as in **j**oy, **jh** as in he**dgeh**og, and **ñ** as in ca**ny**on. The cerebral consonants—**ṭ, ṭh, ḍ, ḍh,** and **ṇ**—are pronounced with the tip of the tongue turned up and drawn back against the dome of the palate. **Ṭ** is pronounced as in **t**ub, **ṭh** as in ligh**t h**eart, **ḍ** as in **d**ove, **ḍh** as in re**d-h**ot, and **ṇ** as in **n**ut. The dental consonants—**t, th, d, dh,** and **n**—are pronounced in the same manner as the cerebrals but with the forepart of the tongue against the teeth. The labial consonants—**p, ph, b, bh,** and **m**—are pronounced with the lips. **P** is pronounced as in **p**ine, **ph** as in u**ph**ill, **b** as in **b**ird, **bh** as in ru**b h**ard, and **m** as in **m**other. The semivowels—**y, r, l,** and **v**—are pronounced as in **y**es, **r**un, **l**ight, and **v**ine respectively. The sibilants—**ś, ṣ,** and **s**—are pronounced, respectively, as in the German word **s***prechen* and the English words **sh**ine and **s**un. The letter **h** is pronounced as in **h**ome.

1 / What Are the Vedas?

Madhva, one of the principal teachers of Vedic philosophy, commenting on the *Vedānta-sūtra* (2.1.6), quotes the *Bhaviṣya Purāṇa* as follows:

ṛg-yajuḥ-sāmārtharvāś ca
bhāratam pañcarātrakam
mūla-rāmāyaṇam caiva
veda ity eva śabditaḥ

purāṇāni ca yānīha
vaiṣṇavāni vido viduḥ

"The *Ṛg Veda, Yajur Veda, Sāma Veda, Atharva Veda, Mahābhārata* [which includes the *Bhagavad-gītā*], *Pañcarātra,* and the original *Rāmāyaṇa* are all considered Vedic literature. . . . The Vaiṣṇava supplements, the *Purāṇas,* are also Vedic literature." We may also include corollary literatures like the *Samhitās,* as well as the commentaries of the great teachers who have guided the course of Vedic thought for centuries.

Some scholars say that only the original four *Vedas—Ṛg, Atharva, Yajur,* and *Sāma*—are genuine Vedic literatures.[1] The *Vedas* themselves, however, do not support this view, nor do the most prominent Vedic teachers, including Śaṅkara, Rāmānuja, and Madhva. The *Chāndogya Upaniṣad* (7.1.4) mentions the *Purāṇas* and *Itihāsas,* which are generally known as histories, as the fifth *Veda: itihāsa-purāṇaḥ pañcamaḥ vedānām vedaḥ.* And *Bhāgavata Purāṇa* (1.4.20) confirms, "The historical facts and authentic stories mentioned in the *Purāṇas* are called the fifth *Veda.*"[2]

In any case, to be accepted as Vedic, a literature must maintain the same purpose as the original Vedic texts. The Vedic scriptures (*śāstras*) comprise a harmonious whole with a harmonious conclusion (*siddhānta*). Consequently, we may accept as a bona fide Vedic writing any work that expands on the Vedic *siddhānta* without changing its meaning, even if the work is not one of the original scriptures. In fact, the Vedic tradition necessitates further authoritative works that convey the

Vedic message according to time and place. However, to be genuine, these extensions of Vedic literature must strictly conform to the doctrines of the *Vedas,* the *Purāṇas,* and the *Vedānta-sūtra.*

Vedic literature is neither dead nor archaic. Nevertheless, any literature—be it ancient or modern—must be considered non-Vedic if it deviates from the Vedic *siddhānta.* Thus Buddhism, Jainism, and Sikhism, though definitely outgrowths of Vedic literature, are not considered Vedic. Even the conception of Hinduism is alien to the Vedic conclusion, as we shall see later.

The Vedic scriptures are vast in scope. The *Ṛg Veda* alone contains 1,017 hymns, the *Mahābhārata* consists of 110,000 couplets, and the eighteen chief *Purāṇas* contain hundreds of thousands of verses. We may ask, "Why do these writings exist? Where did they come from? Who wrote them?" The present book searches out the answers to our questions in the Vedic *śāstras* themselves.

The Purpose of the Vedic Literature

As its main purpose, the Vedic literature imparts knowledge of self-realization and, therefore, liberation (*mokṣa*) from suffering. Generally, scholars agree that the goal of Indian thought is to attain the truth, "the recognition of which leads to freedom."[3] "Every Indian system seeks truth, not as academic, 'knowledge for its own sake,' but to learn the truth which shall make all men free."[4] Indeed, Indian thought strives not for information but for transformation.[5] *Bhagavad-gītā* describes knowledge as "accepting the importance of self-realization, and philosophical search for the Absolute Truth."[6] Yet if people think they are progressing on the path of material happiness, they will not seek to transform themselves. Hence, another important realization—*janma-mṛtyu-jarā-vyādhi-duḥkha-doṣānudarśanam:* "perception of the evil of birth, death, old age, and disease" (*Bhagavad-gītā* 13.9). Uncompromisingly, the Vedic literature asserts that despite its apparent joys, material life means suffering. Vedic knowledge purports to free the sincere inquirer from that suffering.

According to *Bhagavad-gītā* (Bg. 8.16), "From the highest planet in the material world down to the lowest, all are places of misery wherein repeated birth and death take place." Apart from the repeated miseries of birth, old age, disease, and death, the Vedic writings describe another threefold set of miseries: miseries arising from the body itself, miseries inflicted by other living entities, and miseries arising from natural disturbances (such as severe cold, heat, flood, earthquake, or draught). Vedic teachers argue that even if these latter miseries were absent, no one could find happiness in the material world—the forces of time and death force everyone to leave his position. Indeed, the Sanskrit description of the earth is Mṛtyuloka, place of death. It is also *duḥkhālayam* (a place of miseries) and *aśāśvatam* (temporary) (Bg. 8.15).

On hearing this sweeping analysis of life in the material world, Albert Schweitzer termed the Vedic philosophy "world- and life-negation."[7] Others have stated that the *Vedas* teach pessimism and fatalistic resignation. But when we view the *Vedas* closely, we can discern that they teach quite the opposite; they propose that the purpose of human life is not to resign oneself to a temporary and miserable world, but to strive for permanent happiness. For people who follow the Vedic formula, life means an opportunity to attain victory over death. In the Vedic conception, a person negates life precisely when he identifies the illusory body with the self and considers the temporary world to be all-in-all. Such a person misses the opportunity afforded a human being—the opportunity to inquire about the Supreme.

The first verse of the *Vedānta-sūtra* (*athāto brahma-jijñāsā*) is both a declaration and an invitation to everyone: "Now, therefore, let us inquire into the Absolute Truth."[8] The *Vedas* urge that people take to the path of liberation. In one Bengali devotional song we find, "Lord Gaurāṅga is calling, 'Wake up, sleeping souls! How long will you sleep on the lap of the witch called Māyā [material illusion]?' "[9]

The *Vedas* describe liberation as a special prerogative granted to human beings and not to the lower species. For this reason the human body is compared to a boat by which one can cross the ocean of transmigration. A good Vedic instructor who has learned the *Vedas* is like a competent captain, and the Vedic hymns are like favorable breezes. If a person doesn't cross the ocean and attain eternal liberation, he is considered unintelligent, for Vedic philosophy denies the importance of any knowledge that does not lead to the cessation of suffering. The *Garga Upaniṣad* advises, "He is a miserly man who does not solve the problems of life as a human and who quits the world like a cat or a dog, not understanding the science of self-realization."[10]

The Origin of the *Vedas*

The *Bṛhad-āraṇyaka Upaniṣad* (2.4.10) informs us, "The *Ṛg Veda, Yajur Veda, Sāma Veda, Atharva Veda,* and *Itihāsas* [histories like the

Mahābhārata and *Purāṇas*] are all breathed out by the Absolute Truth. Just as one's breath comes easily, these arise from the Supreme Brahman without any effort on His part."[11] According to the Vedic tradition, the *Vedas* are absolute and self-authoritative. They depend on nothing but themselves for explanation. This very principle comes from the mouth of Śrī Kṛṣṇa in *Bhagavad-gītā* (3.15): *brahmākṣara-samudbhavam.* "The *Vedas* are directly manifested from the infallible Supreme Personality of Godhead." The commentator Śrīdhara Svāmī (*Bhāvārtha-dīpikā* 6.1.40) points out that the *Vedas* are supremely authoritative because they arise from Nārāyaṇa Himself. Jīva Gosvāmī notes that the Vedic scripture *Madhyandina-śruti* attributes all the *Vedas* (*Sāma, Atharva, Ṛg* and *Yajur*), as well as the *Purāṇas* and *Itihāsas,* to the breathing of the Supreme Being. Finally, the *Atharva Veda* states that Kṛṣṇa, who in the beginning instructed Brahmā, disseminated Vedic knowledge in the past.

Thus, as we have seen, the Vedic scriptures delineate their own origin. The scriptures describe themselves as *apauruṣeya,* meaning that they do not come from any materially conditioned person but from the Supreme (a source transcendental to mundane duality). Vedic knowledge was imparted to Brahmā at the dawn of creation. Brahmā then instructed Nārada, whose realizations appear throughout Vedic literature.

Vedic knowledge is considered eternal, but because the material cosmos is constantly in flux, Vedic teachings constantly need reassertion. Although the material cosmos is also considered eternal, it goes through stages of creation, maintenance, and annihilation. Formerly the *Vedas* came down by word of mouth, but later the sage Vyāsadeva compiled all the Vedic *śāstras* in written form. In a separate chapter we shall examine Śrīla Vyāsadeva's role and the history of the compilation of the *Vedas.* We shall also consider how scholars try to understand the origins and history of the Vedic literature through the empiric method.

The Vedic Process of Learning

We can see in the Vedic verses an inexorable link between the substance of Vedic knowledge and the means for receiving it (between the Vedic message, we could say, and the Vedic medium). In contrast with Western conceptions, Vedic epistemology favors the process called *śabda* (hearing from Vedic literature), out of three possible knowledge-gaining processes.

The first process, *pratyakṣa* (empiric sensual perception), depends on correction from outside sources. For example, to our eyes the sun may seem no larger than a coin, but from scientific calculation we learn that our senses mislead us—the sun is many times larger than the earth.

The second knowledge-gaining process, *anumāna* (theories based on evidence), cannot give knowledge of what is beyond the range of proof. Charles Darwin's theories and much of archaeology and anthropology rely upon such inductive conjecture ("It may have been like this, or perhaps it was like this"). According to the *Vedas, anumāna* cannot independently lead to perfect knowledge. The *Vedas* assert that objects beyond material nature cannot be known experimentally. These objects are therefore called *acintya.* That which is *acintya* cannot be known by speculation or by argument but only by *śabda,* the process of hearing from Vedic literature.

Indeed, *śabda,* the third knowledge-acquiring process, is considered the most reliable and important. For, since human beings are limited and imperfect, their perception, theories, and speculations cannot be perfect. With the exclusion of *śabda,* the *Vedas* estimate all knowledge to be defective in four ways. First, regardless how bright or precise a person may be, the *Vedas* affirm that he cannot escape mistakes—"to err is human." Second, a human being is subject to illusion. For instance, the *śāstras* mention that every materially conditioned being is under the illusion that the body is the self. Whatever his position in the world, a person is under illusion if he thinks of himself in terms of nationality, religion, race, or family. (A person's first step in transcendental knowledge, according to the *Vedas,* is realizing that his identity is beyond the temporary material body.) Third, every person has limited or imperfect senses. For instance, in a darkened room he cannot see his hand before his face. Finally, the *Vedas* maintain, everyone has a tendency to cheat. For example, a man who presumes to instruct others although defective himself is actually cheating, because his knowledge is imperfect.

Vedic knowledge is *śabda,* knowledge through hearing from higher authority, and it is therefore considered perfect. The Indian scholar Mysore Hiriyanna writes, "The *Vedānta* never dispenses with reason, and the *Upaniṣads* are themselves full of arguments. All that is questioned is the final validity of reason in matters which do not come within its purview."[12] To cite a traditional example, if a child wants to know who his father is, he should ask his mother. He may make a survey of the male population, but much more simply, he can ask his mother, the natural authority. In other words, if a person can accept information given by an authority, he does not have to take the trouble to research independently. The *śabda* method, by which we accept authority, is imperative when we inquire about subject matter beyond the purview of the senses and reason. We may note that in the Vedic conception authority has no Western-styled negative connotations. The term refers not to a dictator but to a deliverer of primary knowledge. For instance, Shakespeare himself is naturally the authority *par excellence* on the works of William Shakespeare.

Aural reception of transcendental knowledge from authority is the Vedic standard. Whereas material knowledge pertains to things within the material universe, transcendental knowledge pertains to things beyond this universe. The *Vedas* point to a supreme original truth unknowable either by direct perception (*pratyakṣa*) or by the inductive method (*anumāna*). When, by aural reception from authority, a person gains transcendental information, he becomes completely fulfilled and happy. He transcends the dualities of the material world. On the other hand, when he follows the empiric tradition, he comes to regard anything outside sensual perception or induction as faith, dogma, intuition, or belief. He concludes, as does A. B. Keith, "Such knowledge as is not empirical is meaningless and should not be described as knowledge."[13]

The Vedic philosophers claim that *śabda* (hearing from an authority) opens up a realm of knowledge beyond scientific methodology. They hold *śabda* to be the only process by which we can know what is unknowable in our present conditioned state. To know his father, a child has no other recourse than to ask his mother. This is a matter not of faith, dogma, or feeling, but simply of hearing from one who knows. If a person can learn from someone who has received perfect knowledge, he can get free from all misery. "Just try to learn the truth by approaching a spiritual master," the *Gītā* (4.34) enjoins. "Inquire from him submissively and render service unto him. The self-realized soul can impart knowledge unto you because he has seen the truth." In the Vedic tradition, only the person who has "seen the truth" can be the ideal teacher, the *guru*. In addition, the *Muṇḍaka Upaniṣad* (1.2.12) enjoins that a sincere student has to approach the ideal *guru* to receive transcendental knowledge and enlightenment.

The *Guru* and *Paramparā*

To learn more about *śabda,* we should examine the Vedic conception of the teacher (*guru*) and the student (*śiṣya*). Not only must the student turn to Vedic literature for perfect knowledge, but also he must receive knowledge personally from a qualified teacher with whom he has a special relationship. Technically the word *guru* means "heavy," and the qualified *guru* must be heavy, or grave, with knowledge. Anyone who is bewildered by the problems of existence must approach a spiritual master for knowledge. Thus *Bhagavad-gītā* presents the ideal teacher-student relationship. Faced with doing battle against his friends and relatives, Arjuna breaks down. A noted psychologist has commented that Arjuna experiences "ontological anxiety," that he loses sight of his identity and his duty. Therefore, he approaches his *guru,* Kṛṣṇa (who is accepted throughout the *Vedas* as the Supreme Person, the knower and compiler of the *Vedas*). "I have lost all composure," Arjuna says. "Please instruct me" (Bg. 2.7). Later, Lord Kṛṣṇa tells Arjuna that everyone should accept a bona fide spiritual master.

In the *Muṇḍaka Upaniṣad* (1.2.12) we find *tad-vijñānārthaṁ sa gurum evābhigacchet samit-pāṇiḥ śrotriyaṁ brahma-niṣṭham:*

> In order to learn the transcendental science, one must submissively approach a bona fide spiritual master, who is coming in disciplic succession and is fixed in the Absolute Truth. [14]

Hiriyanna writes that this Vedic view is not difficult to appreciate. "For self-effort, however valuable in itself, is not an adequate means of grasping a truth so profound. . . . The living voice of a teacher who firmly believes in what he teaches has certainly a better chance of producing conviction than the written word."[15]

Thus, the message of the *Vedas* descends through the spiritual master. As we have mentioned, the *Vedas* maintain that knowledge gained by sense perception or speculation can never enable the student to reach the highest goal. Vedic truth reaches the student by the descending process, from the *Vedas* and through the *guru.* This chain of transmission is called *guru-paramparā,* the disciplic succession. In *Bhagavad-gītā* (4.2) Kṛṣṇa tells Arjuna, *evaṁ paramparā-prāptam:* "This supreme science [*bhakti-yoga,* knowledge through devotional service] was thus received through the chain of disciplic succession." Thus, the student's relationship is not just with his own spiritual master but also with the spiritual master of his spiritual master and the spiritual master of that master and so on, in an unbroken chain of masters. The chain of masters in which a particular *guru* hears and speaks the truth is called his *sampradāya.* For instance, in the Brahma-sampradāya, Vedic knowledge descends from Brahmā, and in the Kumāra-sampradāya it descends from the Kumāra Ṛṣis (sages). In the Vedic conception, these *sampradāyas* began at the creation of the universe and endure to the present moment in the person of the student's own *guru*. Thanks to the consistency of the transmission, all the previous *gurus* are present in the teachings of the present spiritual master. The student receives the pure Vedic message in the same way he might receive a mango from a number of men sitting on the branches of a mango tree. The man at the top of the tree picks the fruit and hands it down carefully to the man below. Thus, it comes down from man to man and reaches the man on the ground, undamaged and unchanged.

One may question whether a line of teachers can accurately pass the message from one to another without change or addition. But not anyone can presume to speak Vedic knowledge in succession from the past teachers—only a perfect *guru*. The Vedic process assures that the transmission remains pure by assuring the qualifications of the transmitter.

The Qualifications of the *Guru*

Since the *guru* must transmit the truths of Vedic knowledge perfectly, he plays a crucial role. Consequently, the *Vedas* admonish the prospective disciple to acquaint himself with the qualifications of a bona fide *guru*. Regrettably, in recent years many Indian and Western teachers at variance with the Vedic version have undermined the *guru's* credibility. Now we have professional *gurus* who charge fees for secret *mantras* and allow their students to disregard all the Vedic regulative austerities, who teach *yoga* as gymnastic exertion and maintain that the purpose of *yoga* is material well-being, and who defy the *Vedas* by declaring themselves or everyone to be God, and so on. It is little wonder that when we hear the word *guru*, we are skeptical.

Nevertheless, according to the Vedic version, the *guru-śiṣya* relationship is an eternal verity that a person can realize only if he sincerely approaches a bona fide *guru*. It is therefore necessary to first understand the symptoms of a bona fide *guru*—that is, of a spiritual master who has received and can impart pure knowledge. Rūpa Gosvāmī, a sixteenth-century Vedic philosopher and disciple of Kṛṣṇa Caitanya, lists in his *Upadeśāmṛta* six symptoms of a *guru:* "Any sober person who can tolerate the urge to speak, the mind's demands, the reactions of anger, and the urges of the tongue, belly, and genitals is qualified to make disciples all over the world."[16]

The spiritual master is also an *ācārya,* one who teaches by personal example. Intellectual brilliance notwithstanding, a man of dubious personal character, who is attached to selfish gratification and self-interest, cannot be a spiritual master. Śrī Kṛṣṇa Caitanya stated, *āpani ācari' bhakti karila pracāra:* "First become perfect, and then you can teach."[17] In other words, the *guru* must be a *svāmī,* or master of the senses, and not a slave to their dictates. No one should assume the titles of *guru, svāmī,* and *sannyāsī* (renounced monk) whimsically. The candidate must actually demonstrate the qualities of *guru, svāmī,* and *sannyāsī.*

By definition, the *guru* imparts instructions consonant with the teachings of Vedic literature. He does not deviate from Vedic teachings through mental speculation, nor is he an atheist, a mundane politician or a humanitarian. He maintains that spiritual knowledge is the ultimate welfare for humanity; therefore he himself lives a life that demonstrates detachment from material pleasure. In other words, he must be blissfully united with the Supreme. Vedic literature admits that such a person is *sudurlabha,* very rarely found (Bg. 7.19).

For his part the *guru* himself has to be a *śiṣya* (student) of a genuine spiritual master in the disciplic succession. There is also a checks-and-balance system called *guru-śāstra-sādhu.*[18] The teachings of *guru* must correspond with the teachings of *sādhu* (the previous spiritual masters in the disciplic succession), which, in turn, must all correspond with the direct meanings of *śāstra* (the scripture).

The Qualifications of the Disciple

A student must also be qualified, and his basic requirements come to light in *Bhagavad-gītā.* The disciple must "inquire from the *guru* submissively and render service unto him" (Bg. 4.34). Faith in the *guru* is of utmost importance and qualifies one for initiation. The *Śvetāśvatara Upaniṣad* (6.23) states:

yasya deve parā bhaktir
yathā deve tathā gurau
tasyaite kathitā hy arthāḥ
prakāśante mahātmanaḥ

"Only unto those great souls who have implicit faith in the Supreme and the spiritual master are all the imports of Vedic knowledge automatically revealed."

Faith in the *guru* is the subject matter in a narration about Śrī Kṛṣṇa from the *Bhāgavata Purāṇa* (10.80). When recalling His boyhood pastimes, Kṛṣṇa recollects that when He once went to collect fuel for His *guru*, He and His friend were lost in the forest during a great rainstorm and spent all night wandering about. In the morning, when the *guru* and other disciples finally found Kṛṣṇa, the *guru* was very pleased, and he blessed Kṛṣṇa:

> It is very wonderful that You have suffered so much trouble for me. Everyone likes to take care of his body as the first consideration, but You are so good and faithful to Your *guru*, that without caring for bodily comforts You have taken so much trouble for the satisfaction of the spiritual master. It is the duty of the disciple to dedicate his life to the service of the spiritual master. My dear best of the twice born, I am greatly pleased by Your action, and I bless You: may all Your desires and ambitions be fulfilled. May the understanding of the *Vedas* which You have learned from me always continue to remain in Your memory, so that at every moment You can remember the teachings of the *Vedas* and quote their instructions without difficulty. Thus You will never be disappointed in this life or in the next.[20]

Kṛṣṇa recalled the incident in this way:

> Without the blessings of the spiritual master, no one can be happy. By the mercy of the spiritual master, and by his blessings, one can achieve peace and prosperity and be able to fulfill the mission of human life.[21]

Obviously, the faith described herein is not simply intellectual agreement on some theological matter. Rather, the disciple must completely surrender himself bodily and mentally as the servant of the *guru* and take up the *guru's* instructions as his life's mission. It is, then, no overstatement that "selection of a *guru* is more significant than the selection of a spouse."[22]

The *Vedas* stress the need for such complete commitment. After all, the *guru* acts as the disciple's savior. He alone can impart Vedic knowledge and thus liberation. The disciple therefore owes a debt to his *guru*, who has personally lifted him out of conditioned ignorance and blessed him with the perfection of eternity, bliss, and knowledge. In his turn, the *guru* must execute his duties humbly as a servitor of the Supreme and of his own *guru* in the disciplic succession.

If one satisfies his *guru* by sincere service and actually understands the Vedic conclusion, he receives initiation as a *brāhmaṇa.* A *brāhmaṇa* is a learned person who is responsible enough to enlighten others. In India there are many *smārta-brāhmaṇas,* or caste-conscious *brāhmaṇas,* who insist that one cannot be elevated to brahminical status unless he is born in a *brāhmaṇa* family. This *brāhmaṇa*-by-birth conception is decidedly non-Vedic. One scholar writes, "In the *Śrīmad Bhagavad-gītā-parvādhyāyāḥ* of the *Mahābhārata,* Vāsudeva-Kṛṣṇa says in very clear terms that the classification of the people into four *varṇas* (castes) is based on *guṇa-karma,* i.e. spiritual quality and conduct."[23]

There is a popular story in the *Chāndogya Upaniṣad* about a boy named Satyakāma who approached a *guru* for enlightenment. "Are you the son of a *brāhmaṇa?*" the *guru* asked. The boy said that he didn't know who his father was. The *guru* then asked him to inquire from his mother, but the boy's mother frankly told him that since she had known many men, she wasn't sure who his father was. The boy then returned to the *guru* and said, "My mother doesn't know." Pleased with the boy's honesty, the spiritual master concluded, "You are a *brāhmaṇa.*"[24]

According to the Vedic standard, anyone can be elevated by training. In the *Hari-bhakti-vilāsa* of Sanātana Gosvāmī, it is stated that one who is properly initiated certainly becomes a *brāhmaṇa,* just as bell metal can be turned into gold when mixed with mercury. In the Seventh Canto of the *Bhāgavata Purāṇa* (7.11.35), Nārada tells King Yudhiṣṭhira that if one has the qualities of a *brāhmaṇa,* he must be accepted as a *brāhmaṇa.* Thus, birth in a particular family, race, or religion is not an essential qualification for a *śiṣya.*

Most important among a disciple's qualifications are faith, service, and submissive inquiry. Yet the disciple should not follow his *guru* blindly. In *Bhagavad-gītā* Arjuna asks a series of probing questions, and Śrī Kṛṣṇa replies with philosophical reasoning and references to *śāstra* and *sādhu.*

In the Vedic tradition the importance of the *guru-śiṣya* relationship cannot be exaggerated. Indeed, the *Padma Puraṇa* stresses that it is impossible to gain spiritual knowledge without a *guru:* "Unless one is initiated by a bona fide spiritual master in the disciplic succession, the *mantra* that one has received is without any effect." Continually the *śāstras* accentuate the inestimable value of association with a saintly person. A moment's association is said to be more valuable than thousands of lifetimes without that association. A *śiṣya's* eagerness to hear from the *guru* is itself a great qualification. After hearing, if he obediently carries out the instructions of the spiritual master, the disciple automatically advances beyond liberation, to the ultimate stage of love of God.

It is necessary that the *śiṣya,* like his *guru,* live according to the high moral standards set forth in the *śāstras.* Śaṅkara states that a student of philosophy must meet the following essential conditions: the student must have the strong will to inquire into the difference between matter and spirit, he must renounce all personal demands and self-interest, and he must restrain his mind and senses.[25] Unless he can give up all material pleasure and be detached from sorrow as well, he cannot qualify for transcendental life. As Kṛṣṇa confirms in *Bhagavad-gītā* (2.41), "Those who are on this path are resolute in purpose, and their aim is one. . . . The intelligence of those who are irresolute is many branched." Traditionally, a disciple must give up the "four pillars of sin": meat-eating, illicit sex, gambling, and intoxication.[26]

Summary

We have described the purpose, the origin, and the process of Vedic knowledge according to the statements of the *Vedas* themselves. The Vedic follower accepts the *śāstras* as the words of the supreme person (*īśvara,* Nārāyaṇa), hence as axiomatic truths. In other words, there is no need to verify those truths that the *Vedas* have already set forth. Further, the follower should understand the cause of all causes not by material knowledge or independent mental conjecture but by hearing faithfully from an authorized spiritual master. The sublime secrets of spiritual life passed on from *guru* to *śiṣya* are open to everyone, regardless of social caste or birth. To become a candidate for spiritual knowledge, the follower must observe the regulations for purification set forth by the *guru.* These are the basic precepts of the *Vedas* regarding the acquisition of transcendental knowledge.

2 / The Empirical Approach to Vedic Literature

In Chapter One we have discussed some of the principles of Vedic learning handed down by the disciplic succession of Vedic teachers. We should also note that in the last two hundred years virtually all Western universities have taken a critical-historical, or empirical, approach. Hinduism and Indian philosophy have become popular subjects in many colleges, and there has arisen a community of established Sanskritists and Indologists. However, if we compare the empirical version of Vedic knowledge with the version of the *Vedas* themselves, we often find the two at opposite poles. Empiric scholars rarely discuss this conflict. They assume, usually correctly, that readers will accept the empiric version because of the scholar's reputation for probing research and analysis. When discrepancies become obvious, the empiric scholars usually represent their own views as the objective picture of Vedic civilization.

Yet these conflicts raise a number of questions. Why do some scholars reject the explanations of the Vedic literature's origin, purpose, and transcendental nature as received from both the texts themselves and the traditional Vedic scholars? Why is the Vedic literature's description of itself necessarily unacceptable? Is it simply that the empiric scholars doubt that the *Vedas* or the *ācāryas* are what they say they are? The *Vedas* claim divine origin, and the scholars deem their origin mythological. The *Vedas* propose to elevate man from suffering and grant him liberation, but the scholars suppose that studying the *Vedas* for spiritual purposes is unscholarly. Although the *Vedas* warn that the Vedic teachings are transcendental to material investigation, scholars reject such injunctions as esoteric taboos and proceed to analyze the *Vedas* in an empirical spirit. They frankly regard the *Vedas* as mythology and assign themselves to the task of demythologizing.

The *Vedas* affirm that Vedic knowledge must be heard from a spiritual master in the disciplic succession, but the scholar who writes books about the *Vedas* is not a *guru,* nor does his scholarly conscience allow him to accept such an approach. Moreover, the scholar surveys the *guru* from what he considers a superior, more objective and academic vantage point. The *Vedas* maintain that one must observe strict moral standards and perform austerities before understanding Vedic literature, but scholars consider such things to be unnecessary.

What is the best way to study the *Vedas?* Should we give credence, after all, to what the *Vedas* say about themselves? Before deciding, we should know something about the substantiality of empiric Vedic scholarship.

Empirical Tools

The tools used by empiric Indologists are the scientific standards of history, anthropology, archaeology, philology, and related disciplines. Since Indological studies began, in the eighteenth century, the research in every field has become increasingly sophisticated. However, the scholars agree that their critical reconstruction of the origin and nature of Vedic culture is highly uncertain.

History

Empiricists generally place great importance on understanding historical development, but for the Vedic period there is no history aside from the *śāstras.* For thousands of years the early Indians kept no such histories, and as O. L. Chavarria-Aguilar writes in his book *Traditional India,* "A more unhistorical people would be difficult to find."[1] *A Sourcebook in Indian Philosophy* informs us, "A historical treatment of Indian philosophy has not been taken up by the great Indian thinkers themselves."[2] Ancient Rome had its Livy and ancient Greece its Herodotus, but India had no great historian to record the Vedic period. According to modern Indologists, the Indian's lack of interest in history was not due to a primitive inability to keep records; rather, he accepted the historical version of the *śāstras* as sufficient.

Scientific historians choose not to accept the historical validity of the *śāstras;* their alternative is to begin the official history of India with the death of Buddha, in 483 B.C. In any case, this is the earliest date empirically settled. Scholars concede that the Vedic period began thousands of years before Christ, but as for the dating of even approximate periods, "everywhere we are on unsafe ground."[3] Nevertheless, scholars have reconstructed various historical periods which they theoretically assign to the thousands of unaccounted years. Pioneer Indologist Max Müller devised a system of classifying the Vedic civilization into periods called

"Chandas, Mantra, Brāhmaṇa, and Sūtra," and a number of scholars have concurred.[4] Others have also given their own divisions. Radhakrishnan, for instance, looks upon the broad divisions of Indian history as Vedic, Epic, Sūtra, and Scholastic.[5] Handbooks on Vedic history differ on specific dates by as much as one or two thousand years. Indeed, Moriz Winternitz, one of the most respected chronologists, argues that any attempt to reconstruct the Vedic period is unscientific. He writes, "The chronology of the history of Indian literature is shrouded in truly terrifying darkness."[6] Winternitz somewhat pointedly notes that it would be pleasant and convenient, especially when preparing a handbook on Vedic literature, to divide the literature into three or four periods and assign dates and categories. "But every attempt of such a kind is bound to fail in the present state of knowledge, and the use of hypothetical dates would only be a delusion, which would do more harm than good."[7] He states that it is even better not to assign dates to the oldest period of Indian literary history. Using discoveries by related field workers and conducting further research into the texts, successive generations of historians continue to develop new pictures of the Vedic past. However, Winternitz quotes a pioneer American Sanskritist who years ago said, "All dates given in Indian literary history are pins set up to be bowled down again."[8] Winternitz remarks, "For the most part this is still the case today."[9] We may thus conclude that there is simply no history of the original Vedic civilization in India, at least none that is acceptable in the strict sense of empiric history.

Archaeology

Archaeology, of course, is especially suitable for finding out about ancient cultures. But what was true for Vedic historical records is also true for archaeological finds, which to date give us no clear picture of Vedic civilization. Of course, many of the geographical sites mentioned in the scriptures are still known, and according to tradition many of the temples in India have been maintained for thousands of years, but these sites have not yielded solid archaeological evidence.

Archaeologists and anthropologists cannot accept the śāstric version that Vedic civilization flourished in India long before fifty thousand years ago—the date which scientists assign as the earliest possible appearance of *homo sapiens* on earth. Consistently the *śāstras* mention that Vedic literature was written down at the beginning of the age of Kali some five thousand years ago, and that philosophers, *yogīs,* and *ṛṣis* lived many millions of years ago. Although empiricists most often discount such sophistication in ancient humanity, they do admit that "the history of the human race is being rewritten with new dating processes and with exciting discoveries around the world."[10] The general trend in the rewriting of human history is to push the theoretical date from the beginning of advanced human civilization further and further back into what has become known as prehistory. As far as the archaeology of India is concerned, the excavations of cities and temples have produced no conclusive empirical data about the Vedic culture's first appearance.

Western archaeology got its start in India early in the nineteenth century, when the surveyors of the East India Company found many temples, shrines, old coins, and inscriptions written in dead scripts. In the 1830's the edicts of Emperor Aśoka were deciphered, and thus Indian civilization was dated at 300 B.C. In the twentieth century, work began on a large scale. The most famous archaeological discoveries relating to the prehistoric period took place under the supervision of archaeologist Sir John Marshall, who in the 1920's uncovered the cities of Harappa and Mohenjaro, located in what is now Pakistan. These were the cities of an efficient, urban social community, now called the Indus civilization, which has been dated at 3,000 B.C.[11] Though a fabulous find for archaeology, Harappa has contributed but little to our understanding of the ancient Vedic period. If it was hoped that the discoveries at Harappa and Mohenjaro might throw some light on the *Vedas,* this hope was not fulfilled. Among the artifacts found at Harappa was a small figure of a seated man who might be Śiva, but this is not definite.

Linguistic research and interpretation of the *Ṛg Veda* have given rise to a hypothesis linking the Indus civilization with the origin of the *Vedas.* As the story has it, the peaceful Draviḍians (the name of the original people of Harappa) were invaded by the Āryan barbarians, who brought with them their tales of Indra (*Ṛg Veda*). This account enjoys wide currency in books, but it is by no means a scientific conclusion.[12] Rather, it is a hypothetical creation set forth to explain what would otherwise be inexplicable. About the Indus civilization, one Indologist comments, "We do not know for certain who the authors of the remarkable civilization were; it is another of those mysteries that make the scholar's life at once interesting and somewhat frustrating."[13] As for the theory that the Draviḍians met their demise under Indra's hordes of plundering Āryans, H. P. Rowlinson writes, "A number of scholars have pointed the finger of accusation at the Āryans... but the guilt of those immigrants is far from established."[14] Thus, although scholars favor various theories, archaeological finds like those of the Indus civilization have to date given evidence insufficient for reconstructing the period in which the Vedic scriptures were composed.

Archaeology gains considerable scientific veracity by allying with other disciplines, such as atomic physics (which produced the carbon 14 dating process). Will archaeologists one day find something that will actually solve the Vedic riddles once and for all? Anthropologist Julian H. Steward writes, "Facts exist only as they are related to theories, and theories are not destroyed by facts—they are replaced by new theories which better explain the facts."[15] In other words, we might say, although archaeologists intend to find out much more, they may never know for sure.

Whatever facts and theories the future may hold, archaeology, the empiricist's main hope, has thus far failed to penetrate the darkness that shrouds the Vedic period; the prime record of Vedic culture is, of course, oral tradition. Hence, in the very area where archaeology alone can give the empiricist knowledge, we can seriously question whether archaeology is even relevant. "Religion is a mental or spiritual phenomenon in which the sacred or supernatural word plays an important part. Obviously this essential expression of religion cannot be investigated archaeologically—the remains are wordless."[16]

Linguistic Research

As we would expect, research has spread to still other disciplines. In fact, among the most important tools in Indological research is the study of linguistics. In the late eighteenth century, linguists in India made a comparative study of Sanskrit, Greek, and Latin and concluded that the languages were so similar in vocabulary and grammar that they must have come from a common ancestral tongue. In 1786, Sir William Jones theorized that Sanskrit and other languages had "sprung from some common source which perhaps no longer exists."[17] This language received the name proto-Indo-European. Although there is no clear evidence that this language was ever spoken, linguists reconstructed a proto-Indo-European language with the help of archaeologists, who contributed evidence on who might have spoken it and where. Stuart Piggot writes: "The location of a possible Indo-European homeland and the identification of the culture implied by the linguistic evidence with a comparable archaeological phenomenon, has been a matter of debate since the idea was first formulated in the last century."[18] From a hypothetical language, a hypothetical human community emerged, its members called Indo-Europeans. Because words like "horse" and "father" were prominent in the vocabulary of proto-Indo-Europeans, the scholars constructed a community of farmers who had domesticated the horse and in whose society the father was dominant.[19] Also, the scholars ascribed to them a religion and rites, although no one can say for certain where these people lived. In a recent history of India we find this assessment:

> The aboriginal home of the Āryans [the Indo-Europeans are supposed to be the predecessors of the Āryans who invaded India] is again a controversial point, and in the face of the hopeless chaos of conflicting views, it seems impossible to come to any definite conclusion. The most probable theory seems to be that the Āryans migrated into India from outside, the exact region from where they came being still a point of discussion.[20]

Professor of linguistics Ward Goddenaugh pointed out that chauvinism and racism definitely entered into historical European interpretations of Indo-European origins. Thus, scholars arbitrarily compiled data to prove that the Āryan forefathers came from Europe.[21]

Despite limited information, linguists tend to construct hypotheses. The prominent Sanskritist A. B. Keith once remarked that by taking the linguistic method too literally, one could conclude that the original Indo-Europeans knew about butter but not milk, snow and feet but not rain and hands.[22]

Already, it appears, the discipline known as linguistic paleontology has fallen out of favor with scholars. In 1971, the eminent linguist Winifred Lehmann asserted, "Clearly, the linguistic paleontologists had overextended themselves to the point of elimination."[23] Dr. Lehmann insists that language cannot be used as a primary source for reconstructing an earlier culture. Still, linguistic theories about the origin and cultural background of the *Vedas* continue to figure prominently in academic accounts of the Vedic period.

In order to date ancient languages, in recent decades Morris Swadesh has devised a linguistic method known as glottochronology. This method arose from the theory that over the millennia, changes in the vocabulary of a language tend to occur at a regular, measurable rate. Scholars have used this method to date the oral tradition of the *Vedas* as well as the appearance of specific literatures. However, linguists themselves report that "no matter how much the technique is refined, the only dating that it can yield will be of the likelihood variety."[24] Glottochronologists have worked out graphs indicating areas in which there is a ninety-percent likelihood that a particular specimen of language can be assigned a correct date. The greater the time period in which the literature *might* have appeared (thousands of years for Vedic literature), the greater the variance in ascribing the approximate date. The variance grows so great as to be no more than an educated guess. Linguistic critic Charles Hockett writes, "Obviously it is not helpful to find that, though the most likely date of an event is forty thousand years ago, the nine-tenths confidence level defines a span running from ninety thousand years ago to a date ten thousand years in our own future."[25] Although regarded as highly imperfect, glottochronology is the best working tool available today for dating ancient languages. It has not, however, revealed anything definite about the origin and real purport of the Vedic literature.

Summary

As we have marked, empirical evidence for the Vedic period seems scanty and fragmentary; the scholars have few hard facts on which to base mature or reliable conclusions. Accordingly, their full and elaborate picture of Vedic history seems hypothetical and conjectural. Of course, drawn as it is from arduous historical, archaeological, and linguistic research, the hypothetical picture surely merits consideration. At the same time, it appears, Indologists would do well to remember that an official photograph is one thing, a hypothetical picture quite another.

Actually, Western scholars have never assessed the Vedic *śāstras* on their own merit. The first studies of the *Vedas,* for example, were clouded by less than objective motivations. In the eighteenth and early nineteenth centuries, pioneer Indologists such as Sir William Jones, Horace H. Wilson, Theodore Goldstücker, and Sir M. Monier-Williams approached the Vedic culture with a view to replacing it with Christian culture.[26] This naturally tainted their investigation of Vedic literature. While the missionary motive declined, an effort was made by the American transcendentalist school (Henry David Thoreau and Ralph Waldo Emerson, etc.) to appreciate the *Vedas* as they are. It would be fair to say, however, that the empirical-historical method eclipsed this endeavor before it could shine forth. And because the Vedic system is intrinsically beyond the range of empirical investigation, modern Indologists have also been unable to study the *Vedas* on the literature's own terms. Thus, it may be appropriate to hear what the *Vedas* say about themselves. As opposed to the fragmented, highly theoretical, or at best partial appreciations of the *Vedas* by Western scholars, this approach will aid us in understanding the wide range of Vedic literatures as a sublime and cohesive whole.

3 / Essential Elements of Vedic Thought

Although he may be unacquainted with Sanskrit, a new student of Vedic literature needs to understand many Sanskirt terms. Simply memorizing words in a glossary cannot fill that need; the *Vedas* themselves prescribe that to understand the meanings of such terms as Bhagavān, Paramātmā, and Brahman, the student must become transcendentally situated, or realized. He must know from personal experience the distinction between matter (*jaḍa*) and spirit (Brahman), and the nature both of illusion (*māyā*) and of the supreme controller (*īśvara*). Since some words, such as *dharma* and *rasa,* have no real English equivalents, the student's need for personal experience and realization becomes so much greater.

To get a clear understanding, the student should first learn the simple, literal meaning of the Sanskrit terms. By avoiding allegorical interpretations and speculation, he will avoid needless confusion. In other words, the student makes easier advancement if he accepts the direct meaning given in the *śāstras* rather than the indirect meanings set forth by imperfect commentators. Vedic literature is not difficult to understand if the student learns the terms of the *śāstras* in their original meanings.

The Three Aspects of the Absolute

The Vedic literatures discuss three aspects of the Absolute Truth: Brahman, Paramātmā, and Bhagavān. The *Upaniṣads* focus upon Brahman; the *yoga* systems, upon Paramātmā; *Bhagavad-gītā* and the *Purāṇas,* upon Bhagavān. *Bhāgavata Purāṇa* (1.2.11) states that all three aspects are actually one, seen from different angles of vision: "Learned transcendentalists who know the Absolute Truth call this nondual substance Brahman, Paramātmā or Bhagavān."[1]

1) Brahman

Brahman refers to the impersonal, all-pervasive aspect of the Absolute Truth. The multifarious manifestations of the cosmos—moving and nonmoving matter, atoms, bodies, planets, space—are not ultimate causes in themselves, nor are they eternal. All of them come from the eternal Brahman. The *Vedānta-sūtra* (1.1.2) clearly states, *janmādy asya yataḥ:* "The Supreme Brahman is the origin of everything."[2] The *Muṇḍaka Upaniṣad* (2.2.10–12) offers elucidation:

> Brilliant is It, the light of lights—
> That which knowers of the soul do know!
> The sun shines not there, nor the moon and stars;
> These lightnings shine not, much less this (earthly) fire!
> After Him, as He shines, doth everything shine.
> This whole world is illumined with His light.
> . . . before, . . . behind, to right and left,
> Stretched forth below and above.[3]

Radhakrishnan writes that Brahman "cannot be defined by logical categories or linguistic symbols. It is the incomprehensible *nirguṇa* ["qualityless"] Brahman, the pure Absolute."[4]

The *Bṛhad-āraṇyaka Upaniṣad* (3.9.26) describes the Brahman philosophers as searching for the root of existence in the components of matter but finding only *neti neti:* "That self is not this, not that."[5] When one realizes Brahman, he knows the impersonal spirit in all things.

2) Paramātmā

Ātmā means "self." Thomas Hopkins writes, "*Ātman* was distinguished from the gross physical body; it was the *inner* self, the principle or energy that gave man his essential nature."[6] Vedic philosophy regards the self as eternal and individual; it is not destroyed when the body is destroyed. On the battlefield of Kurukṣetra, Kṛṣṇa has only encouragement for Arjuna:

> Never was there a time when I did not exist, nor you, nor all these kings; nor in the future shall any of us cease to be. . . . For the soul [*ātmā*] there is never birth nor death. Nor having once been, does he ever cease to be. He is unborn, eternal, ever-existing, undying and primeval. He is not slain when the body is slain.[7]

The *ātmā,* individual soul, is distinct from the Paramātmā (the Supersoul or oversoul, an identity beyond the *ātmā*). The word *parama* means "supreme and transcendental," and, as the *Kaṭha Upaniṣad* (1.2.20) has it, the Paramātmā and the *ātmā* are like two birds sitting on a tree:

> Both the Supersoul [Paramātmā] and the individual atomic soul [*jīva-ātmā*] are situated on the same tree of the body within the same heart of the living being; only one who has become free from all material desires as well as lamentations can, by the grace of the Supreme, understand the glories of the soul.[8]

Awareness of one's eternal relation with the Paramātmā is the goal of the mystic *aṣṭāṅga-yoga* taught by Patañjali (the author of the *Yoga-sūtra*). According to *Bhagavad-gītā,* "That Supersoul [Paramātmā] is perceived by some through meditation. . . ."[9] Perfection in meditation results in the yogic trance called *samādhi:*

> The stage of perfection is called trance, or *samādhi,* when one's mind is completely restrained from material mental activities by practice of *yoga.* This is characterized by one's ability to see the self by the pure mind and to relish and rejoice in the self. In that joyous state, one is situated in boundless transcendental happiness and enjoys himself through transcendental senses. Established thus, one never departs from the truth, and upon gaining this he thinks there is no greater gain. Being situated in such a position, one is never shaken, even in the midst of greatest difficulty. This indeed is actual freedom from all miseries arising from material contact.[10]

This realization occurs when the mystic sees the transcendental form of God within his heart. Although only genuine mystics can see the Supersoul, He is seated in the hearts of all living beings, whether they realize or not. "I am seated in everyone's heart, and from Me come remembrance, knowledge and forgetfulness."[11] The Paramātmā guides the embodied soul, witnesses his activities, and awards him the results of his actions. "The Supersoul enters into the bodies of the created beings who are influenced by the modes of material nature and causes them to enjoy the effects of these by the subtle mind."[12]

Knowing that the Supersoul is present with each soul in each and every material body, the Paramātmā-realized *yogī* sees all beings equally. "The humble sage, by virtue of true knowledge, sees with equal vision a learned and gentle *brāhmaṇa,* a cow, an elephant, a dog and a dog-eater [outcaste]."[13] Indeed, the unified vision of the Paramātmā-realized *yogī* extends to all aspects of existence. "Such a person is situated in transcendence and is self-controlled. He sees everything—whether it be pebbles, stones or gold—as the same. . . . He is a perfect *yogī* who, by comparison to his own self, sees the true equality of all beings, both in their happiness and distress, O Arjuna."[14]

3) Bhagavān

Bhagavān realization is the theistic vision of the Absolute Truth as the Supreme Person possessed of inconceivable attributes.[15] Parāśara Muni defines Bhagavān as the Supreme Person possessing infinite beauty, knowledge, strength, fame, wealth, and renunciation. Although the concept of creation suggests many great personalities (or demigods), in the fullest sense the word *bhagavān* applies only to the Supreme Being, the Godhead Himself.

Bhagavān is the highest feature of the Absolute. He is the Supreme Brahman (Parabrahman) and the source of the Paramātmā. As we have noted previously, the *Vedānta-sūtra* (1.1.2) states that the Absolute Truth is the source of all emanations (*janmādy asya yataḥ*). Further, the *Vedānta* and the *Purāṇas* state that, as the source of everything, the Absolute must possess intelligence and consciousness. These latter attributes imply personality, and the supreme personal feature of the Absolute Truth is termed Bhagavān. Whereas Brahman is devoid of material qualities or attributes, Bhagavān possesses transcendental qualities. All beings rest in Brahman, and Brahman itself rests in the Supreme Person. The *Vedas* regard Brahman as the effulgence (*brahmajyoti*) of the transcendental body of the Supreme Personality of Godhead. The *Brahma-saṁhitā* (5.1) postulates that Bhagavān is *sac-cid-ānanda-vigrahaḥ,* the personal form of eternity, full knowledge, and full bliss.[16]

Impersonal Brahman manifests only the *sat* (eternity) feature of the Absolute. Brahman is to Bhagavān as the sunshine is to the sun. The sunshine is the sun's effulgence, and has no independent existence apart from the sun. Paramātmā manifests the *sat* and *cit* (knowledge) aspects of the Absolute, but Bhagavān alone fully manifests the *sat, cit,* and *ānanda* (bliss) aspects. Thus, Bhagavān is the full embodiment (*vigraha*) of *sac-cid-ānanda.*

Prefacing each of Lord Kṛṣṇa's statements in *Bhagavad-gītā* is the phrase *śrī-bhagavān uvāca*—"The Supreme Personality of Godhead said." Further, the *Gītā* establishes that Bhagavān, Kṛṣṇa, is the ultimate truth: "There is no truth superior to Me."[17] *Brahma-saṁhitā* makes a similar confirmation, *īśvaraḥ paramaḥ kṛṣṇaḥ sac-cid-ānanda-vigrahaḥ:* "The supreme controller is Kṛṣṇa, who has a transcendental form of eternity, bliss, and knowledge."[18] And the *Bhāgavata Purāṇa* (1.3.28) indicates that all *avatāras* proceed from the Supreme Bhagavān (Kṛṣṇa).[19]

In one sense God, or Bhagavān, has no name; yet His activities garner Him many names. The name Kṛṣṇa, meaning "all-attractive," is fundamental because, by Parāśara Muni's definition, the Supreme Person must be all-attractive or all-opulent. To enact various pastimes (*līlā*) for His pleasure and to create and maintain, Bhagavān Kṛṣṇa expands into forms such as Nārāyaṇa, Vāsudeva, and Mahā-Viṣṇu. The name Kṛṣṇa (the all-attractive) also implies Viṣṇu (the all-pervasive). The name Bhagavān (the all-opulent) implies the names *īśvara* (supreme controller) and *puruṣa* (supreme enjoyer). Rūpa Gosvāmī's *Laghu-bhāgavatāmṛta* has this to say about the names given the Absolute:

> According to the intimate relationships between Śrī Kṛṣṇa, the primeval Lord, and His devotees, the *Purāṇas* describe Him by various names. Sometimes He is called Nārāyaṇa; sometimes Upendra [Vāmana], the younger brother of Indra, the King of Heaven [*upa-indra*]; and sometimes Kṣīrodakaśāyī Viṣṇu. Sometimes he is called the thousand-headed Śeṣa Nāga and sometimes the Lord of Vaikuṇṭha.[20]

When the inquirer realizes Bhagavān, the Supreme Personality of Godhead, he simultaneously realizes Brahman and Paramātmā. For we have seen that, far from being separate one from another, the three aspects of the Absolute are all present within Bhagavān.

The Three Energies of the Absolute

1) *Cit*

Cit-śakti is the spiritual energy of the Absolute Truth. Bhagavān, the Supreme Person, is the energetic source, and through His internal *cit* potency He manifests the eternal kingdom of God and His eternal liberated associates. "Just as *māyā* builds this mundane universe with the five material elements, so the spiritual (*cit*) potency has built the spiritual world."[21] The spiritual universe is known as Vaikuṇṭha, "the place without anxiety." *Bhagavad-gītā* describes this separate universe as that eternal nature which remains even after the annihilation of the material universe.

> Yet there is another nature, which is eternal and is transcendental to this manifested and unmanifested matter. It is supreme, and it is never annihilated. When all in this world is annihilated, that part remains as it is. That supreme abode is called unmanifested and infallible, and it is the supreme destination. When one goes there, he never comes back. That is My supreme abode.[22]

The spiritual universe, Vaikuṇṭha, is eternal; that is to say, it is exempt from the strict laws of the material world, wherein all living entities suffer birth, old age, disease and death. When Bhagavān enters the material universe as an incarnation (*avatāra*), He is never subjected to the material laws, but remains situated in His internal spiritual potency (*cit*).

2) *Jīva*

The verbal root *jīv* means "to live, be, or remain alive," and the noun *jīva* refers to the individual living being, or soul. According to the Vedic analysis, the living being (*jīva*) is separate from the body, yet, within each and every body (including those of men, beasts, birds and plants), an individual soul (*jīva*) resides. Individual consciousness is the symptom of the *jīva's* presence.

Although the body is perishable, the *jīva* is eternal. "Know that which pervades the entire body to be indestructible. No one is able to destroy the imperishable soul."[23] The *Bhāgavata Purāṇa* describes the size of the *jīva:* "There are innumerable particles of spiritual atoms, which are measured as one ten-thousandth of the upper portion of the hair."[24] Clearly, the *jīva* defies perception by the material senses.

According to the Vedic conception, consciousness does not arise from a material combination; it is the symptom of the *jīva's* presence within the body. When the *jīva* leaves the body, consciousness also leaves, and the body perishes. It is the *jīva* that is the real self, but in contact with matter, it becomes conditioned. "The empirical individual, the *jīva,* is self-limited by the body and senses."[25] Originally the *jīva* is a spiritual part of the Supreme Bhagavān and shares His qualities of *sac-cid-ānanda* in minute portions. The *jīva's* constitutional position is subordinate to that of the Supreme Bhagavān. Although the Supreme Bhagavān never falls within the control of the material energy, the *jīva,* out of delusion and a misuse of his free will, falls under the control of the material energy and forgets his relationship with the Supreme Bhagavān. Desiring to be an independent enjoyer, the *jīva* enters the material world. The *jīva's* fall from his constitutional position provides the gist, of course, for Western narratives such as Milton's *Paradise Lost.*

Although the *jīva* in the material world suffers in many ways, he remains under the spell of material nature (*māyā*). Actually the *jīva* soul has nothing to do with the material world, but because of *māyā* (illusion) he acts to satisfy himself through the material senses. If he has not attained liberation from his material bodily confinement by the time of universal annihilation, he returns to the body of the Supreme Viṣṇu and takes birth again, in the next creation, to act out his desires (*karma*). When the *jīva* attains liberation, he goes to the *brahmajyoti* or even to Vaikuṇṭha, the spiritual planets where the Supreme resides in His complete, personal form. Real liberation for the *jīva* is to attain his original spiritual identity (*svarūpa*), for in his eternal form the *jīva* can associate with Bhagavān, the Supreme Personality of Godhead.

3) *Māyā*

Material illusion is called *māyā. Māyā* means "unreality, deception, forgetfulness"—"that which is not." Under the influence of *māyā,* a man thinks that he can be happy within the temporary material world. As the deluding energy of the Supreme, *māyā* acts not independently but under His direction. "It is by illusion (*māyā*) the other (*jīva*) is confined. One should know that Nature is illusion (*māyā*) and that the mighty Lord is the illusion-maker."[26]

Māyā's power is such that although a man may be suffering manifold miseries, he will think himself happy. "The cause of man's suffering and impotence is *māyā,* under whose influence he forgets his divine nature."[27] When the *jīva* identifies with the body, he develops thousands of desires and then attempts to fulfill them. It is the nature of the material world that the more the *jīva* tries to exploit the material situation, the more he is bound by *māyā's* complexities. Acting under the influence of *māyā,* the *jīva* subjects himself to the law of *karma* (cause and effect).

As for the origin of *māyā,* Bhagavān Kṛṣṇa states, "This divine energy of Mine [*māyā*], consisting of the three modes of material nature, is difficult to overcome."[28] The *Vedas* further enjoin: "Although *māyā* [illusion] is false or temporary, the background of *māyā* is the supreme magician, the Personality of Godhead, who is Maheśvara, the supreme controller."[29]

In sum, *māyā* is a delusion, a trick, a mirage that bewilders a person into thinking that eternality and happiness abide in the activities of the material world (which in actuality is temporary and miserable). Even a highly educated or intelligent man may be under the spell of *māyā; Bhagavad-gītā* designates such a person as *māyayāpahṛta-jñāna,* "one whose knowledge is stolen by *māyā*."[30] Vedic literature purports to free all beings from the clutches of *māyā*. "To be delivered from this illusion which has somehow come to dominate the race of man is the end of all endeavor."[31] According to *Bhagavad-gītā,* it is very difficult for the *jīva* to break free from the bondage of *māyā:* "This divine energy of Mine, consisting of the three modes of material nature, is difficult to overcome. But those who have surrendered unto Me can easily cross beyond it."[32]

Karma

Western science and philosophy commonly hold that the law of causality governs all action and events in the universe, that there can be no actions or events without corresponding causes, at least on the material platform. The Vedic literature calls this law of cause and effect the law of *karma*. From time immemorial, the *jīva* has been acting in the material world and enjoying or suffering the reactions of his actions. His actions bring about his transmigration from one material body to another. In other words, the *jīva* takes off and puts on bodies just as one takes off old and useless garments and puts on new ones. As the *jīva* transmigrates, he suffers or enjoys the results of his past activities (*karma*).

In one sense, all *karma* is bondage. Even pious activities, or "good *karma,*" bind a person to the wheel of transmigration. One has to be freed from all *karma* if he is to transcend *saṁsāra,* repeated birth and death. The *jīva* creates his own *karma* out of his particular desires to enjoy this world in different ways. Thus, neither Bhagavān nor material nature is responsible for the *karma* of the *jīva;* he makes his own destiny. According to the *jīva's* activities (and under the supervision of the Supreme), material nature simply awards the *jīva* his next body to carry out his desires. Freedom from the great chain of *karma* comes through knowledge. "As the blazing fire turns firewood to ashes, O Arjuna, so does the fire of knowledge burn to ashes all reactions [*sarva-karmāṇi*] to material activities."[33] This "fire of knowledge" refers to the *jīva's* awareness of his constitutional position as the eternal servant of the Supreme. When one surrenders to Bhagavān, he transcends all past, present, and future *karma.*

The *jīva* cannot become free from *karma* merely by refraining from action. The *Vedas* portray the soul as eternally and irrevocably active. "It is indeed impossible for an embodied being to give up all activities. Therefore, it is said that he who renounces the fruits of action [*karma-phala-tyāgī*] is he who has truly renounced."[34] In other words, one has to learn the art of working without accruing *karma.*

In *Bhagavad-gītā,* Bhagavān Kṛṣṇa explains this art of *karma-yoga* in detail. Briefly, one who performs his activities as a sacrifice to the Supreme Bhagavān avoids *karma,* bondage within the material world. Such refined, sacrificial activity is called *akarma,* that is, action without reaction. The *Nārada-pañcarātra* explains that the art of *karma-yoga* is *hṛṣīkeṇa hṛṣīkeśa-sevanam:* "serving the Lord of the senses with one's senses." It is the function of the *guru* to teach his students this elusive art of *akarma,* action without reaction.

Saṁsāra

Saṁsāra means repeated birth and death, or transmigration. As a result of *karma,* a person may take his birth in a family of wealthy merchants or in a family of insects. The *Padma Purāṇa* delineates that there are 8,400,000 species, and that the fallen *jīva* has to undergo birth in every one of them. After evolving through many thousands of births, the *jīva* at last reaches the human form, a chance to cultivate self-realization for his ultimate liberation from the cycle of *saṁsāra.*

Guṇas

Literally, the word *guṇa* means "rope." There are three *guṇas* (modes of material nature)—goodness (*sattva*), passion (*rajas*), and ignorance (*tamas*)—which bind one to nature like three strong ropes. Consequently, the material world of *māyā* is sometimes called *tri-guṇa-mayī.*

The *jīva* attains different bodies according to the *guṇas* in which he has acted in the past, and each body in turn induces him to act according to its predominant *guṇa.* Let us consider a man influenced by the mode of goodness (as, for example, a philosopher, a physician, or a poet). This man lives with a sense of knowledge and, therefore, happiness. By cultivating knowledge of the material world, he makes his life pleasant; bound to that pleasant feeling by the rope of mundane goodness, he does not attempt spiritual elevation. As long as a person is attached to an advanced state of material happiness and works simply to improve material conditions, he cannot attain liberation (though he may continue to attain bodies in the mode of goodness). Whatever his material opulence, he nonetheless faces the inevitable fourfold miseries of birth, old age, disease, and death.

Bhagavad-gītā describes the mode of passion (*rajo-guṇa*) as being "born of unlimited desires and longings."[35] Typifying this *guṇa* are sexual attraction and enjoyment. The *jīva* hankers for sex, and on achieving his desires he forms a hard knot of attachment to material life. Gradually, his gross desires expand into subtler longings for honor, family enjoyment, money, and so forth. The *jīva* has to work hard constantly to acquire and maintain these things. According to the Vedic analysis, the achievements of great materialistic civilizations spring from *rajo-guṇa*.

Lastly, *tamo-guṇa*, the mode of ignorance, conditions the *jīva* to laziness and excessive sleep and, generally, to dejection and dependence on intoxicants. "The result of this mode is madness."[36]

At any given time, not one mode alone but some combination of the modes influences the *jīva's* actions. At one time, *rajas* may dominate over *tamas;* at another, *sattva* over *rajas;* at still another, *tamas* over *rajas;* and so forth. At the moment of death, a *jīva* in the mode of goodness transmigrates to a body in the higher planets, a *jīva* in the mode of passion transmigrates to a body in a middle planet like the earth, and a *jīva* in the mode of ignorance transmigrates to a body in the animal species.[37]

Everything in the material world arises from interacting mixtures of the modes of nature. "The *guṇas* are the primal elements which combine in different proportions to constitute all objects of the world."[38] Like a puppet, the *jīva* seems to dance but in fact dangles on these three ropes, *tri-guṇa-mayī.* The *śāstras* explain everything in terms of the *guṇas*—including types of faiths, determination, the kind of food one eats, and the kind of charity one performs. The transcendentalist is one who can rise above the modes. An important difference between Bhagavān, the supreme soul, and the *jīva* soul, the infinitesimal soul, is that Bhagavān is never under the influence of the *guṇas*. At all times He is their master, whereas the *jīva* falls under their influence. By following the Vedic injunctions, the *jīva* can gradually transcend the three material modes and attain his pure transcendental consciousness. Hence, Kṛṣṇa exhorts Arjuna in *Bhagavad-gītā* to "rise above these modes" by turning to the Supreme.[39]

Puruṣa and *Prakṛti*

Puruṣa (referring to Bhagavān, the Supreme Lord) means the supreme predominator and enjoyer. *Prakṛti* means the predominated nature. The living beings (*jīvas*) and the material energy (*māyā*) are, respectively, higher and lower forms of *prakṛti*. *Puruṣa* corresponds to the male (the enjoyer); and *prakṛti* corresponds to the female (the enjoyed). Both, of course, enjoy the relationship.

The *Śvetāśvatara Upaniṣad* (6.7) describes the *puruṣa* aspect of the Absolute Truth in this way: "We know Him who is the Supreme Lord of lords, the Ruler of rulers."[40] Bhagavān Kṛṣṇa affirms, "Of all that is material and all that is spiritual in this world, know for certain that I am both its origin and dissolution."[41] The *puruṣa* is the cause of all causes, the energetic source of all energies. Even when the *jīva* attains liberation, he cannot assume the position of the whole, of the *puruṣa,* because the *jīva* is an eternally fragmental part of the *puruṣa*. *Bhāgavata Purāṇa* (10.87.30) sums up the situation:

> O Supreme Eternal! If the embodied living entities were eternal and all-pervading like You, they would not be under Your control. But if the living entities are accepted as minute energies of Your Lordship, they are at once subject to Your supreme control. Therefore real liberation entails surrender by the living entities to Your control, and that surrender will make them happy. In that constitutional position only can they be controllers. Therefore, men with limited knowledge who advocate the monistic theory that the Supreme and the living entities are equal in all respects are actually misleading themselves and others.[42]

Since the supreme *puruṣa* alone is all-predominant, the independent controller and enjoyer, He is called *asamaurdhva,* "the greatest of all." By learning to meditate on the *puruṣa* or Puruṣottama (supreme living being) in His various manifestations as Nārāyaṇa, Kṛṣṇa, Vāsudeva, and

Viṣṇu, the conditioned *jīva* will attain purification and the supreme liberation from transmigration.

Parā prakṛti and *Aparā prakṛti*

There are two types of *prakṛti: parā prakṛti* and *aparā prakṛti.* The *jīva* is called *parā,* or superior, *prakṛti:* the *jīva* is above the inferior energy, dead matter, which is called *aparā prakṛti.* The *jīva* is also called the marginal energy, because, although purely spiritual, he comes sometimes under the influence of *aparā prakṛti* (*māyā*) and sometimes under the influence of the spiritual energy.

Bhagavān Kṛṣṇa describes the energies of the Supreme in this way:

> Earth, water, fire, air, space, mind, intelligence, and false ego—altogether these eight comprise my separated material energies [*prakṛti*]. Besides this inferior nature, O mighty-armed Arjuna, there is a superior energy of Mine, which are all living entities who are struggling with material nature and are sustaining the universe.[43]

The *jīvas* "sustain the universe," for they are the superior energy (*parā prakṛti*) working within matter (*aparā prakṛti*). The *jīvas* can manipulate matter for their enjoyment. Of itself, *aparā prakṛti* (earth, water, fire and so on) has no potency to generate the innumerable manifestations within the universe. The activities of the universe result from the active *jīvas* moving inert matter. Thus, the Vedic version opposes the conception of a universe operating mechanistically, without any spiritual touch. Because they are the superior spiritual energy, the *jīvas* can create many things; but in no case are they the supreme *puruṣa.* Thus, they cannot create matter out of nothing; nor can they create life from matter. They can only manipulate what they have received.

The *jīva* simply imitates the real *puruṣa,* who is Bhagavān, the Supreme Personality of Godhead. Because in reality the *jīva* is not the *puruṣa,* by imitating the *puruṣa* he brings endless trouble on himself. In material life, every *jīva* thinks, "I am the *puruṣa,* the lord, the enjoyer." This is called illusion (*māyā*). The *jīva* does have a certain degree of controlling power, but in all cases this is limited. The Vedic literatures advocate that the *jīva* abandon his futile attempt to become God by manipulating *aparā prakṛti.*

Brahmā—Śiva—Viṣṇu

There are many misconceptions current about the "Hindu trinity" of Brahmā, Śiva, and Viṣṇu. Generally, dictionaries define Brahmā as "the chief member of the Hindu trinity,"[44] and other sources describe a triumvirate Godhead with all gods being equal. The very term "trinity" suggests an attempt to apply Christian theology to Vedic literature in the manner of the early Christian missionaries. The pioneer Indologist Sir William Jones once made this comment:

> Very respectable natives have assured me that one or two missionaries have been absurd enough, in their zeal for the conversion of the Gentiles, to urge that the Hindus were even now almost Christians because their Brahmā, Viṣṇu, and Maheśa [Śiva] were no other than the Christian trinity; a sentence in which we can only wonder whether folly, ignorance, or impiety predominates.[45]

In any case, the *Vedas* do not support these widespread theories. All three personalities are classified as *guṇa-avatāras,* controllers of the modes of nature. Brahmā creates the material universe and controls the mode of passion. Viṣṇu maintains the universe and controls the mode of goodness, and Śiva destroys the universe and controls the mode of ignorance.

Brahmā, a very powerful *jīva,* is the first living being born in the universe. His life endures for the entire life-span of the universe, and when the universe is annihilated, he dies. Compared to humans, his life span is long indeed:

> By human calculation, a thousand ages taken together is the duration of Brahmā's one day. And such also is the duration of his night. When Brahmā's day is manifest, this multitude of living entities come into being, and at the arrival of Brahmā's night they are all annihilated.[46]

Yet *Brahma-saṁhitā* compares Brahmā to a jewel whose brilliance merely reflects the light of the sun.[47] Brahmā creates the cosmos under the direction and inspiration of Bhagavān, the Supreme Personality of Godhead.

Śiva is in charge of the destruction of the universe at the time of annihilation. He is also in charge of the *tamo-guṇa* (the mode of ignorance), although we should not conclude that he is ignorant. One of his names is Āśutoṣa, which indicates that he is easily pleased. Śiva accepts worshipers among the most fallen beings, including ghosts and demons, who worship him for material benedictions (which are easy to obtain). *Bhāgavata Purāṇa* (12.13.16) states, *vaiṣṇavānāṁ yathā śambhuḥ:* "Śiva is the greatest Vaiṣṇava [devotee of Viṣṇu]." In *Padma Purāṇa,* Śiva makes this remark to his wife:

> My dear Pārvatī, there are different methods of worship, and, out of all, the worship of the Supreme Person [Bhagavān] is considered the highest. But even higher than the worship of the Supreme Bhagavān is the worship of His devotees.[48]

Viṣṇu is an expansion of Bhagavān Kṛṣṇa, the source of all incarnations. There are many expansions of Viṣṇu, and all are the one Supreme Person, Bhagavān. One Viṣṇu expansion maintains the universe and controls *sattva-guṇa,* the mode of goodness. Of the three *guṇa-avatāras,* Viṣṇu is the only one who can award liberation from *saṁsāra* (*hariṁ vinā naiva sṛtiṁ taranti*). It is therefore imprecise to regard devotion to Brahmā or Śiva as providing commensurate benefit; for from the platform of *tamas* and *rajas* one can hardly realize the Absolute Truth. The mode of goodness serves as a springboard from which one can transcend all the modes and realize his pure relationship with the supreme transcendental Bhagavān. Since Brahmā and Śiva are expansions of Viṣṇu, we can appreciate Louis Renou's observation, "In fact, as a religion in the strict sense of the term, Hinduism can almost be summarized as Viṣṇuism."[49]

Śruti and *Smṛti*

Vedic authorities accept three sources of Vedic knowledge, called *prasthāna-traya. Śruti-prasthāna* refers to the four *Vedas* and the *Upaniṣads. Nyāya-prasthāna* refers to the *Vedānta-sūtra,* and *smṛti-prasthāna* refers to the *Purāṇas, Bhagavad-gītā,* and *Mahābhārata.* Some empiric scholars argue that whereas *śruti* is acceptable, *smṛti* is not. They contend that the *Vedas* (*śruti*) constitute original knowledge and that the *Purāṇas* are recent collections of imaginary stories. Others say that *Vedānta* (*nyāya* or logical argument) can be accepted, but not the *Purāṇas* (*smṛti*). Indeed, they even question whether *smṛti*—which includes *Bhagavad-gītā*—can be acceptable as Vedic authority.

We have already pointed out that the *ācārya* Madhva deems that the *Vedas, Vedānta, Purāṇas,* and *Mahābhārata* are Vedic *śāstra* and that whatever these literatures enunciate is valid evidence. The *ācārya* Śaṅkara also accepts *Bhagavad-gītā* and compares the *Gītā* to a cow that delivers the essence of the *Vedas* and the *Upaniṣads.* Jīva Gosvāmī, in his *Kṛṣṇa-sandarbha,* quotes from *śruti* that *aitihāsya-purāṇa* (historical *Purāṇas*) must be accepted especially for this age. Rūpa Gosvāmī, in his *Bhakti-rasāmṛta-sindhu* (1.2.101), postulates that by adhering to the *śrutis* alone one is simply mouthing the words of the scriptures and not understanding or practicing them.

It is the empiric scholars, not the *ācāryas,* who contest the authority of *smṛti.* The four original *Vedas* are *śruti*—they came down orally. (*Śruti* means "hearing"; *smṛti* means "remembering" [what was originally spoken].) Whereas *śruti* is compared to the mother, *smṛti* is compared to the sister; after a child hears from his mother, he again learns from the descriptions given by his sister. One cannot deny the authority of *Bhagavad-gītā* or *Bhāgavata Purāṇa* simply because they are *smṛti.* The Vedic teacher Vācaspati Miśra states in the *Bhāmatī* that this would be *śruti-smṛti-virodhaḥ:* in conflict with both the *śruti* and the *smṛti.* Śaṅkara, Rāmānuja, and Madhva presented *smṛti* as valid evidence and wrote commentaries on *Bhagavad-gītā.* As we shall see in the next chapter, Vedic literature stands as a single, comprehensive whole meant for transcendental understanding. When we reject major portions, the Vedic literatures appear incomplete, incoherent, and inconclusive. Consequently, the Vedic tradition prompts the student of these literatures to hear the *śāstra* from a fully realized *ācārya* (*guru*).

4 / Vedic Literature—Siddhānta and History

The word *siddhānta* means "conclusion." We might ask whether the Vedic literature actually has a *siddhānta.* Does a comprehensive theme unite the many books? If the purpose is ultimately one, why do the *śāstras* appear to present many different philosophies? Why do they stress so many different forms of worship and meditation? Do the *śāstras* themselves give a plausible history of the Vedic literature?

Generally, scholars base their answers to these questions upon the historical order in which they believe the books appeared. Thus, there has arisen the theory that the *Ṛg Veda* appeared before the *Upaniṣads* and the *Purāṇas.* As hundreds and thousands of years passed and people's attitudes changed, different philosophies and sects are supposed to have developed. Many scholars conclude that around 200 B.C. monotheism arose. From this view it appears that Vedic literature comes from no single master plan.

Vedic literature, however, has its own version of the Vedic *siddhānta* and history. To understand the Vedic version, we have simply to let the writings speak for themselves.

The Vedic *Siddhānta*

Where should we look for the Vedic *siddhānta?* Is there any one work epitomizing and clarifying the different thematic strains, their relative positions and conclusions? Clearly, such a compendium of the *Vedas* would have to be authoritative and acceptable to all schools of thought. And clearly, of all works, *Bhagavad-gītā* best meets these qualifications. For this reason alone the *Gītā* has become the best known and most frequently translated of all Vedic writings. Here, indeed, is an instance in which the academic scholars and Vedic *ācāryas* agree. Śaṅkara described the *Gītā* as "an epitome of the essentials of the whole Vedic teachings." Rāmānuja put the keystone of his entire philosophy in his *Gītā-bhāṣya* (commentary on *Bhagavad-gītā*). Śrīdhara Svāmī declared, "The *Gītā,* which issued from the lotuslike lips of Padmanābha Himself [Bhagavān

Kṛṣṇa] must be well assimilated; what is the use of the multiplicity of other scriptures?"[1] Thomas Hopkins observed, "The greatness and continuing importance of the *Gītā* lies in its success in achieving a complex and multipurpose synthesis."[2] The prominent *Gītā* commentator His Divine Grace A. C. Bhaktivedanta Swami Prabhupāda writes that the *Gītā* is "the essence of Vedic knowledge. Because *Bhagavad-gītā* is spoken by the Supreme Personality of Godhead, one need not read any other Vedic literature."[3] He adds that if one is so fortunate as to read the *Gītā* without motivated interpretation, he surpasses all studies of Vedic wisdom and all scriptures.

It is also of this great work that Louis Renou writes, "For almost everyone the *Bhagavad-gītā* is the book par excellence."[4] Ananda K. Coomerswamy describes the *Gītā* as "a compendium of the whole Vedic doctrine to be found in the earlier *Vedas, Brāhmaṇas* and *Upaniṣads,* and being therefore the basis of all later developments, it can be regarded as the focus of all Indian religion."[5] About two hundred years ago, translations began appearing in the West, and, among others, Immanuel Kant, Henry David Thoreau, Ralph Waldo Emerson, and Aldous Huxley have accepted the *Gītā* as their introduction to Vedic wisdom.

Within its seven hundred verses, *Bhagavad-gītā* contains the main issues of Vedic philosophy. If one reads the *Gītā* in the proper spirit, he can gain Vedic knowledge through the natural process of *śabda.* In the *Gītā* the crisis-ridden disciple Arjuna accepts Kṛṣṇa as his spiritual master. Arjuna is a warrior, and his dialogue with Kṛṣṇa takes place just before a huge battle is to begin on the field of Kurukṣetra. Seeing his friends and relatives on the other side, Arjuna suddenly loses his desire to fight and becomes confused about his duty. Bhagavān Kṛṣṇa then begins to give His instructions, which are consonant with the totality of Vedic knowledge. Indeed, Kṛṣṇa often alludes to and even quotes *śāstras* such as the *Vedānta-sūtra.*

If we use *Bhagavad-gītā* as a guide to the *siddhānta* of all the *śāstras*—if it is, as Śaṅkara says, "the epitome of essentials"—we may next ask, "What is the essence of *Bhagavad-gītā?*" Not a difficult question, really. For Kṛṣṇa repeatedly declares the highest *yogī* to be he who is exclusively devoted in love to Bhagavān, the Supreme Personality of Godhead. Kṛṣṇa affirms that this doctrine of devotion to and love for the Supreme is "the most confidential part of the Vedic scriptures."[6] In the final verses Kṛṣṇa concludes that Arjuna should abandon all other *dharmas* and simply surrender unto Him. "I shall deliver you from all sinful reaction. Do not fear."[7]

The student should not confuse the Kṛṣṇa of *Bhagavad-gītā* with the "rural, sectarian god" envisioned by many scholars. Of the *Gītā's* Bhagavān Kṛṣṇa, Hopkins writes, "Kṛṣṇa has been revealed as the Supreme Lord [in the *Bhagavad-gītā*], identified with the Vedic Brahman and Puruṣa and with the universal form of Viṣṇu. He is the culmination of all the religious forms of the *Vedas*."[8] Ainslee Embree comments, "Throughout the *Gītā* is the assumption that transcending and completing the disciplines of work and knowledge is the way of devotion to Kṛṣṇa as the Supreme Lord. To surrender to Him, men find the final end they seek—the realization of their true self. It is this emphasis on devotion that has made the *Gītā* the scripture that appeals most directly to the heart of the Indian people."[9]

When we turn to the history of the compilation of the *śāstras,* we can see how the great themes of *Bhagavad-gītā* resound harmoniously throughout the entirety of Vedic literature.

Vedic History

We have already pointed out that there is no accurate empirical reckoning of Vedic literature's oral tradition. Moriz Winternitz concludes, "Vedic literature extends from an unknown past (say *x*) to 500 B.C."[10] However, it is generally admitted that the teachings are indeed very ancient and were committed to writing centuries after their actual composition. Dr. Radhakrishnan writes, "An historical treatment of Indian philosophy has not been taken up by the great Indian thinkers themselves."[11] This was because the Vedic *ācāryas* themselves saw no need for further investigation, since the scriptures substantiate the basic history of their origin as follows: (1) The oral tradition began simultaneous to the cosmic creation, when the Supreme Being spoke Vedic knowledge to the first living being, Brahmā.[12] (2) Vyāsadeva, a powerful literary incarnation of Bhagavān, recorded the *Vedas* at the beginning of the Kali millennium, some five thousand years ago.

Bhāgavata Purāṇa (1.4.17–25) describes the sage Vyāsadeva in this way:

> The great sage, who was fully equipped in knowledge, could see through his transcendental vision the deterioration of everything material due to the influence of the age [Kali-yuga]. He could see also that the faithless people in general would be reduced in duration of life and would be impatient due to lack of

> goodness. . . . He saw that the sacrifices mentioned in the *Vedas* were means by which the people's occupations could be purified. And to simplify the process he divided the one *Veda* into four in order to expand them among men. . . . The historical facts and authentic stories mentioned in the *Purāṇas* are called the fifth *Veda.* After the *Vedas* were divided into four divisions, Paila Ṛṣi became the professor of the *Ṛg Veda,* Jaimini the professor of the *Sāma Veda,* and Vaiśampāyana alone became glorified by the *Yajur Veda.* The Sumantu Muni Āṅgirasa . . . was entrusted with the *Atharva Veda* . . . and Romaharṣaṇa was entrusted with the *Purāṇas* and historical records. All these learned scholars, in their turn, rendered their entrusted *Vedas* unto their many disciples, grand-disciples, and great-grand-disciples, and thus the respective branches of the followers of the *Vedas* came into being. Thus, the great sage Vyāsadeva . . . edited the *Vedas* so they might be assimilated by less intellectual men. Out of compassion, the great sage thought it wise that this would enable men to achieve the ultimate goal of life. Thus, he compiled the great historical narration called the *Mahābhārata* for women, laborers, and friends of the twice-born [unqualified relatives of *brāhmaṇas*].[13]

According to this version, the *śāstras* are not the works of many hands over thousands of years. Of course, scholars disagree with this account because it contradicts our present conception of ancient civilizations, but the followers of the *Vedas* accept the śāstric statements as correct. Whatever version one accepts, a significant question remains. If the *śāstras* are harmonious, why do they appear to highlight different aspects of the Absolute Truth? Bearing this question in mind, we now look at different parts of the *Vedas* themselves.

The Four *Vedas*

The word *veda* means "know" and denotes divine knowledge. The *Vedas* are mainly hymns, chanted by priests, in praise of the gods. For many centuries these hymns were not written down. The *Ṛg Veda,* "the *Veda* of praise," consists of 1,017 hymns arranged in ten books. Most of the verses are in praise of Agni, the god of fire, and Indra, the god of rain and the heavens. Their use is confined to those trained in the disciplines of spiritual life. Known as the "sacrificial *Veda,*" the *Yajur Veda* contains instructions for performing sacrifices. The *Sāma Veda* is the "*Veda* of chants" and consists of 1,549 verses, many of which also appear, in different contexts, within the *Ṛg Veda.* In particular, the *Sāma Veda* praises the heavenly beverage, *soma.* The *Atharva Veda* contains chants and rites, often for healing sickness. Although the Vedic rituals are challengingly intricate, many scholars pass them off as savage incantations. Seeking to correct this view, Ainslee Embree writes, "*Vedas* means 'hymns.' They are not, then, the spiritual outpourings of the heart of primitive men at the dawn of history, as has sometimes been suggested; they are the achievement of a highly developed religious system."[14]

Generally, people are attracted to the *karma-kāṇḍa* portion, which deals mainly with fruitive activity for elevation to heavenly planets. It is stated that if one wants such material opulence one must perform the Vedic sacrifices. Ignorant of the actual Vedic *siddhānta,* many people have thought the *karma-kāṇḍa* portions to be the ultimate.

The four *Vedas* encourage satisfaction of material desires through worship of the demigods. For instance, one who desires sex should worship the heavenly king Indra, and one who desires good progeny should worship the great progenitors called the Prajāpatis. One who desires good fortune should worship Durgādevī, and one who desires power should worship Agni, the god of fire. One who aspires for money should worship the Vasus, and one who desires a strong body should worship the earth. In any case, the Vedic literature depicts the demigods not as imaginary but as authorized agents of the supreme will who administer universal affairs. The functions of nature do not go on willy-nilly; for each aspect there is a personality in charge. Indra, for instance, allots rainfall, and Varuṇa presides over the oceans.

We should note, however, that none of these gods—they number some thirty-three million—are ever equated with Bhagavān, the Supreme. Sacrificial hymns offered to the demigods generally conclude with the words *oṁ tat sat. Ṛg Veda* (1.2.22.20) states, *oṁ tad viṣṇoḥ paramaṁ padaṁ sadā paśyanti sūrayaḥ:* "The demigods are always looking to that supreme abode of Viṣṇu."[15] *Bhagavad-gītā* gives confirmation:

oṁ-tat-sad iti nirdeśo
brahmaṇas tri-vidhaḥ smṛtaḥ
brāhmaṇās tena vedāś ca
yajñāś ca vihitāḥ purā

> From the beginning of creation, the three syllables *oṁ tat sat* have been used to indicate the Supreme Absolute Truth [Brahman]. They were uttered by *brāhmaṇas* while chanting the Vedic hymns and during sacrifices, for the satisfaction of the Supreme.[16]

The three words *oṁ tat sat* indicate the Absolute Truth, the Supreme, Bhagavān (Viṣṇu). These words are uttered to assure the perfection of the sacrifice. Some scholars are surprised to find that the *Purāṇas* describe Lord Viṣṇu (or, Lord Kṛṣṇa) as the highest aspect of the Absolute Truth when supposedly the *Vedas* do not stress the point. And consequently many scholars conclude that Viṣṇu grew in popularity over the centuries. But actually the *Vedas* do stress the words *oṁ tat sat, oṁ tad viṣṇoḥ.* Whenever someone worshiped a demigod (Indra or Varuṇa or whomever) he made obeisances to Viṣṇu for success. In *Bhagavad-gītā,* Kṛṣṇa asserts that the benefits of the demigods are in actuality "bestowed by Me alone."[17] Because the four *Vedas* deal mainly with material elevation, and because Viṣṇu is the Lord of liberation from material illusion, most sacrifices are to the demigods and not to Viṣṇu. Yet by reciting *oṁ* and *oṁ tad viṣṇoḥ,* even the followers of the *karma-kāṇḍa* acknowledge Viṣṇu as the ultimate benefactor.

In *Bhagavad-gītā* Kṛṣṇa criticizes the followers of the four *Vedas* who do not know the ultimate purpose of sacrifice—*veda-vāda-ratāḥ pārtha nānyad astīti vādinaḥ:*

> Men of small knowledge are very much attached to the flowery words of the *Vedas,* which recommend various fruitive activities for elevation to heavenly planets, resultant good birth, power, and so forth. Being desirous of sense gratification and opulent life, they say that there is nothing more than this.[18]

The Vedic *siddhānta* established in *Bhagavad-gītā* corresponds to that of the four *Vedas,* although in the *Vedas* it is not so thoroughly developed. Nonetheless, there are many references in the four *Vedas* to the supremacy of the Supreme Bhagavān. *Atharva Veda* makes this statement: "The Supreme Person desired to create living entities, and thus Nārāyaṇa created all living beings. From Nārāyaṇa, Brahmā was born. Nārāyaṇa created all the Prajāpatis [the patriarchs]. Nārāyaṇa created Indra."[19] Also, *yo brahmāṇaṁ vidadhāti pūrvaṁ yo vai vedāṁś ca gāpayati sma kṛṣṇaḥ:* "It was Kṛṣṇa who in the beginning instructed Brahmā in the Vedic knowledge and who disseminated Vedic knowledge in the past."[20] The *Vedas* specify, *brahmaṇyo devakī-putraḥ:* "The son of Devakī, Kṛṣṇa, is the Supreme Personality."[21] We also find, "In the beginning of the creation there was only the Supreme Personality Nārāyaṇa. There was no Brahmā, no Śiva, no fire, no moon, no stars in the sky, no sun. There was only Kṛṣṇa, who creates all and enjoys all."[22]

Bhagavān Kṛṣṇa assessed the four *Vedas* in this way:

> The *Vedas* mainly deal with the subject of the three modes of material nature. Rise above these modes, O Arjuna. Be transcendental to all of them. Be free from all dualities and from all anxieties for gain and safety, and be established in the self.[23]

Although the *karma-kāṇḍa* portions of the *Vedas* give direction for material aggrandizement, the *Vedas* are actually meant for elevation to transcendental life. When the *karma-kāṇḍa* activities of sense gratification are finished, the chance for spiritual realization is offered in the form of the *Upaniṣads.*

The *Upaniṣads*

The *Upaniṣads* are a collection of 108 philosophical dissertations. The word *upa-ni-ṣat* means "sit closely" and refers to the disciple sitting closely beside his *guru* in order to receive transcendental Vedic wisdom. Thus, the *Upaniṣads* mark the beginning of transcendental life.

The *Upaniṣads'* main contribution is that they establish the Absolute as nonmaterial. The *Upaniṣads* describe Brahman as eternal, unmanifest reality from which all manifestations issue and in which they rest. Being inconceivable to material senses, Brahman is described as *nirguṇa* (without qualities) and *rūpa* (formless). In the words of *Bṛhad-āraṇyaka Upaniṣad* (3.9.26), Brahman "is incomprehensible, for it is not comprehended."[24] Thus, the wisdom of the *Upaniṣads* clearly transcends the *karma-kāṇḍa* portions of the four *Vedas,* for "the religious aim is no longer the obtaining of earthly and heavenly happiness by sacrificing correctly to the gods, but the release, as a result of true knowledge, from rebirth by absorption in the Brahman."[25] Although the *Upaniṣads* emphasize meditation upon the impersonal Brahman, they do not contradict the *siddhānta* epitomized in *Bhagavad-gītā;* the *Upaniṣads* do not deny that the Absolute Truth has personality. While denying that the

Godhead has material personality, the *Upaniṣads* do assert the Godhead's spiritual personality. For instance, the *Śvetāśvatara Upaniṣad* (3.19) clearly explains that the Absolute Truth has no material legs and hands but has spiritual hands with which He accepts everything offered to Him; and that, similarly, Bhagavān has no material eyes, but He does have spiritual eyes that see all. Further, although He has no material ears, He hears all, and, possessing all-perfect spiritual senses, He knows past, present, and future.

There are many similar Vedic hymns establishing the Supreme Absolute Truth as a person beyond the material world. For instance, the *Hayaśīrṣa Pañcarātra* explains that although every *Upaniṣad* first presents the Supreme Brahman as impersonal, at the end the personal form of Bhagavān emerges. As *Īśa Upaniṣad* indicates, the Supreme Absolute Truth is eternally both impersonal and personal. The invocation of the *Bṛhad-āraṇyaka Upaniṣad* states, "That [Supreme Being] is the whole—this [universe] is the whole. From the whole the whole comes forth."[26] *Śvetāśvatara Upaniṣad* (3.8) states, "I know the great Puruṣa, who is luminous, like the sun, and beyond darkness."[27] The *Aitareya Upaniṣad* (1.1.2) describes the supreme controller as the energetic cause of the creation: "He created these worlds. . . ."[28] The *Praśna Upaniṣad* (6.3) corroborates. The *Kaṭha Upaniṣad* affirms, "The Eternal among the eternals, the Consciousness among all consciousnesses . . . bestows the fruits [of activities to all the] *jīvas*. . . ."[29]

In addition to Brahman and Bhagavān realization, the *Upaniṣads* also speak about realization of the intermediate, localized form, the Paramātmā (Supersoul). The *Muṇḍaka, Śvetāśvatara,* and *Kaṭha Upaniṣads* state that within the heart of every living entity there reside both the individual atomic *jīva* and the Supersoul, the Paramātmā. They are like two birds sitting in the tree of the body. One of the birds (the individual *jīva*) is eating the fruit of the tree (that is, enjoying the senses), and the other bird (Paramātmā) is simply witnessing. The *jīva's* forgetfulness of his relationship with the Paramātmā causes him to change his position from one tree to another (the process of transmigration). Both the *Kaṭha* and *Śvetāśvatara Upaniṣads* give a further comment: Although the two birds are in the same tree, the bird that is eating is fully engrossed as the enjoyer of the fruits of the tree. If, in some way or other, he turns his face to his friend, who is the Lord, and recognizes His glories, he is at once delivered from all anxieties.[30]

Throughout the *Upaniṣads* we see that the individual *jīva* and the Paramātmā, the Supersoul, retain their separate individuality, although they attain a kind of oneness when the *jīva* agrees to act according to the Paramātmā's will. Whatever the case, neither the Supreme Paramātmā nor the individual *jīva* ever loses individuality. This is important, because as we will later see, the concept of *bhakti* stressed in *Bhagavad-gītā* is lost if the *jīva* becomes one with the Supreme Brahman in all respects. In *bhakti,* a loving relationship develops between the individual *jīva* and the Supreme Person, Bhagavān. In no instance should we confuse the *jīva* with the supreme *puruṣa.* If one confuses these or attempts to merge them into one, he loses the ultimate *siddhānta* of the Vedic literature.

By describing the antimaterial quality (*nirguṇatva*) of the Absolute, the *Upaniṣads* prepare the way for a proper understanding of the transcendental personality (Bhagavān) who possesses all spiritual opulences and is the ultimate object of all meditation and *bhakti* (devotion).

Vedānta-sūtra

Vedānta-sūtra consists of codes revealing the method of understanding Vedic knowledge, and it is the most concise form of all Vedic knowledge. According to the *Vāyu* and *Skanda Purāṇas,* "A *sūtra* is a code that expresses the essence of all knowledge in a minimum of words. It must be universally applicable and faultless in its linguistic presentation."[31]

Scholars know the *Vedānta-sūtra* by a variety of names, including (1) *Brahma-sūtra,* (2) *Śārīraka,* (3) *Vyāsa-sūtra,* (4) *Bādarāyaṇa-sūtra,* (5) *Uttara-mīmāṁsā* and (6) *Vedānta-darśana.* There are four chapters (*adhyāyas*) in the *Vedānta-sūtra* and four divisions (*padas*) in each chapter. Thus, *Vedānta-sūtra* is known as *ṣoḍaśa-pada* because it contains sixteen divisions of codes. The theme of each division is fully described in terms of five different subject matters (*adhikaraṇas*), which are technically called *pratijñā, hetu, udāharaṇa, upanaya,* and *nigamana.* Every theme must necessarily be explained with reference to *pratijñā,* or a solemn declaration of the purpose of the treatise. At the beginning of the *Vedānta-sūtra* there is the solemn declaration of purpose, *athato brahma-jijñāsā:* "Now is the time to inquire about the Absolute Truth." Reasons (*hetu*) must be expressed, examples (*udāharaṇa*) must be given in terms of various facts, the theme (*upanaya*) must gradually be brought nearer for understanding, and finally it must be supported by authoritative quotations (*nigamana*) from the Vedic *śāstras.*

According to the great lexicographer Hemacandra (also known as Kośakāra), *Vedānta* comprises the purport of the *Upaniṣads,* which are themselves part of the *Brāhmaṇa* portions of the *Vedas.*[32] As Professor

Apte describes in his dictionary, the *Brāhmaṇa* portion provides the rules for employing hymns at various sacrifices and gives detailed accounts of the hymns' origins.[33] (The *mantra* portion, on the other hand, contains the hymns themselves.) So Hemacandra said that the *Vedānta-sūtra* forms the supplement of the *Vedas*. Since *Veda* means "knowledge," and *anta* means "the end," *Vedānta* provides the proper understanding of the *Vedas'* ultimate purpose. We may again note that the *Upaniṣads,* which are themselves parts of the *Vedas' Brāhmaṇa* portion, support the knowledge given in the codes of the *Vedānta-sūtra*.

The Histories (*Itihāsas*)

The histories, or *Itihāsas,* are supplementary Vedic literatures. They include the *Mahābhārata* and the *Purāṇas*. Because the Vedic rituals are hard to understand and the *Vedānta-sūtra* is compressed and highly philosophical, the histories offer Vedic knowledge in the form of stories and historical incidents. The *Chāndogya Upaniṣad* refers to the *Mahābhārata* and *Purāṇas* as the fifth *Veda*.[34]

The Vedic *ācāryas* consider the stories in the *Purāṇas* to be actual histories, not just of this planet but of many planets within the universe. Undoubtedly, some of the historical data taken from other planets does not accord with life on this planet (for example, fabulously long life spans or the ability to fly without mechanical aid). But there is no reason for regarding the *Purāṇas* as later additions. What may be incomprehensible is not necessarily inauthentic. A. Embree writes, "The *Purāṇas*. . . were depicting their understanding of the universe, where the supernatural was commonplace, miraculous births were ordinary."[35] Followers of the *Purāṇas* argue that considering the situations of different planets and differences in time and circumstance, one should not find the *Purāṇas* difficult to understand. In other words, "It is high time that the scholars give up their prejudices and give the *Purāṇas* a due place as a source on ancient Indian history."[36] Advocates of the *Purāṇas* argue that the great *ṛṣi* Vyāsadeva did not inject imaginary tales in his literature. Vyāsadeva and the great *ācāryas* contemporary to and following him—Śukadeva, Sūta, Maitreya, and, more recently, Rāmānuja and Madhva—accepted the *Purāṇas* as authentic Vedic literature.

The *Purāṇas* mainly deal with the superhuman activities of Bhagavān and His various incarnations in various ages. Also chronicled are the activities of the sages and devotees of Bhagavān. Although there is no strict historical chronology to these Purāṇic stories, the Vedic *ācāryas* do not consider them imaginary. Modern historians look in vain for a key to understanding them, and ultimately frustrated, the historians at last offer theories about their compilation.

The *Mahābhārata,* the story of "the greater kingdom of Bhārata-varṣa," describes the history of the ancient world empire. Comprising some 100,000 four-line stanzas, the *Mahābhārata* is the longest poem in world literature, and Vedic tradition certifies it as the work of Vyāsadeva. This epic relates how the pious Pāṇḍavas overthrew the demoniac dynasty of the Kurus. The Kurus cheated the Pāṇḍava brothers of their right to the throne, exiled them to a forest, and on their return denied them their land. The work centers on the ensuing eighteen-day battle between the sons of Kuru and their cousins, the sons of Pāṇḍu. Sometimes called the "*Veda* of Kṛṣṇa," the *Mahābhārata* highlights Bhagavān Kṛṣṇa—especially in its main segment, *Bhagavad-gītā.*

There are eighteen major *Purāṇas,* six composed for people in the mode of ignorance, six for those in the mode of passion, and six for those in the mode of goodness. Of all the *Purāṇas,* the *Bhāgavata Purāṇa* is foremost and most widely read. Also, the *Bhāgavata Purāṇa* (*Śrīmad-Bhāgavatam*) is considered the most direct commentary on the *Vedānta-sūtra,* since Vyāsadeva is the author of both.

As its main subject matter, the *Bhāgavatam* portrays Bhagavān Kṛṣṇa and His associates and devotees. The other *Purāṇas* also delineate different methods by which one can worship the demigods, but *Bhāgavatam* discusses only the Supreme Bhagavān. Its opening verse (*janmādy asya yataḥ*) corresponds to the opening verse of *Vedānta-sūtra* and indicates that Vyāsadeva is writing directly about the Absolute Truth, the source of all emanations.[37] Since it centers on the worship of the Supreme Personality of Godhead, Bhagavān Śrī Kṛṣṇa, one may say that *Śrīmad-Bhāgavatam* transcends the *karma-kāṇḍa* sections of the *Vedas* (dealing with sacrifices for material gain), the *jñāna-kāṇḍa* sections (dealing with philosophical inquiries), and the *upāsanā-kāṇḍa* sections (dealing with demigod worship). *Śrīmad-Bhāgavatam* (1.2.6) itself defines the highest path in this way: "That religion is best which causes its followers to become ecstatic in love of God, which is unmotivated and free from material impediments, for this only can satisfy the self."[38]

Sometimes the *bhakti* path indicated by this verse draws the criticism that it is intended for those who cannot pursue higher philosophy. But according to the *Bhāgavatam* itself (1.2.12), real *bhakti* must be based on a realization of all Vedic literature (in other words, *bhakti* must develop in pursuance of Vedānta philosophy): "The Absolute Truth is realized by the seriously inquisitive student or sage who is well-equipped with knowledge and who has become detached by rendering devotional service and hearing the *Vedānta-sūtra.*"[39]

As George Hart writes, "The *Bhāgavata Purāṇa* is among the finest works of devotion ever written, being equalled in my opinion only by other works in the Indian language."[40] Nonetheless, one must understand *Śrīmad-Bhāgavatam* in the light of Vedānta philosophy. *Vedānta-sūtra* explains the Absolute Truth through impeccable logic and argument, and *Śrīmad-Bhāgavatam* is an elaborate commentary upon the *Vedānta-sūtra.* Generally, professional reciters of *Śrīmad-Bhāgavatam* dwell upon the *rāsa-līlā* section, which describes Kṛṣṇa's famous dance with the damsels of Vṛndāvana. Taken out of context, this section (Tenth Canto, Chapters 29–35) actually becomes an obstacle to one's understanding of Bhagavān Kṛṣṇa and the Vedic *siddhānta.*

Śrīmad-Bhāgavatam takes up where *Bhagavad-gītā* leaves off. *Bhagavad-gītā* affirms that if one knows about the transcendental appearance and activities of Bhagavān Kṛṣṇa, he can be liberated from the cycle of birth and death.[41] *Śrīmad-Bhāgavatam* begins with the acknowledgement of Bhagavān Kṛṣṇa as the cause of all causes and then goes on to narrate the transcendental pastimes from Kṛṣṇa's appearance to His disappearance. Thus, *Śrīmad-Bhāgavatam* is sometimes called the postgraduate study of *Bhagavad-gītā.*

Śrīmad-Bhāgavatam centers on Bhagavān Kṛṣṇa as the ultimate Vedic and Vedāntic conclusion. Since only Bhagavān Kṛṣṇa exhibits the complete features of the Godhead, He is confirmed as the source of all incarnations, including the expansions of Viṣṇu. *Ete cāṁśa-kalāḥ puṁsaḥ kṛṣṇas tu bhagavān svayam*—Bhagavān Kṛṣṇa is the *summum bonum.* That is *Bhāgavatam's* predominant theme.[42] Now let us see how this *siddhānta* corresponds to the teachings of the *ācāryas.*

5 / The Teachings of the Ācāryas

An *ācārya* is a teacher of Vedic knowledge. He imparts the teachings of the *śāstras* and himself lives by those teachings. For centuries the *ācāryas* have guided the destiny of the Vedic culture. Generally, people trust the instructions of the Vedic *ācāryas* because these teachers afford perfect examples in their own actions. In addition, the care of the Vedic *paramparā* (the passing down of Vedic knowledge) has always been entrusted to the *ācāryas;* therefore, they are the personal representatives of that knowledge. Although an *ācārya* speaks according to the time and circumstance in which he appears, he upholds the original conclusion, or *siddhānta,* of the Vedic literature.

Śaṅkara

Śaṅkara (A.D. 788–820) was a Shaivite (follower of Śiva) born in an orthodox South Indian *brāhmaṇa* family. When still a young boy, he became an ascetic and, it appears, compiled his two major works (*Viveka-cuḍāmaṇi* and *Śārīraka-bhāṣya*). He traveled widely over India and died in the Himalayas at age thirty-two.

At the time Śaṅkara appeared, Buddhism had received the patronage of the Indian emperor Aśoka and had thus spread throughout India. Śaṅkara sought to reform and purify religious life by reasserting the authority of the Vedic scriptures, which Buddha had completely rejected.

Śaṅkara's interpretation of Vedic literature is known as *advaita-vedānta* (nondualistic Vedānta) because he posited that the *jīva* is identical with God. Although there are many śāstric statements describing the Absolute Truth as the Supreme Person and the *jīvas* as His subordinate, eternal parts, Śaṅkara taught that the *jīvas* are themselves the Absolute Truth (Parabrahman) and that there is ultimately no variety, individuality, or personality in spiritual existence. He taught that the supposed individuality of both the Supreme Being and the *jīva* is false.

In denying the plurality of *jīvas,* Śaṅkara differed from all orthodox Vedic schools. Further, Śaṅkara held that questions about the origin of the cosmos are unanswerable and that the nature of *māyā* is inexplicable. To account for the Vedic verses describing *īśvara,* the Supreme Person, as the cause of all causes, Śaṅkara developed a twofold theory of Brahman. For him, there were two aspects of Brahman—the pure impersonal Brahman and the Brahman manifest in the universe as the Lord. In order to arrive at this conclusion, Śaṅkara reinterpreted or rejected most of the Vedic *smṛti,* and he pointedly contradicted *Bhagavad-gītā* and the *Purāṇas* by equating *jīva* and Bhagavān. Ostensibly, Śaṅkara accepted the authority of *Bhagavad-gītā,* but his interpretations of the verses opposed the clear *siddhānta* of the *Gīta.*

Thus, Śaṅkara's philosophy is sometimes considered a compromise between theism and atheism. Since it would have been impossible to restore the Vedic literature's theistic conception just after the Buddhists' complete atheism, Śaṅkara made a logical compromise to fit the time and circumstance. His interpretations resemble Buddhism, but he rested his case on the authority of Vedic literature. Śaṅkara lived only thirty-two years, but wherever in India he traveled, his philosophy prevailed and Buddhism bowed.

Over a long period, Śaṅkara's *Śārīraka-bhāṣya* was for many the definitive rendition of *Vedānta,* and for some scholars (notably Radhakrishnan and Moore in *A Source Book in Indian Philosophy*) it remains so. Troy Organ expresses another viewpoint:

> This line of thought has unfortunately been given support by many philosophers of the West who have been advised that nondual Vedānta is a true picture and the supreme development of Hinduism. This must be written off as a form of special pleading of a noble and brash form of living Hinduism.[1]

Rāmānuja

Rāmānuja (A.D. 1017–1137) was a South Indian *brāhmaṇa* who taught and traveled widely. For a time he was the chief priest of the Vaiṣṇava temple of Śrī Raṅga, in southern India. This temple is located on an island at the confluence of the Kāverī and Kolirana rivers, near Tricinapallī, in the district of Tāñjora. Rāmānuja wrote three major commentaries: *Vedārtha-saṅgraha* (on the *Vedas*), *Śrī-bhāṣya* (on *Vedānta-sūtra*), and *Bhagavad-gītā-bhāṣya* (on the *Bhagavad-gītā*). He is best known for his robust presentation of Vaiṣṇavism (worship of Viṣṇu, or Bhagavān) and for his opposition to the impersonal monism of Śaṅkara.

Rāmānuja expounded *viśiṣṭādvaita,* or qualified nondualism. He taught that there is a difference between Parabrahman (Supreme Brahman) and the *jīvas* (eternally fragmentary souls). Not accepting Śaṅkara's elimination of the loving relationship (*bhakti*) between the Supreme and the *jīvas,* Rāmānuja sought to expose Śaṅkara's philosophical contradictions and his defiance of the Vedic *siddhānta.* On the other hand, Rāmānuja accepted the Vedic statements concerning the qualitative oneness of the Supreme and the *jīvas.* He thus presented his philosophy of qualified oneness by giving logical reasons to show that the Absolute includes both what is changing (the material world and the *jīvas* caught up in *saṁsāra*) and what is changeless (the transcendental Lord).

By way of analogy, Rāmānuja discussed the relation between the body and the soul: just as the *jīva* controls his body, God controls the material world and the *jīvas* within it; just as the body is an instrument for the *jīva,* the material cosmos is an instrument for God. After liberation, the self exists eternally in a spiritual body; whereas the soul experiences events, the material body simply determines the kind of experiences the soul goes through. Rāmānuja also described that the body and soul cannot be separated; either materially every living body has a self (*ātmā*), or by his *karma* every self has a certain type of body. After liberation, the self also exists eternally in a spiritual body. The soul experiences, but the body doesn't, although the body determines the kind of experiences the soul goes through. By the analogy of inseparable body and soul, the Supreme Lord is understood to be both Supreme Soul and the cosmos. In this way, adhering to Vedic principles, Rāmānuja explained the variegated material world as part of the Absolute Truth. The eternal, unchanging nature of the Absolute (that is, of the Supreme Lord) does not contradict His maintaining the changing material world. Rāmānuja taught that through God's grace the *jīva* can transcend the material world and attain the eternal abode of Viṣṇu.

Madhva

Like Rāmānuja, Madhva (A.D. 1239–1319) belonged to the Vaiṣṇava tradition and devoted himself to combating Śaṅkara's impersonal philosophy. Madhvācārya's *Pūrṇaprajña-bhāṣya* establishes a type of Vedānta philosophy called *śuddha-dvaita* (pure dualism). In his teachings Madhva describes three entities—the Supreme Lord, the *jīva,* and the material world. Even more emphatically than Rāmānuja, Madhva maintained that God and the *jīvas* are eternally distinct. Whereas Śaṅkara had described the Lord as the material cause of the cosmos, Madhva accepted the direct meaning of the *smṛti-śāstras* and held that the Lord is transcendental to the material world, which is the product of His inferior energy (*aparā prakṛti*). In other words, God is distinct from His material creation. At the same time, the *jīvas* are also distinct from matter, for they are the superior, spiritual energy of the Lord.

Madhva maintained that although the *jīvas* are superior to matter, they are distinct from the Lord and are His servitors. Whereas the Lord is independent, the *jīvas* are totally dependent on Him. Madhva taught that the Lord creates, maintains, and annihilates the cosmos, and at the same time, in His original eternal form as Bhagavān Kṛṣṇa, the Lord remains superior to manifest and unmanifest matter. In addition, Madhva explained that each person molds his own *karma,* and that through *bhakti* one can eliminate all his *karma* and return to his original position of serving the Lord in the eternal spiritual world.

Caitanya

In the late sixteenth century, with the advent of Kṛṣṇa Caitanya, in Bengal, Rāmānuja's and Madhva's theistic philosophy of Vaiṣṇavism (worship of Viṣṇu, or Bhagavān) reached its climax. Caitanya's philosophy of *acintya-bhedābheda-tattva* completed the progression to devotional theism. Rāmānuja had agreed with Śaṅkara that the Absolute is one only, but he had disagreed by affirming individual variety within that oneness. Madhva had underscored the eternal duality of the Supreme and the *jīva:* he had maintained that this duality endures even after liberation. Caitanya, in turn, specified that the Supreme and the *jīvas* are "inconceivably, simultaneously one and different" (*acintya-bheda-abheda*). He strongly opposed Śaṅkara's philosophy for its defiance of Vyāsadeva's *siddhānta.*

In rejecting impersonalism, Caitanya said that it clouds the Vedic literature's meaning. He explained the direct meaning of the *śāstras* as devotion (*bhakti*) to Bhagavān Kṛṣṇa. Thus, Caitanya made an unprecedented contribution. Here was the possibility of a devotional relationship between God and man. Rūpa Gosvāmī, an early disciple, described Caitanya's unique gift: "O most munificent incarnation! You are Kṛṣṇa Himself appearing as Śrī Kṛṣṇa Caitanya Mahāprabhu. . . . You are widely distributing pure love of Kṛṣṇa. We offer our respectful obeisances unto You."[2]

We know more about Kṛṣṇa Caitanya than about the earlier *ācāryas,* thanks to such biographical sources as *Śrī Caitanya-caritāmṛta* (A.D. 1616), by Kṛṣṇadāsa Kavirāja Gosvāmī. Caitanya (A.D. 1486–

1534) was born in Navadvīpa, Bengal. He took the renounced order (*sannyāsa*) at the age of twenty-four. His spiritual master, Īśvara Purī, was a disciple of Mādhavendra Purī, who came in the line of Madhva. Caitanya's immediate followers (the six Gosvāmīs: Rūpa, Sanātana, Jīva, Gopāla Bhaṭṭa, Raghunātha Bhaṭṭa and Raghunātha dāsa) compiled extensive Sanskrit literatures and thus documented Caitanya's philosophical system according to Vedic evidence. Himself, Caitanya wrote only eight verses, on the ecstasy of devotion to Kṛṣṇa. His disciples understood Caitanya to be Bhagavān Kṛṣṇa Himself appearing in the form of a devotee.

Some observers have charged Caitanya with introducing an erotic element into *bhakti* philosophy. What Caitanya actually taught was that the original and pure sex psychology exists in the person of the Absolute Truth, Bhagavān Kṛṣṇa. The pure exchange of pleasure between the Supreme Bhagavān and His liberated servitors is characteristic of the highest spiritual relationship. This exchange is not tainted by mundane sex and cannot even be understood by a person still affected by material desire. When conditioned *jīvas* try to understand the loving affairs of Bhagavān Kṛṣṇa, they misconstrue Bhagavān Kṛṣṇa as a mundane "god of love." Himself a *sannyāsī* noted for strict avoidance of women and worldly affairs, Caitanya pointed out that the *jīva's* relationship with Bhagavān Kṛṣṇa is eternally pure and transcendental. His personality demonstrated conjugal longing for Kṛṣṇa. Further, Caitanya taught that this conjugal mood is one of five original relationships between the *jīvas* and Bhagavān. Finally, in Caitanya's view anyone can attain transcendental devotion to Bhagavān (God) if he absorbs himself in chanting Bhagavān's names.

6 / Impersonalism Versus Theism

In his *Vedānta* commentary *Śārīraka-bhāṣya,* Śaṅkara accepts the Vedic principle that beyond matter there is eternal, spiritual existence. Yet he insists that this existence is impersonal. So, as some have observed, Śaṅkara at once accepts and rejects Vedic literature.

Basic Tenets of Śaṅkara's Vedānta Commentary:

1) The Absolute Truth As Impersonal

According to the Vaiṣṇava *ācāryas,* the Absolute Truth would be incomplete without personality. *Vedānta-sūtra* proposes, *athāto brahma-jijñāsā:* "Let us inquire into the Absolute Truth." Then *Vedānta-sūtra* defines the Absolute Truth thus: *janmādy asya yataḥ:* "The Absolute Truth is that from which everything is emanating." So the Vaiṣṇava *ācāryas* deduce that the Absolute Truth, the source of all cosmic variety (living beings, planets, space, time, and so on) must also possess the qualities that are emanating. One such quality, of course, is personality. In other words, the Absolute Truth, or the complete whole (*oṁ pūrṇam*), must possess all the qualities of its parts.[1] The Vaiṣṇavas thus accept the threefold aspects of Brahman, Paramātmā, and Bhagavān (as defined in Chapter Three).

However, Śaṅkara portrays the impersonal Brahman as ultimate, to the exclusion of Paramātmā and Bhagavān. He asserts that eternal existence is devoid of form, senses, activity, and individual consciousness. He disregards the Vedic account of a positive spiritual relationship between the liberated *jīva* and the Supreme Brahman, Parameśvara.

Some Śaṅkarites maintain that a novice may think of the Absolute Truth as a person to facilitate meditation. In any case, Śaṅkarites maintain that ultimately Brahman is formless. For Śaṅkara and the Śaṅkarites, the empirical world is an illusion, and Brahman alone is truth. Śaṅkara advertised *nirguṇa* (qualityless) Brahman as the only reality, but even the *Upaniṣads,* which stress the impersonal Brahman, affirm the spiritual form, name, and personality of the Absolute Truth.

In *Bhagavad-gītā* Bhagavān Kṛṣṇa affirms that He is the source of everything material and spiritual and that Brahman rests in Him.[2] The

Śaṅkarites interpret the *aham* ("I") of *Bhagavad-gītā* to refer to the impersonal Brahman, but the Vaiṣṇava theists contend that *aham* directly refers to the person Bhagavān. In other words, *aham* has a specific meaning and is not a vague term subject to interpretation.

Whereas the Vaiṣṇava followers of *Vedānta* embrace the philosophical method called *mukhya-vṛtti* (explanation by direct meaning), the Śaṅkarite philosophers employ the method called *gauṇa-vṛtti* (explanation by indirect meaning). *Mukhya-vṛtti* means exact dictionary definition, whereas *gauṇa-vṛtti,* when misapplied, degenerates into word jugglery. The Vaiṣṇavas argue that if one accepts the Vedic authority on its own terms (as emanating from Nārāyaṇa Himself), there will be no scope for fanciful interpretation or indirect meaning. They consider the Vedic *śāstras* to be *apauruṣeya,* above the four defects of illusion, error, and so on; but Śaṅkara boldly implies that in some of *Vedānta-sūtra's* codes, Vyāsadeva betrays a poor understanding of logic and grammar. On this basis, Śaṅkara changes prefixes and suffixes in the original codes in order to make them consistent with the philosophy of *Śārīraka-bhāṣya.*

The Śaṅkarites try to negate material distress by merging with Brahman and extinguishing individual existence. Thus, according to the Vaiṣṇava theists, the Śaṅkarites deny the *jīva* the opportunity to enjoy eternal variegated pleasure on the spiritual platform. For Śaṅkara, after one becomes free from all material desires and realizes his spiritual identity he can merge with Brahman. According to the Vaiṣṇava theists, the *jīva* cannot remain merged in Brahman eternally. *Āruhya kṛcchreṇa paraṁ padaṁ tataḥ patanty adho 'nādṛta-yuṣmad-aṅghrayaḥ:* Although by severe austerities impersonalist philosophers attain liberation from material activities and rise to Brahman, they must come down again to the material world due to having imperfect knowledge of the Absolute Truth.[3] The Vaiṣṇavas contend that because the personal identity of the *jīva* is eternal, the *jīva* must either take up personal relationships birth after birth in material bodies or transcend material life and reestablish himself in his eternal personal relationship with the Supreme Bhagavān. In other words, the Vaiṣṇavas contend that eternal *mokṣa* is not possible outside one's personal relationship with the Supreme Bhagavān.

2) *Ātmā* and Brahman Are One

Śaṅkara gave great emphasis to the Sanskrit phrase *tat tvam asi* ("You are that also"), which alludes to the *jīva's* qualitative oneness with the

Supreme. To support his monistic interpretation, Śaṅkara concluded that the living entity (*ātmā* or *jīva*) is equal in every respect to the Supreme Brahman. He therefore defined liberation (*mokṣa*) in terms of the *jīva's* abandonment of his illusory sense of individuality and his subsequent merging into Brahman. Vedic literature does affirm that the *jīva* is not the body and that the sense of material individuality is due to *māyā's* influence. All transcendentalists proclaim *ahaṁ brahmāsmi:* "I am not the body; I am spirit soul," as stated in the *Bṛhad-āraṇyaka Upaniṣad* (1.4.10). The theists, however, maintain that although the *jīva* is spirit, he is not identical in all ways with the all-pervading, omniscient Parabrahman. They maintain that although all *jīvas* are Brahman, Bhagavān is the principal eternal amongst eternals (*nityo nityānām*) and is beyond both the fallible and infallible.[4] This is the philosophy of *acintya-bhedābheda-tattva,* simultaneous oneness and difference. For the theist, the *jīvas* are one in quality with the Supreme Brahman, but His quantity is infinite and theirs infinitesimal.

Śaṅkara posited that all such distinctions are products of illusion and are false because the only truth is Brahman, the impersonal Absolute. Vaiṣṇava theists maintain that to substantiate this point, Śaṅkara repeatedly defied the śāstric *siddhānta.* Madhva elaborated the eternal distinction between the finite spirit soul and the Supreme Spirit and contested the theory of an impersonal Absolute in great detail. Rāmānuja likened the supreme *īśvara* to a great fire and all the individual *jīvas* to sparks in that fire. The theists maintain that the Vedic literature makes a clear distinction between the *jīvas* and the Supreme, who are one in quality but not in quantity. The Vaiṣṇavas liken the individual *jīva* to a gold earring made of gold but at the same time distinct from the reservoir of gold, the gold mine. The theists maintain that Bhagavān Kṛṣṇa proclaims eternal, spiritual individuality in *Bhagavad-gītā* when He tells Arjuna, "Never was there a time when I did not exist, nor you, nor all these kings; nor in the future shall any of us cease to be."[5]

The Vaiṣṇavas also maintain that bliss (*ānanda*) cannot exist outside a relationship. The *Vedānta-sūtra* (1.1.12) states *ānandamayo 'bhyāsāt,* which intimates that the Supreme Absolute is blissful in His loving exchanges with His parts and parcels. Richard Lannoy writes, "According to the *bhakti* mystics, perfect identity of *ātman* with Brahman in a state of pure isolation precludes the further possibility of a relation of love to God and can only lead to a condition of spiritual sterility."[6]

Śaṅkara also encouraged worshiping the deity form of various demigods (five in particular) for realizing the ultimate equality of the living being and the Supreme Lord. By worshiping a form composed of material energy, Śaṅkara believed, one could realize the quality of Brahman behind the various forms. For Śaṅkara, worship was a passing process meant to elevate one to impersonal unity. Of course, the Vaiṣṇava theists reject this position. They believe that one cannot equate the Supreme Bhagavān with the demigods or with one's own self (*ātmā*). They distinguish between worship of the self, worship of the demigods, and worship of the Supreme Bhagavān. They cite the twelfth and thirteenth *mantras* of *Īśa Upaniṣad* to substantiate this position.[7]

The Vaiṣṇava theists argue that if the *ātmā* were actually the same as the Supreme, the *ātmā* could never fall into the illusion of material identity. In other words, "If I am Brahman, the greatest, why am I covered by ignorance?" Since the Vedic literatures do not admit that the Supreme is subject to such delusion, the Vaiṣṇava theists call the Śaṅkarites Māyāvādīs, indicating that they have inadvertently stated that *māyā* (illusion) covers the potency of the Supreme. The theists maintain that it is impossible for the Supreme Bhagavān to be illusioned.

3) The Theory of Emanations Denied

Śaṅkara denied that the Absolute Truth is the source of the material cosmos. In his refutation of Vyāsadeva's original *pariṇāma-vāda* (the theory of the emanation of all existences from the Supreme Brahman), Śaṅkara said that if the Absolute Truth expanded into the *jīvas,* the universes, and all-pervading souls, His original nature would change. Since the Absolute Truth must be changeless, He cannot expand into different energies. In other words, if one tears a piece of paper into many pieces, the paper no longer exists as an individual entity. The Vaiṣṇava theists counter by citing the *acintya-śakti,* the inconceivable potencies of the Absolute. According to the Vedic version, the Supreme possesses inconceivable potencies by which He can distribute Himself throughout the universe as all-pervasive energy and yet remain the complete whole. In the words of *Īśa Upaniṣad,* "Because He is the complete whole, even though so many complete units emanate from Him, He remains the complete balance."[8]

The Vaiṣṇava *ācāryas* maintain that the Supreme Brahman must exist both as infinite whole and also as finite parts. If He were only infinite, He could not be perfectly complete to reciprocate with His parts in transcendental bliss. If the *puruṣa* were formless and one, He would be like a king without subjects. Thus, the Vaiṣṇava *ācāryas* hold that the Supreme Bhagavān is the energetic source of all energies (*janmādy asya*) and that His energies are constantly changing, or transforming. Through his indirect interpretation, Śaṅkara contended that if the Absolute Truth were in any way transformed, His oneness would be no more. The Vaiṣṇava theists point out that Śaṅkara contradicts Vyāsadeva: according to the latter's version, it is the by-product or energy of the Supreme that is transformed, and not the Supreme; the Supreme always remains whole and complete. Thus, in the Vaiṣṇava view, Śaṅkara's alteration of the theory of emanations was an attempt to establish impersonalism by discrediting the Vedic conception.

4) The Theory of Illusion

Śaṅkara substituted for *pariṇāma-vāda* his own *vivarta-vāda,* or theory of illusion. Maintaining that the material world has no reality, he stated *brahma satyaṁ jagan mithyā:* "Brahman is real; the universe is false." Śaṅkarites often give the example that seeing the world as real is like mistaking a rope for a snake, but Vaiṣṇavas object that the nonreality of the material cosmos is not substantiated by Vedic *śāstra.* In *Bhagavad-gītā* Kṛṣṇa explicitly states that material nature is His "divine energy" and is under His control. Practically speaking, the conditioned soul has to deal with the material world; he cannot simply say that it does not exist. For the Vaiṣṇavas, the universe has a dual purpose. The *jīvas* can enjoy their senses under the spell of *māyā,* and eventually they can see their folly, reform, attain liberation, and finally return to their spiritual nature. The material world is a stage for this drama. It is real in that it is the energy of the Supreme, and it is illusory in that it is temporary. A mirage presupposes the existence of real water. A rope mistaken for a snake presupposes the existence of a real snake. The conditioned *jīvas* mistakenly consider the material world their real home, but the Vaiṣṇavas maintain that their eternal home of friendship and love is the spiritual world of the Supreme Bhagavān. In his *Gītā-bhāṣya,* Śaṅkara himself called Bhagavān Kṛṣṇa transcendental to the material cosmos (*nārāyaṇaḥ paro 'vyaktāt*). But rallying around the theory of illusion and virtually rejecting the supremacy of Bhagavān, the Śaṅkarites (Māyāvādīs) have created a subtle form of atheism garbed as Vedic knowledge.

Although the Śaṅkarites do not accept the original *Vedānta-sūtra* without Śaṅkara's commentaries, there are a number of other major commentaries to *Vedānta,* including those of Rāmānuja and Madhva and the *acintya-bhedābheda-tattva* of Caitanya. Apart from these, as the Vaiṣṇavas point out, the most direct commentary on *Vedānta-sūtra* comes from its author, Vyāsadeva. That is the *Bhāgavata Purāṇa.* Supportive evidence is found in the *Garuḍa Purāṇa: sarva-vedānta-sāraṁ hi śrī-bhāgavatam iṣyate.*

The Real Śaṅkara

The *Padma Purāṇa* discloses that Śaṅkara is an incarnation of Lord Śiva. In that work, Lord Śiva makes this intimation to his wife Pārvatī:

> My dear wife, hear my explanations of how I have spread ignorance through Māyāvāda philosophy. Simply by hearing it, even an advanced scholar will fall down. In this philosophy, which is certainly very inauspicious for people in general, I have misrepresented the real meaning of the *Vedas* and recommended that one give up all activities in order to achieve freedom from *karma.* In this Māyāvāda philosophy I have described the *jīvātmā* and Paramātmā to be one and the same. The Māyāvāda philosophy is impious. It is covered Buddhism. My dear Pārvatī, in the form of a *brāhmaṇa* in Kali-yuga I teach this imagined Māyāvāda philosophy. In order to cheat the atheists, I describe the Supreme Personality of Godhead to be without form and without qualities. Similarly, in explaining *Vedānta* I describe the same Māyāvāda philosophy in order to mislead the entire population toward atheism by denying the personal form of the Lord.[9]

Naturally, the question arises, "Why would Lord Śiva do such a thing?" According to the *śāstras,* he was simply following orders. In the *Śiva Purāṇa,* the Supreme Bhagavān told Lord Śiva, "In Kali-yuga, mislead the people in general by propounding imaginary meanings from the *Vedas* to bewilder them."[10]

Thus, the *Vedas* indicate, Śaṅkara took up the impersonalist guise so that he could discharge the duty given him by the Supreme Lord: to discredit the Buddhists and to reassert Vedic authority. Within his lifetime, Śaṅkara revealed a number of times that he was actually a highly advanced devotee of the Supreme Bhagavān. He never denied the spiritual form known as *sac-cid-ānanda-vigraha,* the eternal, all-blissful form of knowledge existing before the material creation. Indeed, in the very first verse of his *Gītā-bhāṣya,* he asserts that Nārāyaṇa, the Supreme Bhagavan, is transcendental to the material creation. In his *Meditation on the Bhagavad-gītā,* he writes, *namo 'stu te vyāsa:* "Salutations to thee, O Vyāsa. Thou art of mighty intellect, and thine eyes are as large as the petals of the full-blown lotus. It was thou who brightened this lamp of wisdom, filling it with the oil of the *Mahābhārata.*"[11] He describes Bhagavān Kṛṣṇa as the *guru* of the universe and teacher of all the worlds and offers his obeisances, *kṛṣṇāya gītāmṛta-duhe namaḥ:* "Salutations to thee, O Supreme Lord, for Thou art the milker of the ambrosia of the *Gītā.*"[12] As Śaṅkara also points out, *vedaiḥ sāṅga-pada-kramopaniṣādaiḥ:* it is Bhagavān Kṛṣṇa "whose glories are sung by the verses of the *Vedas,* of whom the singers of the *Sāma* sing, and of whose glories the *Upaniṣads* proclaim in full choir."[13]

There are also a number of works, such as *Prayers for Kṛṣṇa,* in which Śaṅkara discloses his knowledge of *bhakti-yoga* in relation to Bhagavān. One of his last statements has become famous:

bhaja govindaṁ bhaja govindaṁ
bhaja govindaṁ mūḍha-mate
samprāpte sannihite kāle na hi
na hi rakṣati ḍukṛṅ-karaṇe

He is saying, "You intellectual fools, just worship Govinda, just worship Govinda, just worship Govinda. Your grammatical knowledge and word jugglery will not save you at the time of death." This was Śaṅkara's last advice; it was for all those who would become confused by intellectual wrangling and miss the actual Vedic *siddhānta.*

7 / The Vedic Social Philosophy

Hinduism

As Ainslee T. Embree has noted, the words "Hindu" and "Hinduism" are not found in the Vedic literature:

> The physical setting is the land known to the Western world since ancient times as India, a word borrowed by the Greeks from the Persians, who, because of the difficulty they had with the initial "s" called the great Sindhu River (the modern Indus) the "Hindu." It was this word that came to be applied by foreigners to the religion and culture of the people who lived in the land watered by the two rivers, the Indus and the Ganges, although the people themselves did not use the term.[1]

Of course, "Hindu" and "Hinduism" have come into very wide use, and every dictionary defines Viṣṇu as "the Hindu god," although no *ācārya* or scripture ever used the word. "Hindu religion" is also the name applied to describe all kinds of social, cultural, nationalistic, and religious activities, many of which are non-Vedic. To denote genuine Vedic society, the *śāstras* use the word "Āryan." For the followers of the *Vedas,* human advancement meant advancing toward spiritual realization, and a community with spiritual goals was known as an Āryan community. The Āryan social institution became known as *varṇāśrama-dharma,* which arranges society in eight groupings. We shall now examine Vedic social philosophy in the practical terms of *varṇāśrama-dharma.*

The God-centered Society

Sociologist Pitirim Sorokin might describe *varṇāśrama* society in his own terminology as an "ideational culture," that is, a culture whose world view is primarily metaphysical instead of sensate or sensual. The first *mantra* of *Īśa Upaniṣad* provides this ideational culture's basic idea:

> Everything animate or inanimate within the universe is controlled and owned by the Lord. One should therefore accept only those things necessary for himself, which are set aside as his quota, and one should not accept other things, knowing well to whom they belong.[2]

This is the motto of the *īśāvāsya,* God-centered, society. *Īśa* refers to the Supreme Absolute Person, Bhagavān.

According to this view, the *jīvas* do not own anything. Nor can the community or state assume ownership. As *Īśa Upaniṣad* explains, nature has designated for each species an allotment ample both for survival and for peace and happiness. By instinct, animals adhere to these natural regulations in their eating, sleeping, mating, and defending, but human beings have the unique propensity to enjoy and possess things beyond their natural allotment. The *Vedas* direct man to follow the natural regulations. *Varṇāśrama-dharma* upholds that by divine arrangement everyone will receive his necessities, and that there will be no scarcity, provided that humanity lives in its natural, sane condition.

Houston Smith points out that religions have to become socially active if they are to remain relevant, but that they must not break away from "religion's earlier concerns" if they are to remain religious.[3] According to the conception of *īśāvāsya,* found in *Īśa Upaniṣad,* both material needs and transcendental aspirations find fulfillment in a God-centered society. There was no problem of hunger or unemployment under the rule of the Vedic *rājarṣis* (saintly kings), nor was there heavy industrialization that created artificial needs. The goal of the *īśāvāsya* society was not merely peaceful material life but full opportunity for all to attain liberation from *saṁsāra.*

Dharma—Artha—Kāma—Mokṣa

Vedic literature prescribes religion (*dharma*), economic development (*artha*), sense gratification (*kāma*), and liberation (*mokṣa*). A society is not considered civilized if it does not pursue these goals in a regulated fashion. The *Bhāgavata Purāṇa* (4.22.34) clarifies:

> Those who strongly desire to cross the ocean of nescience must not associate with the modes of ignorance [*tamas*] because hedonistic activities are the greatest obstructions to realization of religious principles, economic development, regulated sense

> gratification and, at last, liberation. The Vedic literature describes eating, sleeping, mating, and defending as being common to the human being and the animal. *Dharma,* however, is the human being's special prerogative.[4]

Those who desire material gain execute pious activities and perform religious functions recommended in the *Vedas.* Petitioning God for material benefit may not be pure *bhakti,* but it is a common phenomenon. The *Vedas* encourage recognition of Bhagavān's proprietorship, and *artha,* economic development, as the goal of religion in the material context. Economic gain is necessary for increased sense gratification (*kāma*), and liberation from material life (*mokṣa*) becomes attractive when one is disillusioned with the temporary happiness of sense gratification. Of the four activities, liberation is considered most important. "Out of the four principles—namely, religion, economic development, sense gratification, and liberation—liberation has to be taken very seriously. The other three are subject to destruction by the stringent law of nature—death."[5]

Varṇāśrama-dharma

The Vedic literature confirms that *varṇāśrama-dharma* has been existing since time immemorial. It proceeds not from man but from Bhagavān Kṛṣṇa Himself, who states in *Bhagavad-gītā, cātur-varṇyam mayā sṛṣṭaṁ guṇa-karma-vibhāgaśaḥ:* "According to the three modes of material nature and the work ascribed to them, the four divisions of human society were created by Me."[6] In other words, the *varṇāśrama* system has existed from the dawn of civilization. The *Viṣṇu Purāṇa* explains further:

varṇāśramācāravatā
puruṣeṇa paraḥ pumān
viṣṇur ārādhyate panthā
nānyat tat-toṣa-kāraṇam

"The Supreme Personality of Godhead, Lord Viṣṇu, is worshiped by the proper execution of prescribed duties in the system of *varṇa* and *āśrama.* There is no other way to satisfy the Supreme Personality of Godhead. One must be situated in the institution of the four *varṇas* and *āśramas*" (*Viṣṇu Purāṇa* 3.8.9).[7]

The four *varṇas* (social orders) include (1) the *brāhmaṇas,* teachers and spiritual advisors; (2) the *kṣatriyas,* administrators and warriors;

(3) the *vaiśyas,* farmers and businessmen; and (4) the *śūdras,* laborers and craftsmen. These *varṇas* are not political or social factions; they are natural categories to be found in every human civilization.

According to the Vedic conception, in every community throughout the world there are intellectuals (those motivated by goodness, or *sattva-guṇa*), militarists and politicians (those motivated by passion, or *rajo-guṇa*), farmers and businessmen (those motivated by both passion and ignorance), and common laborers (those motivated by ignorance, or *tamo-guṇa*). The advocates of *varṇāśrama-dharma* maintain that although the system may deteriorate into hereditary casteism, its original form emanates from the Supreme Bhagavān and is therefore sound and congenial. In fact, society becomes successful only when these natural orders cooperate for spiritual realization. The *Bhāgavata Purāṇa* (1.2.13) says this: "it is therefore concluded that the highest perfection one can achieve, by discharging his prescribed duties [*dharma*] according to caste divisions and order of life, is to please the Lord Hari [the Supreme Bhagavān]."[8]

In addition to the four *varṇas,* there are four *āśramas,* or spiritual orders. These are (1) *brahmacarya* (celibate student life), (2) *gṛhastha* (married householder life), (3) *vānaprastha* (retired life), and (4) *sannyāsa* (renounced life).

The Āryans regarded the *varṇāśrama* institution as the ideal material instrument by which mankind could rise to the spiritual platform. If everyone pleased God by his occupational service, there would be peace and prosperity in society, and the individual could finally attain *mokṣa.* As *varṇāśrama-dharma* exists in its present corrupt form in India, people claim to be *brāhmaṇas* and *kṣatriyas* by birth alone, even though they may not personally possess the qualities of *brāhmaṇas* or *kṣatriyas.* In *Bhagavad-gītā* Kṛṣṇa specifically states that He created the four orders according to *guṇa* and *karma,* not according to birth. By these criteria, it is safe to say that in the present age of Kali a pure *varṇāśrama-dharma* society has not yet existed.

According to the Vedic literature, in ages past the *varṇāśrama-dharma* was not simply a token conception but a worldwide system. Its most important ingredient for success was a strong, pious king who accepted advice from the *brāhmaṇas.* The Vedic histories relate that kings such as Pṛthu, Prahlāda, Dhruva, Rāmacandra, Yudhiṣṭhira and Parīkṣit ruled ideally for thousands of years. But, as foretold in the *śāstras,* the present age of Kali has corrupted the pure *varṇāśrama-dharma* outlined in the Vedic literature.

Duties in the Four Social Orders

In the Vedic conception, the social body is analogous to the human body, or to the body of *īśvara* (Bhagavān). Accordingly, the *brāhmaṇas* are the head, the *kṣatriyas* the arms, the *vaiśyas* the waist, and the *śūdras* the legs. In the social body, as in any other body, all parts are important, and no one neglects any part, yet the brain is especially important because it delivers information to the other parts.

Among the brahminical qualities, the *śāstras* mention control of the mind and the senses, tolerance, simplicity, cleanliness, knowledge, truthfulness, devotion, and faith in the Vedic wisdom. The *brāhmaṇas* were teachers of all departments of Vedic knowledge, priests of Vedic functions, and recipients of charity. There is nothing in these descriptions to support Max Weber's view that the *brāhmaṇa* was "similar . . . to the ancient sorcerer."[9] Weber creates an occult, primitive aura around the *brāhmaṇa,* whom he consistently described as using "magic" and "charisma."[10]

According to *varṇāśrama* philosophy, the *brāhmaṇa* was not a strange, spell-casting wizard but a gentleman of perfect behavior and genuine spiritual knowledge. Lannoy has this to say:

> The spiritually perfected individual, however, is probably as widely idealized in India today as he ever was, even if few live up to the model. Nothing of comparable mass appeal has replaced him as the symbolic hub of the social wheel.[11]

Bhagavad-gītā also outlines the duties of the *kṣatriya* (warrior and administrator): "Heroism, power, determination, resourcefulness, courage in battle, generosity and leadership. . . ."[12] The *kṣatriyas* protected the helpless and gave gifts in charity. Although they were learned in the *śāstras,* they never assumed the position of teachers. Their duty was to fight for a righteous cause. In *Bhagavad-gītā,* for instance, Arjuna did not want to fight, but Kṛṣṇa urged him to fight because it was his duty as a *kṣatriya.*

The *śastra* also describes the duties of the *vaiśyas* and *śūdras:* "Farming, protection of cows, and business are the qualities of work for the *vaiśyas,* and for the *śūdras,* there is labor and service to others."[13] According to Vedic *śāstra,* the cow is associated with Bhagavān Kṛṣṇa and His pastimes and is also one of man's seven mothers. Therefore, by Āryan standards cow-killing is barbaric. As a king protects his human subjects, the *vaiśyas* protect the cows. The *vaiśya* is primarily an agriculturalist who raises grains and vegetables in village farms and tends cow herds. Vedic society was not advanced in industry and urbanization. According to the Vedic conception, one can live happily with a little land for growing his grains and grazing his cows. In this way, one's economic problems are solved. For the *vaiśyas,* wealth meant not money but cows, grain, butter, and milk. Apparently these people were accustomed to jewelry, fine clothing, and even gold, and they often exchanged these things for agricultural products.

The *śūdras* rendered service to the other three classes. *Śūdras* were men without propensities for intellectual, military, or mercantile life. Nonetheless, in *Bhagavad-gītā* Kṛṣṇa assures that every social order can attain the supreme goal: "Those who take shelter in Me, although they may be of lower birth—women, *vaiśyas* [merchants] as well as *śūdras* [workers]—can approach the supreme destination."[14]

According to his *karma,* the *jīva* attains a body situated in the modes of nature. Spiritually, the caste distinctions—as well as all other material distinctions—do not exist. At the same time, such material distinctions enable everyone in society to engage fully in serving and satisfying the Supreme Bhagavān.

Duties in the Four Spiritual Orders

The first order one enters is *brahmacarya,* celibate student life. According to the Vedic teacher Yājñavalkya, "The vow of *brahmacarya* helps one to abstain from sex indulgence in works, words, and mind—at all times, under all circumstances, and in all places." Therefore, one observes *brahmacarya* from childhood, when he has no knowledge of sex. At age five, children go to *gurukula,* the residence of the spiritual master, and the master trains them in the strict discipline of *brahmacarya.*

Brahmacārī training forms one's character for his whole life. During these early years, the spiritual master takes note of the student's propensities and determines the *varṇa* for which he is best suited. When a boy reaches twenty-five, he may leave *brahmacārī* life and the protection of the spiritual master in order to get married and take up household life. The idea is that, having undergone *brahmacārī* training, he will in no circumstance become the victim of unrestricted sex.

The Vedic moralist Cāṇakya Paṇḍita says that the educated man sees every woman except his own wife as his mother, he sees others' property as garbage in the street, and he treats everyone as he would like to be treated himself.

In the Vedic conception, restriction of sex is vital, because the sex drive is the most binding material desire. Because of sex attachment, one returns to the material world and undergoes material miseries in lifetime after lifetime. To be sure, the *varṇāśrama* system does accommodate the *jīva's* deep-rooted desire for sense gratification. In essence, the *varṇāśrama* system provides a life pattern in which one can satisfy his desires and in which also, through regulation, one can gradually detach himself from material bondage.

The *gṛhastha* (householder) has some license for sense pleasure not allowed in the other three *āśramas,* but everything is regulated so that he can fulfill his desires and yet become spiritually purified. In a *gṛhastha* marriage, sex is allowed only for producing good children. Although the *gṛhastha-āśrama* provides license for sex pleasure, the *Vedas* enjoin that one should not become a mother or father unless one can free his dependents from death. Purification of the child's existence begins at the time of conception in the mother's womb. In the *garbhādhāna-saṁskāra* ritual, the parents express their intention to beget a child, and they perform a ceremony to purify their consciousness prior to conception.

The third *āśrama* is called *vānaprastha,* or retired life. Even if one is ideally situated in the *gṛhastha-āśrama,* one is advised to free oneself from all family connection at the age of fifty in order to prepare for the next life. *Vānaprastha* is an intermediate stage between *gṛhastha* life and complete renunciation. In the *vānaprastha-āśrama,* the husband and wife discontinue sexual relations, but the wife may remain with the husband as his assistant. Ideally, they travel together to holy places of pilgrimage such as Hardwar, Hṛṣīkeśa, Vṛndāvana, and Purī. By traveling to these sanctified places, the *vānaprasthas* become detached from their home, family, and business affairs. Finally, the man breaks all family connections and takes up *sannyāsa,* the renounced order.

The *sannyāsī* is the spiritual master of all the *varṇas* and *āśramas,* and one who follows the Vedic injunctions is duty-bound to show him respect. Because he is the embodiment of renunciation, the *sannyāsī* is held in the highest esteem. If one is prepared to take *sannyāsa,* he approaches a *sannyāsī* and asks to receive the renounced order by Vedic ceremony. After he formally takes *sannyāsa,* he shaves his head, wears simple saffron robes, and carries a *sannyāsī's* staff (*daṇḍa*). He is considered civilly dead, and his wife, left in the charge of her older children, officially becomes a widow.

However, family ties are so strong that the new *sannyāsī* is first allowed to live in a cottage some distance from his home and accept food sent by his family. Hence, *kuṭīcaka* is the first of the four progressive stages of *sannyāsa* (*kuṭīcaka* means "one who lives in a cottage"). In the second stage (*bahūdaka*) one no longer accepts food from home, but goes to another village to preach Vedic knowledge. At this time he secures his meals by begging from door to door. In the third stage (*parivrājakācārya*) the *sannyāsī* places himself completely at the mercy of the Supreme Bhagavān and travels extensively to give spiritual instruction to whomever he meets. In the final stage (*paramahaṁsa,* or "swanlike man") one has completely realized himself as the eternal servant of the Supreme Bhagavān and is able to instruct others in the art of *bhakti-yoga,* love of God.

The *sannyāsī* who remains alone and constantly meditates on the Supreme Bhagavān is called *bhajanānandī.* The *sannyāsī* who accepts disciples is called *goṣṭhy-ānandī.* Of the *goṣṭhy-ānandī sannyāsī,* Bhagavān Kṛṣṇa makes this appraisal: "For one who explains the supreme secret to the devotees, devotional service is guaranteed, and at the end he will come back to Me. There is no servant in this world more dear to Me than he, nor will there ever be one more dear."[15]

Taking into account people's various positions in the modes of material nature, *varṇāśrama-dharma* provides a scientific arrangement to elevate everyone. The ultimate goal of Vedic culture is surrender to the Supreme Bhagavān, and this surrender is the *siddhānta* governing Vedic literature and tradition.

Readings

ŚRĪ ĪŚA UPANIṢAD

INVOCATION. The Personality of Godhead is perfect and complete, and because He is completely perfect, all emanations from Him, such as this phenomenal world, are perfectly equipped as complete wholes. Whatever is produced of the complete whole is also complete in itself. Because He is the complete whole, even though so many complete units emanate from Him, He remains the complete balance.

1. Everything animate or inanimate that is within the universe is controlled and owned by the Lord. One should therefore accept only those things necessary for himself, which are set aside as his quota, and one should not accept other things, knowing well to whom they belong.

2. One may aspire to live for hundreds of years if he continuously goes on working in that way, for that sort of work will not bind him to the law of *karma*. There is no alternative to this way for man.

3. The killer of the soul, whoever he may be, must enter into the planets known as the worlds of the faithless, full of darkness and ignorance.

4. Although fixed in His abode, the Personality of Godhead is swifter than the mind and can overcome all others running. The powerful demigods cannot approach Him. Although in one place, He controls those who supply the air and rain. He surpasses all in excellence.

5. The Supreme Lord walks and does not walk. He is far away, but He is very near as well. He is within everything, and yet He is outside of everything.

6. He who sees everything in relation to the Supreme Lord, who sees all entities as His parts and parcels and who sees the Supreme Lord within everything, never hates any thing nor any being.

7. One who always sees all living entities as spiritual sparks, in quality one with the Lord, becomes a true knower of things. What, then, can be illusion or anxiety for him?

8. Such a person must factually know the greatest of all, who is unembodied, omniscient, beyond reproach, without veins, pure and uncontaminated, the self-sufficient philosopher who has been fulfilling everyone's desire since time immemorial.

9. Those who engage in the culture of nescient activities shall enter into the darkest region of ignorance. Worse still are those engaged in the culture of so-called knowledge.

10. The wise have explained that one result is derived from the culture of knowledge and that a different result is obtained from the culture of nescience.

11. Only one who can learn the process of nescience and that of transcendental knowledge side by side can transcend the influence of repeated birth and death and enjoy the full blessing of immortality.

12. Those who are engaged in the worship of demigods enter into the darkest region of ignorance, and still more so do the worshipers of the impersonal Absolute.

13. It is said that one result is obtained by worshiping the supreme cause of all causes and that another result is obtained by worshiping that which is not supreme. All this is heard from the undisturbed authorities who clearly explained it.

14. One should know perfectly the Personality of Godhead and His transcendental name, as well as the temporary material creation with its temporary demigods, men and animals. When one knows these, he surpasses death and the ephemeral cosmic manifestation with it, and in the eternal kingdom of God he enjoys his eternal life of bliss and knowledge.

15. O my Lord, sustainer of all that lives, Your face is covered by Your dazzling effulgence. Please remove that covering and exhibit Yourself to Your pure devotee.

16. O my Lord, O primeval philosopher, maintainer of the universe, O regulating principle, destination of the pure devotees, well-wisher of the progenitors of mankind—please remove the effulgence of Your transcen-

dental rays so that I can see Your form of bliss. You are the eternal Supreme Personality of Godhead, like unto the sun, as am I.

17. Let this temporary body be burnt to ashes, and let the air of life be merged with the totality of air. Now, O my Lord, please remember all my sacrifices, and, because You are the ultimate beneficiary, please remember all that I have done for You.

18. O my Lord, powerful as fire, omnipotent one, now I offer You all obeisances and fall on the ground at Your feet. O my Lord, please lead me on the right path to reach You, and, since You know all that I have done in the past, please free me from the reactions to my past sins so that there will be no hindrance to my progress.

BHAGAVAD-GĪTĀ

1/ Observing the Armies on the Battlefield of Kurukṣetra

*Comparing the opposing armies.**

1. Dhṛtarāṣṭra said: O Sañjaya, after my sons and the sons of Pāṇḍu assembled in the place of pilgrimage at Kurukṣetra, desiring to fight, what did they do?
2. Sañjaya said: O King, after looking over the army arranged in military formation by the sons of Pāṇḍu, King Duryodhana went to his teacher and spoke the following words.
3. O my teacher, behold the great army of the sons of Pāṇḍu, so expertly arranged by your intelligent disciple the son of Drupada.
4. Here in this army are many heroic bowmen equal in fighting to Bhīma and Arjuna: great fighters like Yuyudhāna, Virāṭa and Drupada.
5. There are also great heroic, powerful fighters like Dhṛṣṭaketu, Cekitāna, Kāśirāja, Purujit, Kuntibhoja and Śaibya.
6. There are the mighty Yudhāmanyu, the very powerful Uttamaujā, the son of Subhadrā and the sons of Draupadī. All these warriors are great chariot fighters.
7. But for your information, O best of the *brāhmaṇas,* let me tell you about the captains who are especially qualified to lead my military force.
8. There are personalities like you, Bhīṣma, Karṇa, Kṛpa, Aśvatthāmā, Vikarṇa and the son of Somadatta called Bhūriśravā, who are always victorious in battle.

---

*The Kurus are led by the sons of Dhṛtarāṣṭra, chief of whom is Duryodhana; opposing them is the army led by the five Pāṇḍavas, chief of whom is Arjuna, who is befriended by Kṛṣṇa who is acting as Arjuna's chariot driver. The *Mahābhārata* relates that the Pāṇḍavas were unlawfully cheated out of their kingdom and forced to battle by Dhṛtarāṣṭra and his sons.

9. There are many other heroes who are prepared to lay down their lives for my sake. All of them are well equipped with different kinds of weapons, and all are experienced in military science.
10. Our strength is immeasurable, and we are perfectly protected by Grandfather Bhīṣma, whereas the strength of the Pāṇḍavas, carefully protected by Bhīma, is limited.
11. All of you must now give full support to Grandfather Bhīṣma, as you stand at your respective strategic points of entrance into the phalanx of the army.
12. Then Bhīṣma, the great valiant grandsire of the Kuru dynasty, the grandfather of the fighters, blew his conchshell very loudly, making a sound like the roar of a lion, giving Duryodhana joy.
13. After that, the conchshells, drums, bugles, trumpets and horns were all suddenly sounded, and the combined sound was tumultuous.
14. On the other side, both Lord Kṛṣṇa and Arjuna, stationed on a great chariot drawn by white horses, sounded their transcendental conchshells.
15. Lord Kṛṣṇa blew His conchshell, called Pāñcajanya; Arjuna blew his, the Devadatta; and Bhīma, the voracious eater and performer of herculean tasks, blew his terrific conchshell, called Pauṇḍra.
16–18. King Yudhiṣṭhira, the son of Kuntī, blew his conchshell, the Anantavijaya, and Nakula and Sahadeva blew the Sughoṣa and Maṇipuṣpaka. That great archer the King of Kāśī, the great fighter Śikhandī, Dhṛṣṭadyumna, Virāṭa, the unconquerable Sātyaki, Drupada, the sons of Draupadī, and the others, O King, such as the mighty-armed son of Subhadrā, all blew their respective conchshells.
19. The blowing of these different conchshells became uproarious. Vibrating both in the sky and on the earth, it shattered the hearts of the sons of Dhṛtarāṣṭra.
20. At that time Arjuna, the son of Pāṇḍu, seated in the chariot bearing the flag marked with Hanumān, took up his bow and prepared to shoot his arrows. O King, after looking at the sons of Dhṛtarāṣṭra drawn in military array, Arjuna then spoke to Lord Kṛṣṇa these words.

Arjuna overwhelmed, refuses to fight, and gives his reasons.

21–22. Arjuna said: O infallible one, please draw my chariot between the two armies so that I may see those present here who desire to fight and with whom I must contend in this great trial of arms.

23. Let me see those who have come here to fight, wishing to please the evil-minded son of Dhṛtarāṣṭra.
24. Sañjaya said: O descendant of Bharata, having thus been addressed by Arjuna, Lord Kṛṣṇa drew up the fine chariot in the midst of the armies of both parties.
25. In the presence of Bhīṣma, Droṇa and all the other chieftains of the world, the Lord said: Just behold, Pārtha, all the Kurus assembled here.
26. There Arjuna could see, within the midst of the armies of both parties, his fathers, grandfathers, teachers, maternal uncles, brothers, sons, grandsons, friends, and also his fathers-in-law and well-wishers.
27. When the son of Kuntī, Arjuna, saw all these different grades of friends and relatives, he became overwhelmed with compassion and spoke thus.
28. Arjuna said: My dear Kṛṣṇa, seeing my friends and relatives present before me in such a fighting spirit, I feel the limbs of my body quivering and my mouth drying up.
29. My whole body is trembling, my hair is standing on end, my bow Gāṇḍīva is slipping from my hand, and my skin is burning.
30. I am now unable to stand here any longer. I am forgetting myself, and my mind is reeling. I see only causes of misfortune, O Kṛṣṇa, killer of the Keśī demon.
31. I do not see how any good can come from killing my own kinsmen in this battle, nor can I, my dear Kṛṣṇa, desire any subsequent victory, kingdom, or happiness.
32–35. O Govinda, of what avail to us are a kingdom, happiness or even life itself when all those for whom we may desire them are now arrayed on this battlefield? O Madhusūdana, when teachers, fathers, sons, grandfathers, maternal uncles, fathers-in-law, grandsons, brothers-in-law and other relatives are ready to give up their lives and properties and are standing before me, why should I wish to kill them, even though they might otherwise kill me? O maintainer of all living entities, I am not prepared to fight with them even in exchange for the three worlds, let alone this earth. What pleasure will we derive from killing the sons of Dhṛtarāṣṭra?
36. Sin will overcome us if we slay such aggressors. Therefore it is not proper for us to kill the sons of Dhṛtarāṣṭra and our friends. What should we gain, O Kṛṣṇa, husband of the goddess of fortune, and how could we be happy by killing our own kinsmen?
37–38. O Janārdana, although these men, their hearts overtaken by greed, see no fault in killing one's family or quarreling with friends,

why should we, who can see the crime in destroying a family, engage in these acts of sin?

39. With the destruction of dynasty, the eternal family tradition is vanquished, and thus the rest of the family becomes involved in irreligion.

40. When irreligion is prominent in the family, O Kṛṣṇa, the women of the family become polluted, and from the degradation of womanhood, O descendant of Vṛṣṇi, comes unwanted progeny.

41. An increase of unwanted population certainly causes hellish life both for the family and for those who destroy the family tradition. The ancestors of such corrupt families fall down, because the performances for offering them food and water are entirely stopped.

42. By the evil deeds of those who destroy the family tradition and thus give rise to unwanted children, all kinds of community projects and family welfare activities are devastated.

43. O Kṛṣṇa, maintainer of the people, I have heard by disciplic succession that those who destroy family traditions dwell always in hell.

44. Alas, how strange it is that we are preparing to commit greatly sinful acts; driven by the desire to enjoy royal happiness, we are intent on killing our own kinsmen.

45. Better for me if the sons of Dhṛtarāṣṭra, weapons in hand, were to kill me unarmed and unresisting on the battlefield.

46. Sañjaya said: Arjuna, having thus spoken on the battlefield, cast aside his bow and arrows and sat down on the chariot, his mind overwhelmed with grief.

2/ Contents of the Gītā Summarized

Arjuna surrenders to Kṛṣṇa for instruction.

1. Sañjaya said: Seeing Arjuna full of compassion, his mind depressed, his eyes full of tears, Madhusūdana, Kṛṣṇa, spoke the following words.

2. The Supreme Personality of Godhead said: My dear Arjuna, how have these impurities come upon you? They are not at all befitting a man who knows the value of life. They lead not to higher planets but to infamy.

3. O son of Pṛthā, do not yield to this degrading impotence. It does not become you. Give up such petty weakness of heart and arise, O chastiser of the enemy.

4. Arjuna said: O killer of enemies, O killer of Madhu, how can I counterattack with arrows in battle men like Bhīṣma and Droṇa, who are worthy of my worship?

5. It would be better to live in this world by begging than to live at the cost of the lives of great souls who are my teachers. Even though desiring worldly gain, they are superiors. If they are killed, everything we enjoy will be tainted with blood.

6. Nor do we know which is better—conquering them or being conquered by them. The sons of Dhṛtarāṣṭra, whom if we killed we should not care to live, are now standing before us on this battlefield.

7. Now I am confused about my duty and have lost all composure because of miserly weakness. In this condition I am asking You to tell me for certain what is best for me. Now I am Your disciple, and a soul surrendered unto You. Please instruct me.

8. I can find no means to drive away this grief which is drying up my senses. I will not be able to dispel it even if I win a prosperous, unrivaled kingdom on earth with sovereignty like the demigods in heaven.

9. Sañjaya said: Having spoken thus, Arjuna, chastiser of enemies, told Kṛṣṇa, "Govinda, I shall not fight," and fell silent.

Kṛṣṇa instructs: one should not grieve for the real self which is eternal.

10. O descendant of Bharata, at that time Kṛṣṇa, smiling, in the midst of both the armies, spoke the following words to the grief-stricken Arjuna.

11. The Supreme Personality of Godhead said: While speaking learned words, you are mourning for what is not worthy of grief. Those who are wise lament neither for the living nor for the dead.

12. Never was there a time when I did not exist, nor you, nor all these kings; nor in the future shall any of us cease to be.

13. As the embodied soul continuously passes, in this body, from boyhood to youth to old age, the soul similarly passes into another body at death. A sober person is not bewildered by such a change.

14. O son of Kuntī, the nonpermanent appearance of happiness and distress, and their disappearance in due course, are like the appearance and disappearance of winter and summer seasons. They arise from sense perception, O scion of Bharata, and one must learn to tolerate them without being disturbed.

15. O best among men [Arjuna], the person who is not disturbed by happiness and distress and is steady in both is certainly eligible for liberation.

16. Those who are seers of the truth have concluded that of the nonexistent [the material body] there is no endurance and of the eternal [the soul] there is no change. This they have concluded by studying the nature of both.
17. That which pervades the entire body you should know to be indestructible. No one is able to destroy that imperishable soul.
18. The material body of the indestructible, immeasurable and eternal living entity is sure to come to an end; therefore, fight, O descendant of Bharata.
19. Neither he who thinks the living entity is the slayer nor he who thinks it slain is in knowledge, for the self slays not nor is slain.
20. For the soul there is neither birth nor death at any time. He has not come into being, does not come into being, and will not come into being. He is unborn, eternal, ever-existing and primeval. He is not slain when the body is slain.
21. O Pārtha, how can a person who knows that the soul is indestructible, eternal, unborn and immutable kill anyone or cause anyone to kill?
22. As a person puts on new garments, giving up old ones, the soul similarly accepts new material bodies, giving up the old and useless ones.
23. The soul can never be cut to pieces by any weapon, nor burned by fire, nor moistened by water, nor withered by the wind.
24. This individual soul is unbreakable and insoluble, and can be neither burned nor dried. He is everlasting, present everywhere, unchangeable, immovable and eternally the same.
25. It is said that the soul is invisible, inconceivable and immutable. Knowing this, you should not grieve for the body.
26. If, however, you think that the soul [or the symptoms of life] is always born and dies forever, you still have no reason to lament, O mighty-armed.
27. One who has taken his birth is sure to die, and after death one is sure to take birth again. Therefore, in the unavoidable discharge of your duty, you should not lament.
28. All created beings are unmanifest in their beginning, manifest in their interim state, and unmanifest again when annihilated. So what need is there for lamentation?
29. Some look on the soul as amazing, some describe him as amazing, and some hear of him as amazing, while others, even after hearing about him, cannot understand him at all.

30. O descendant of Bharata, he who dwells in the body can never be slain. Therefore you need not grieve for any living being.

Why Arjuna must fight.

31. Considering your specific duty as a *kṣatriya,* you should know that there is no better engagement for you than fighting on religious principles; and so there is no need for hesitation.
32. O Pārtha, happy are the *kṣatriyas* to whom such fighting opportunities come unsought, opening for them the doors of the heavenly planets.
33. If, however, you do not perform your religious duty of fighting, then you will certainly incur sins for neglecting your duties and thus lose your reputation as a fighter.
34. People will always speak of your infamy, and for a respectable person, dishonor is worse than death.
35. The great generals who have highly esteemed your name and fame will think that you have left the battlefield out of fear only, and thus they will consider you insignificant.
36. Your enemies will describe you in many unkind words and scorn your ability. What could be more painful for you?
37. O son of Kuntī, either you will be killed on the battlefield and attain the heavenly planets, or you will conquer and enjoy the earthly kingdom. Therefore, get up with determination and fight.
38. Do thou fight for the sake of fighting, without considering happiness or distress, loss or gain, victory or defeat—and by so doing you shall never incur sin.

How to act without reaction.

39. Thus far I have described this knowledge to you through analytical study. Now listen as I explain it in terms of working without fruitive results. O son of Pṛthā, when you act in such knowledge you can free yourself from the bondage of works.
40. In this endeavor there is no loss or diminution, and a little advancement on this path can protect one from the most dangerous type of fear.
41. Those who are on this path are resolute in purpose, and their aim is one. O beloved child of the Kurus, the intelligence of those who are irresolute is many-branched.
42–43. Men of small knowledge are very much attached to the flowery words of the *Vedas,* which recommend various fruitive activi-

ties for elevation to heavenly planets, resultant good birth, power, and so forth. Being desirous of sense gratification and opulent life, they say that there is nothing more than this.

44. In the minds of those who are too attached to sense enjoyment and material opulence, and who are bewildered by such things, the resolute determination for devotional service to the Supreme Lord does not take place.

45. The *Vedas* deal mainly with the subject of the three modes of material nature. O Arjuna, become transcendental to these three modes. Be free from all dualities and from all anxieties for gain and safety, and be established in the self.

46. All purposes served by a small well can at once be served by a great reservoir of water. Similarly, all the purposes of the *Vedas* can be served to one who knows the purpose behind them.

47. You have a right to perform your prescribed duty, but you are not entitled to the fruits of action. Never consider yourself the cause of the result of your activities, and never be attached to not doing your duty.

48. Perform your duty equipoised, O Arjuna, abandoning all attachment to success or failure. Such equanimity is called *yoga.*

49. O Dhanañjaya, keep all abominable activities far distant by devotional service, and in that consciousness surrender unto the Lord. Those who want to enjoy the fruits of their work are misers.

50. A man engaged in devotional service rids himself of both good and bad actions even in this life. Therefore strive for *yoga,* which is the art of all work.

51. By thus engaging in devotional service to the Lord, great sages or devotees free themselves from the results of work in the material world. In this way they become free from the cycle of birth and death and attain the state beyond all miseries [by going back to Godhead].

52. When your intelligence has passed out of the dense forest of delusion, you shall become indifferent to all that has been heard and all that is to be heard.

53. When your mind is no longer disturbed by the flowery language of the *Vedas,* and when it remains fixed in the trance of self-realization, then you will have attained the divine consciousness.

The symptoms of one in transcendental consciousness.

54. Arjuna said: O Kṛṣṇa, what are the symptoms of one whose consciousness is thus merged in transcendence? How does he speak, and what is his language? How does he sit, and how does he walk?

55. The Supreme Personality of Godhead said: O Pārtha, when a man gives up all varieties of desire for sense gratification, which arise from mental concoction, and when his mind, thus purified, finds satisfaction in the self alone, then he is said to be in pure transcendental consciousness.

56. One who is not disturbed in mind even amidst the threefold miseries or elated when there is happiness, and who is free from attachment, fear and anger, is called a sage of steady mind.

57. In the material world, one who is unaffected by whatever good or evil he may obtain, neither praising it nor despising it, is firmly fixed in perfect knowledge.

58. One who is able to withdraw his senses from sense objects, as the tortoise draws its limbs within the shell, is firmly fixed in perfect consciousness.

59. The embodied soul may be restricted from sense enjoyment, though the taste for sense objects remains. But, ceasing such engagements by experiencing a higher taste, he is fixed in consciousness.

60. The senses are so strong and impetuous, O Arjuna, that they forcibly carry away the mind even of a man of discrimination who is endeavoring to control them.

61. One who restrains his senses, keeping them under full control, and fixes his consciousness upon Me, is known as a man of steady intelligence.

62. While contemplating the objects of the senses, a person develops attachment for them, and from such attachment lust develops, and from lust anger arises.

63. From anger, complete delusion arises, and from delusion bewilderment of memory. When memory is bewildered, intelligence is lost, and when intelligence is lost one falls down again into the material pool.

64. But a person free from all attachment and aversion and able to control his senses through regulative principles of freedom can obtain the complete mercy of the Lord.

65. For one who is thus satisfied [in Kṛṣṇa consciousness], the threefold miseries of material existence exist no longer; in such satisfied consciousness, one's intelligence is soon well established.

66. One who is not connected with the Supreme [in Kṛṣṇa consciousness] can have neither transcendental intelligence nor a steady mind, without which there is no possibility of peace. And how can there be any happiness without peace?

67. As a boat on the water is swept away by a strong wind, even one of the roaming senses on which the mind focuses can carry away a man's intelligence.
68. Therefore, O mighty-armed, one whose senses are restrained from their objects is certainly of steady intelligence.
69. What is night for all beings is the time of awakening for the self-controlled; and the time of awakening for all beings is night for the introspective sage.
70. A person who is not disturbed by the incessant flow of desires—that enter like rivers into the ocean, which is ever being filled but is always still—can alone achieve peace, and not the man who strives to satisfy such desires.
71. A person who has given up all desires for sense gratification, who lives free from desires, who has given up all sense of proprietorship and is devoid of false ego—he alone can attain real peace.
72. That is the way of the spiritual and godly life, after attaining which a man is not bewildered. If one is thus situated even at the hour of death, one can enter into the kingdom of God.

3/ Karma-yoga

Not renunciation alone, but action in devotion brings freedom

1. Arjuna said: O Janārdana, O Keśava, why do You want to engage me in this ghastly warfare, if You think that intelligence is better than fruitive work?
2. My intelligence is bewildered by Your equivocal instructions. Therefore, please tell me decisively which will be most beneficial for me.
3. The Supreme Personality of Godhead said: O sinless Arjuna, I have already explained that there are two classes of men who try to realize the self. Some are inclined to understand it by empirical, philosophical speculation, and others by devotional service.
4. Not by merely abstaining from work can one achieve freedom from reaction, nor by renunciation alone can one attain perfection.
5. Everyone is forced to act helplessly according to the qualities he has acquired from the modes of material nature; therefore no one can refrain from doing something, not even for a moment.

6. One who restrains the senses of action but whose mind dwells on sense objects certainly deludes himself and is called a pretender.
7. On the other hand, if a sincere person tries to control the active senses by the mind and begins *karma-yoga* [in Kṛṣṇa consciousness] without attachment, he is by far superior.
8. Perform your prescribed duty, for doing so is better than not working. One cannot even maintain one's physical body without work.

Sacrifice for Viṣṇu.

9. Work done as a sacrifice for Viṣṇu has to be performed, otherwise work causes bondage in this material world. Therefore, O son of Kuntī, perform your prescribed duties for His satisfaction, and in that way you will always remain free from bondage.
10. In the beginning of creation, the Lord of all creatures sent forth generations of men and demigods, along with sacrifices for Viṣṇu, and blessed them by saying, "Be thou happy by this *yajña* [sacrifice] because its performance will bestow upon you everything desirable for living happily and achieving liberation."
11. The demigods, being pleased by sacrifices, will also please you, and thus, by cooperation between men and demigods, prosperity will reign for all.
12. In charge of the various necessities of life, the demigods, being satisfied by the performance of *yajña* [sacrifice], will supply all necessities to you. But he who enjoys such gifts without offering them to the demigods in return is certainly a thief.
13. The devotees of the Lord are released from all kinds of sins because they eat food which is offered first for sacrifice. Others, who prepare food for personal sense enjoyment, verily eat only sin.
14. All living bodies subsist on food grains, which are produced from rains. Rains are produced by performance of *Yajña* [sacrifice], and *yajña* is born of prescribed duties.
15. Regulated activities are prescribed in the *Vedas,* and the *Vedas* are directly manifested from the Supreme Personality of Godhead. Consequently the all-pervading Transcendence is eternally situated in acts of sacrifice.
16. My dear Arjuna, one who in human life does not follow the prescribed cycle of sacrifice thus established by the *Vedas* certainly leads a life full of sin. Living only for the satisfaction of the senses, such a person lives in vain.

17. But for one who takes pleasure in the self, whose human life is one of self-realization, and who is satisfied in the self only, fully satiated—for him there is no duty.
18. A self-realized man has no purpose to fulfill in the discharge of his prescribed duties, nor has he any reason not to perform such work. Nor has he any need to depend on any other living being.
19. Therefore, without being attached to the fruits of activities, one should act as a matter of duty, for by working without attachment one attains the Supreme.
20. Kings such as Janaka attained perfection solely by performance of prescribed duties. Therefore, just for the sake of educating the people in general, you should perform your work.

The leader must act as an example.

21. Whatever action a great man performs, common men follow. And whatever standards he sets by exemplary acts, all the world pursues.
22. O son of Pṛthā, there is no work prescribed for Me within all the three planetary systems. Nor am I in want of anything, nor have I a need to obtain anything—and yet I am engaged in prescribed duties.
23. For if I ever failed to engage in carefully performing prescribed duties, O Pārtha, certainly all men would follow My path.
24. If I did not perform prescribed duties, all these worlds would be put to ruination. I would be the cause of creating unwanted population, and I would thereby destroy the peace of all living beings.
25. As the ignorant perform their duties with attachment to results, the learned may similarly act, but without attachment, for the sake of leading people on the right path.
26. So as not to disrupt the minds of ignorant men attached to the fruitive results of prescribed duties, a learned person should not induce them to stop work. Rather, by working in the spirit of devotion, he should engage them in all sorts of activities [for the gradual development of Kṛṣṇa consciousness].
27. The spirit soul bewildered by the influence of false ego thinks himself the doer of activities that are in actuality carried out by the three modes of material nature.
28. One who is in knowledge of the Absolute Truth, O mighty-armed, does not engage himself in the senses and sense gratification, knowing well the differences between work in devotion and work for fruitive results.

29. Bewildered by the modes of material nature, the ignorant fully engage themselves in material activities and become attached. But the wise should not unsettle them, although these duties are inferior due to the performers' lack of knowledge.
30. Therefore, O Arjuna, surrendering all your works unto Me, with full knowledge of Me, without desires for profit, with no claims to proprietorship, and free from lethargy, fight.
31. Those persons who execute their duties according to My injunctions and who follow this teaching faithfully, without envy, become free from the bondage of fruitive actions.
32. But those who, out of envy, do not regularly follow these teachings are to be considered bereft of all knowledge, befooled, and ruined in their endeavors for perfection.
33. Even a man of knowledge acts according to his own nature, for everyone follows the nature he has acquired from the three modes. What can repression accomplish?
34. There are principles to regulate attachment and aversion pertaining to the senses and their objects. One should not come under the control of such attachment and aversion, because they are stumbling blocks on the path of self-realization.
35. It is far better to discharge one's prescribed duties, even though faultily, than another's duties perfectly. Destruction in the course of performing one's own duty is better than engaging in another's duties, for to follow another's path is dangerous.

Lust, the great enemy of the world.

36. Arjuna said: O descendant of Vṛṣṇi, by what is one impelled to sinful acts, even unwillingly, as if engaged by force?
37. The Supreme Personality of Godhead said: It is lust only, Arjuna, which is born of contact with the material mode of passion and later transformed into wrath, and which is the all-devouring sinful enemy of this world.
38. As fire is covered by smoke, as a mirror is covered by dust, or as the embryo is covered by the womb, the living entity is similarly covered by different degrees of this lust.
39. Thus the wise living entity's pure consciousness becomes covered by his eternal enemy in the form of lust, which is never satisfied and which burns like fire.
40. The senses, the mind and the intelligence are the sitting places of this lust. Through them lust covers the real knowledge of the living entity and bewilders him.

41. Therefore, O Arjuna, best of the Bharatas, in the very beginning curb this great symbol of sin [lust] by regulating the senses, and slay this destroyer of knowledge and self-realization.

42. The working senses are superior to dull matter; mind is higher than the senses; intelligence is still higher than the mind; and he [the soul] is even higher than the intelligence.

43. Thus knowing oneself to be transcendental to the material senses, mind and intelligence, O mighty-armed Arjuna, one should steady the mind by deliberate spiritual intelligence [Kṛṣṇa consciousness] and thus—by spiritual strength—conquer this insatiable enemy known as lust.

4/ Transcendental Knowledge

The disciplic succession.

1. The Personality of Godhead, Lord Śrī Kṛṣṇa, said: I instructed this imperishable science of *yoga* to the sun-god, Vivasvān, and Vivasvān instructed it to Manu, the father of mankind, and Manu in turn instructed it to Ikṣvāku.

2. This supreme science was thus received through the chain of disciplic succession, and the saintly kings understood it in that way. But in course of time the succession was broken, and therefore the science as it is appears to be lost.

3. That very ancient science of the relationship with the Supreme is today told by Me to you because you are My devotee as well as My friend and can therefore understand the transcendental mystery of this science.

Kṛṣṇa speaks of His transcendental nature and His mission.

4. Arjuna said: The sun-god Vivasvān is senior by birth to You. How am I to understand that in the beginning You instructed this science to him?

5. The Personality of Godhead said: Many, many births both you and I have passed. I can remember all of them, but you cannot, O subduer of the enemy!

6. Although I am unborn and My transcendental body never deteriorates, and although I am the Lord of all living entities, I still appear in every millennium in My original transcendental form.

7. Whenever and wherever there is a decline in religious practice, O descendant of Bharata, and a predominant rise of irreligion—at that time I descend Myself.
8. To deliver the pious and to annihilate the miscreants, as well as to reestablish the principles of religion, I Myself appear, millennium after millennium.
9. One who knows the transcendental nature of My appearance and activities does not, upon leaving the body, take his birth again in this material world, but attains My eternal abode, O Arjuna.
10. Being freed from attachment, fear and anger, being fully absorbed in Me and taking refuge in Me, many, many persons in the past became purified by knowledge of Me—and thus they all attained transcendental love for Me.
11. As all surrender unto Me, I reward them accordingly. Everyone follows My path in all respects, O son of Pṛthā.
12. Men in this world desire success in fruitive activities, and therefore they worship the demigods. Quickly, of course, men get results from fruitive work in this world.
13. According to the three modes of material nature and the work associated with them, the four divisions of human society are created by Me. And although I am the creator of this system, you should know that I am yet the nondoer, being unchangeable.
14. There is no work that affects Me; nor do I aspire for the fruits of action. One who understands this truth about Me also does not become entangled in the fruitive reactions of work.
15. All the liberated souls in ancient times acted with this understanding of My transcendental nature. Therefore you should perform your duty, following in their footsteps.

The intricacies of action.

16. Even the intelligent are bewildered in determining what is action and what is inaction. Now I shall explain to you what action is, knowing which you shall be liberated from all misfortune.
17. The intricacies of action are very hard to understand. Therefore one should know properly what action is, what forbidden action is, and what inaction is.
18. One who sees inaction in action, and action in inaction, is intelligent among men, and he is in the transcendental position, although engaged in all sorts of activities.

19. One is understood to be in full knowledge whose every endeavor is devoid of desire for sense gratification. He is said by sages to be a worker for whom the reactions of work have been burned up by the fire of perfect knowledge.
20. Abandoning all attachment to the results of his activities, ever satisfied and independent, he performs no fruitive action, although engaged in all kinds of undertakings.
21. Such a man of understanding acts with mind and intelligence perfectly controlled, gives up all sense of proprietorship over his possessions and acts only for the bare necessities of life. Thus working, he is not affected by sinful reactions.
22. He who is satisfied with gain which comes of its own accord, who is free from duality and does not envy, who is steady both in success and failure, is never entangled, although performing actions.
23. The work of a man who is unattached to the modes of material nature and who is fully situated in transcendental knowledge merges entirely into transcendence.
24. A person who is fully absorbed in Kṛṣṇa consciousness is sure to attain the spiritual kingdom because of his full contribution to spiritual activities, in which the consummation is absolute and that which is offered is of the same spiritual nature.

Divisions of sacrifice.

25. Some *yogīs* perfectly worship the demigods by offering different sacrifices to them, and some of them offer sacrifices in the fire of the Supreme Brahman.
26. Some [the unadulterated *brahmacārīs*] sacrifice the hearing process and the senses in the fire of mental control, and others [the regulated householders] sacrifice the objects of the senses in the fire of the senses.
27. Others, who are interested in achieving self-realization through control of the mind and senses, offer the functions of all the senses, and of the life breath, as oblations into the fire of the controlled mind.
28. Having accepted strict vows, some become enlightened by sacrificing their possessions, and others by performing severe austerities, by practicing the *yoga* of eightfold mysticism, or by studying the *Vedas* to advance in transcendental knowledge.
29. Still others, who are inclined to the process of breath restraint to remain in trance, practice by offering the movement of the outgoing breath into the incoming, and the incoming breath into the outgoing,

and thus at last remain in trance, stopping all breathing. Others, curtailing the eating process, offer the outgoing breath into itself as a sacrifice.

30. All these performers who know the meaning of sacrifice become cleansed of sinful reactions, and, having tasted the nectar of the results of sacrifices, they advance toward the supreme eternal atmosphere.

31. O best of the Kuru dynasty, without sacrifice one can never live happily on this planet or in this life: what then of the next?

32. All these different types of sacrifice are approved by the *Vedas,* and all of them are born of different types of work. Knowing them as such, you will become liberated.

33. O chastiser of the enemy, the sacrifice performed in knowledge is better than the sacrifice of material possessions. After all, O son of Pṛthā, all sacrifices of work culminate in transcendental knowledge.

Approach a spiritual master and learn the truth.

34. Just try to learn the truth by approaching a spiritual master. Inquire from him submissively and render service unto him. The self-realized souls can impart knowledge unto you because they have seen the truth.

35. Having obtained real knowledge from a self-realized soul, you will never fall again into such illusion, for by this knowledge you will see that all living beings are but part of the Supreme, or, in other words, that they are Mine.

36. Even if you are considered to be the most sinful of all sinners, when you are situated in the boat of transcendental knowledge you will be able to cross over the ocean of miseries.

37. As a blazing fire turns firewood to ashes, O Arjuna, so does the fire of knowledge burn to ashes all reactions to material activities.

38. In this world, there is nothing so sublime and pure as transcendental knowledge. Such knowledge is the mature fruit of all mysticism. And one who has become accomplished in the practice of devotional service enjoys this knowledge within himself in due course of time.

39. A faithful man who is dedicated to transcendental knowledge and who subdues his senses is eligible to achieve such knowledge, and having achieved it he quickly attains the supreme spiritual peace.

40. But ignorant and faithless persons who doubt the revealed scriptures do not attain God consciousness; they fall down. For the doubting soul there is happiness neither in this world nor in the next.
41. One who acts in devotional service, renouncing the fruits of his actions, and whose doubts have been destroyed by transcendental knowledge, is situated factually in the self. Thus he is not bound by the reactions of work, O conqueror of riches.
42. Therefore the doubts which have arisen in your heart out of ignorance should be slashed by the weapon of knowledge. Armed with *yoga,* O Bhārata, stand and fight.

5/ Karma-yoga—Action in Kṛṣṇa Consciousness

Which is better? Renunciation or work in devotion?

1. Arjuna said: O Kṛṣṇa, first of all You ask me to renounce work, and then again You recommend work with devotion. Now will You kindly tell me definitely which of the two is more beneficial?
2. The Personality of Godhead replied: The renunciation of work and work in devotion are both good for liberation. But, of the two, work in devotional service is better than renunciation of work.
3. One who neither hates nor desires the fruits of his activities is known to be always renounced. Such a person, free from all dualities, easily overcomes material bondage and is completely liberated, O mighty-armed Arjuna.

The goal of both is the same.

4. Only the ignorant speak of devotional service [*karma-yoga*] as being different from the analytical study of the material world [Sāṅkhya]. Those who are actually learned say that he who applies himself well to one of these paths achieves the results of both.
5. One who knows that the position reached by means of analytical study can also be attained by devotional service, and who therefore sees analytical study and devotional service to be on the same level, sees things as they are.
6. Merely renouncing all activities yet not engaging in the devotional service of the Lord cannot make one happy. But a thoughtful person engaged in devotional service can achieve the Supreme without delay.

7. One who works in devotion, who is a pure soul, and who controls his mind and senses is dear to everyone, and everyone is dear to him. Though always working, such a man is never entangled.

8-9. A person in the divine consciousness, although engaged in seeing, hearing, touching, smelling, eating, moving about, sleeping and breathing, always knows within himself that he actually does nothing at all. Because while speaking, evacuating, receiving, or opening or closing his eyes, he always knows that only the material senses are engaged with their objects and that he is aloof from them.

10. One who performs his duty without attachment, surrendering the results unto the Supreme Lord, is unaffected by sinful action, as the lotus leaf is untouched by water.

11. The *yogīs,* abandoning attachment, act with body, mind, intelligence and even with the senses, only for the purpose of purification.

12. The steadily devoted soul attains unadulterated peace because he offers the result of all activities to Me; whereas a person who is not in union with the Divine, who is greedy for the fruits of his labor, becomes entangled.

13. When the embodied living being controls his nature and mentally renounces all actions, he resides happily in the city of nine gates [the material body], neither working nor causing work to be done.

14. The embodied spirit, master of the city of his body, does not create activities, nor does he induce people to act, nor does he create the fruits of action. All this is enacted by the modes of material nature.

15. Nor does the Supreme Lord assume anyone's sinful or pious activities. Embodied beings, however, are bewildered because of the ignorance which covers their real knowledge.

16. When, however, one is enlightened with the knowledge by which nescience is destroyed, then his knowledge reveals everything, as the sun lights up everything in the daytime.

17. When one's intelligence, mind, faith and refuge are all fixed in the Supreme, then one becomes fully cleansed of misgivings through complete knowledge and thus proceeds straight on the path of liberation.

The sage sees with equal vision.

18. The humble sages, by virtue of true knowledge, see with equal vision a learned and gentle *brāhmaṇa,* a cow, an elephant, a dog and a dog-eater [outcaste].

19. Those whose minds are established in sameness and equanimity have already conquered the conditions of birth and death. They are flawless like Brahman, and thus they are already situated in Brahman.

20. A person who neither rejoices upon achieving something pleasant nor laments upon obtaining something unpleasant, who is self-intelligent, who is unbewildered, and who knows the science of God, is already situated in transcendence.

21. Such a liberated person is not attracted to material sense pleasure but is always in trance, enjoying the pleasure within. In this way the self-realized person enjoys unlimited happiness, for he concentrates on the Supreme.

22. An intelligent person does not take part in the sources of misery, which are due to contact with the material senses. O son of Kuntī, such pleasures have a beginning and an end, and so the wise man does not delight in them.

23. Before giving up this present body, if one is able to tolerate the urges of the material senses and check the force of desire and anger, he is well situated and is happy in this world.

24. One whose happiness is within, who is active and rejoices within, and whose aim is inward is actually the perfect mystic. He is liberated in the Supreme, and ultimately he attains the Supreme.

25. Those who are beyond the dualities that arise from doubts, whose minds are engaged within, who are always busy working for the welfare of all living beings, and who are free from all sins achieve liberation in the Supreme.

26. Those who are free from anger and all material desires, who are self-realized, self-disciplined and constantly endeavoring for perfection, are assured of liberation in the Supreme in the very near future.

27–28. Shutting out all external sense objects, keeping the eyes and vision concentrated between the two eyebrows, suspending the inward and outward breaths within the nostrils, and thus controlling the mind, senses and intelligence, the transcendentalist aiming at liberation becomes free from desire, fear and anger. One who is always in this state is certainly liberated.

The peace formula.

29. A person in full consciousness of Me, knowing Me to be the ultimate beneficiary of all sacrifices and austerities, the Supreme Lord of all planets and demigods, and the benefactor and well-wisher of all living entities, attains peace from the pangs of material miseries.

6/ Dhyāna-yoga

To be a yogī *one must renounce sense gratification.*

1. The Supreme Personality of Godhead said: One who is unattached to the fruits of his work and who works as he is obligated is in the renounced order of life, and he is the true mystic, not he who lights no fire and performs no duty.
2. What is called renunciation you should know to be the same as *yoga,* or linking oneself with the Supreme, O son of Pāṇḍu, for one can never become a *yogī* unless he renounces the desire for sense gratification.
3. For one who is a neophyte in the eightfold *yoga* system, work is said to be the means; and for one who is already elevated in *yoga,* cessation of all material activities is said to be the means.
4. A person is said to be elevated in *yoga* when, having renounced all material desires, he neither acts for sense gratification nor engages in fruitive activities.

Controlling the mind.

5. One must deliver himself with the help of his mind, and not degrade himself. The mind is the friend of the conditioned soul, and his enemy as well.
6. For him who has conquered the mind, the mind is the best of friends; but for one who has failed to do so, his mind will remain the greatest enemy.
7. For one who has conquered the mind, the Supersoul is already reached, for he has attained tranquillity. To such a man happiness and distress, heat and cold, honor and dishonor are all the same.
8. A person is said to be established in self-realization and is called a *yogī* [or mystic] when he is fully satisfied by virtue of acquired knowledge and realization. Such a person is situated in transcendence and is self-controlled. He sees everything—whether it be pebbles, stones or gold—as the same.
9. A person is considered still further advanced when he regards honest well-wishers, affectionate benefactors, the neutral, mediators, the envious, friends and enemies, the pious and the sinners all with an equal mind.
10. A transcendentalist should always engage his body, mind and self in relationship with the Supreme; he should live alone in a

secluded place and should always carefully control his mind. He should be free from desires and feelings of possessiveness.

The rules and goals of yoga *practice.*

11–12. To practice *yoga,* one should go to a secluded place and should lay *kuśa* grass on the ground and then cover it with a deerskin and a soft cloth. The seat should be neither too high nor too low and should be situated in a sacred place. The *yogī* should then sit on it very firmly and practice *yoga* to purify the heart by controlling his mind, senses and activities and fixing the mind on one point.

13–14. One should hold one's body, neck and head erect in a straight line and stare steadily at the tip of the nose. Thus, with an unagitated, subdued mind, devoid of fear, completely free from sex life, one should meditate upon Me within the heart and make Me the ultimate goal of life.

15. Thus practicing constant control of the body, mind and activities, the mystic transcendentalist, his mind regulated, attains to the kingdom of God [or the abode of Kṛṣṇa] by cessation of material existence.

16. There is no possibility of one's becoming a *yogī,* O Arjuna, if one eats too much or eats too little, sleeps too much or does not sleep enough.

17. He who is regulated in his habits of eating, sleeping, recreation and work can mitigate all material pains by practicing the *yoga* system.

18. When the *yogī,* by practice of *yoga,* disciplines his mental activities and becomes situated in transcendence—devoid of all material desires—he is said to be well established in *yoga.*

19. As a lamp in a windless place does not waver, so the transcendentalist, whose mind is controlled, remains always steady in his meditation on the transcendent self.

20–23. In the stage of perfection called trance, or *samādhi,* one's mind is completely restrained from material mental activities by practice of *yoga.* This perfection is characterized by one's ability to see the self by the pure mind and to relish and rejoice in the self. In that joyous state, one is situated in boundless transcendental happiness, realized through transcendental senses. Established thus, one never departs from the truth, and upon gaining this he thinks there is no greater gain. Being situated in such a position, one is never shaken, even in the midst of greatest difficulty. This indeed is actual freedom from all miseries arising from material contact.

24. One should engage oneself in the practice of *yoga* with determination and faith and not be deviated from the path. One should abandon, without exception, all material desires born of mental speculation and thus control all the senses on all sides by the mind.
25. Gradually, step by step, one should become situated in trance by means of intelligence sustained by full conviction, and thus the mind should be fixed on the self alone and should think of nothing else.
26. From wherever the mind wanders due to its flickering and unsteady nature, one must certainly withdraw it and bring it back under the control of the self.
27. The *yogī* whose mind is fixed on Me verily attains the highest perfection of transcendental happiness. He is beyond the mode of passion, he realizes his qualitative identity with the Supreme, and thus he is freed from all reactions to past deeds.
28. Thus the self-controlled *yogī,* constantly engaged in *yoga* practice, becomes free from all material contamination and achieves the highest stage of perfect happiness in transcendental loving service to the Lord.

A true yogī *see Kṛṣṇa.*

29. A true *yogī* observes Me in all beings and also sees every being in Me. Indeed, the self-realized person sees Me, the same Supreme Lord, everywhere.
30. For one who sees Me everywhere and sees everything in Me, I am never lost, nor is he ever lost to Me.
31. Such a *yogī,* who engages in the worshipful service of the Supersoul, knowing that I and the Supersoul are one, remains always in Me in all circumstances.
32. He is a perfect *yogī* who, by comparison to his own self, sees the true equality of all beings, in both their happiness and their distress, O Arjuna!

Arjuna rejects the yoga *practice.*

33. Arjuna said: O Madhusūdana, the system of *yoga* which You have summarized appears impractical and unendurable to me, for the mind is restless and unsteady.
34. For the mind is restless, turbulent, obstinate and very strong, O Kṛṣṇa, and to subdue it, I think, is more difficult than controlling the wind.

35. Lord Śrī Kṛṣṇa said: O mighty-armed son of Kuntī, it is undoubtedly very difficult to curb the restless mind, but it is possible by suitable practice and by detachment.
36. For one whose mind is unbridled, self-realization is difficult work. But he whose mind is controlled and who strives by appropriate means is assured of success. That is My opinion.

What happens to one who tries but fails in yoga?

37. Arjuna said: O Kṛṣṇa, what is the destination of the unsuccessful transcendentalist, who in the beginning takes to the process of self-realization with faith but who later desists due to worldly-mindedness and thus does not attain perfection in mysticism?
38. O mighty-armed Kṛṣṇa, does not such a man, who is bewildered from the path of transcendence, fall away from both spiritual and material success and perish like a riven cloud, with no position in any sphere?
39. This is my doubt, O Kṛṣṇa, and I ask You to dispel it completely. But for You, no one is to be found who can destroy this doubt.
40. The Supreme Personality of Godhead said: Son of Pṛthā, a transcendentalist engaged in auspicious activities does not meet with destruction either in this world or in the spiritual world; one who does good, My friend, is never overcome by evil.
41. The unsuccessful *yogī,* after many, many years of enjoyment on the planets of the pious living entities, is born into a family of righteous people, or into a family of rich aristocracy.
42. Or [if unsuccessful after long practice of *yoga*] he takes his birth in a family of transcendentalists who are surely great in wisdom. Certainly, such a birth is rare in this world.
43. On taking such a birth, he again revives the divine consciousness of his previous life, and he again tries to make further progress in order to achieve complete success, O son of Kuru.
44. By virtue of the divine consciousness of his previous life, he automatically becomes attracted to the yogic principles—even without seeking them. Such an inquisitive transcendentalist stands always above the ritualistic principles of the scriptures.
45. And when the *yogī* engages himself with sincere endeavor in making further progress, being washed of all contaminations, then ultimately, achieving perfection after many, many births of practice, he attains the supreme goal.

46. A *yogī* is greater than the ascetic, greater than the empiricist and greater than the fruitive worker. Therefore, O Arjuna, in all circumstances, be a *yogī*.

The highest of all yogīs.

47. And of all *yogīs,* the one with great faith who always abides in Me, thinks of Me within himself, and renders transcendental loving service to Me—he is the most intimately united with Me in *yoga* and is the highest of all. That is My opinion.

7/ Knowledge of the Absolute

Hear from Me and know Me in full.

1. The Supreme Personality of Godhead said: Now hear, O son of Pṛthā, how by practicing *yoga* in full consciousness of Me, with mind attached to Me, you can know Me in full, free from doubt.
2. I shall now declare unto you in full this knowledge, both phenomenal and numinous. This being known, nothing further shall remain for you to know.
3. Out of many thousands among men, one may endeavor for perfection, and of those who have achieved perfection, hardly one knows Me in truth.
4. Earth, water, fire, air, ether, mind, intelligence and false ego—all together these eight constitute My separated material energies.
5. Besides these, O mighty-armed Arjuna, there is another, superior energy of Mine, which comprises the living entities who are exploiting the resources of this material, inferior nature.
6. All created beings have their source in these two natures. Of all that is material and all that is spiritual in this world, know for certain that I am both the origin and the dissolution.

Kṛṣṇa speaks for Himself.

7. O conqueror of wealth, there is no truth superior to Me. Everything rests upon Me, as pearls are strung on a thread.
8. O son of Kuntī, I am the taste of water, the light of the sun and the moon, the syllable *oṁ* in the Vedic *mantras;* I am the sound in ether and ability in man.
9. I am the original fragrance of the earth, and I am the heat in fire. I am the life of all that lives, and I am the penances of all ascetics.

10. O son of Pṛthā, know that I am the original seed of all existences, the intelligence of the intelligent, and the prowess of all powerful men.
11. I am the strength of the strong, devoid of passion and desire. I am sex life which is not contrary to religious principles, O lord of the Bhāratas [Arjuna].
12. Know that all states of being—be they of goodness, passion or ignorance—are manifested by My energy. I am, in one sense, everything, but I am independent. I am not under the modes of material nature, for they, on the contrary, are within Me.

The world is deluded by the modes of nature.

13. Deluded by the three modes [goodness, passion and ignorance], the whole world does not know Me, who am above the modes and inexhaustible.
14. This divine energy of Mine, consisting of the three modes of material nature, is difficult to overcome. But those who have surrendered unto Me can easily cross beyond it.

Four kinds of men who approach God.

15. Those miscreants who are grossly foolish, who are lowest among mankind, whose knowledge is stolen by illusion, and who partake of the atheistic nature of demons do not surrender unto Me.
16. O best among the Bhāratas, four kinds of pious men begin to render devotional service unto Me—the distressed, the desirer of wealth, the inquisitive, and he who is searching for knowledge of the Absolute.
17. Of these, the one who is in full knowledge and who is always engaged in pure devotional service is the best. For I am very dear to him, and he is dear to Me.
18. All these devotees are undoubtedly magnanimous souls, but he who is situated in knowledge of Me I consider to be just like My own self. Being engaged in My transcendental service, he is sure to attain Me, the highest and most perfect goal.
19. After many births and deaths, he who is actually in knowledge surrenders unto Me, knowing Me to be the cause of all causes and all that is. Such a great soul is very rare.

The worship of demigods.

20. Those whose intelligence has been stolen by material desires surrender unto demigods and follow the particular rules and regulations of worship according to their own natures.

21. I am in everyone's heart as the Supersoul. As soon as one desires to worship some demigod, I make his faith steady so that he can devote himself to that particular deity.

22. Endowed with such a faith, he endeavors to worship a particular demigod and obtains his desires. But in actuality these benefits are bestowed by Me alone.

23. Men of small intelligence worship the demigods, and their fruits are limited and temporary. Those who worship the demigods go to the planets of the demigods, but My devotees ultimately reach My supreme planet.

Worship of the Supreme Lord.

24. Unintelligent men, who do not know Me perfectly, think that I, the Supreme Personality of Godhead, Kṛṣṇa, was impersonal before and have now assumed this personality. Due to their small knowledge, they do not know My higher nature, which is imperishable and supreme.

25. I am never manifest to the foolish and unintelligent. For them I am covered by My internal potency, and therefore they do not know that I am unborn and infallible.

26. O Arjuna, as the Supreme Personality of Godhead, I know everything that has happened in the past, all that is happening in the present, and all things that are yet to come. I also know all living entities; but Me no one knows.

27. O scion of Bharata, O conqueror of the foe, all living entities are born into delusion, bewildered by dualities arisen from desire and hate.

28. Persons who have acted piously in previous lives and in this life and whose sinful actions are completely eradicated are freed from the dualities of delusion, and they engage themselves in My service with determination.

29. Intelligent persons who are endeavoring for liberation from old age and death take refuge in Me in devotional service. They are actually Brahman because they entirely know everything about transcendental activities.

30. Those in full consciousness of Me, who know Me, the Supreme Lord, to be the governing principle of the material manifestation, of the demigods, and of all methods of sacrifice, can understand and know Me, the Supreme Personality of Godhead, even at the time of death.

8/ Attaining the Supreme

Arjuna inquires, Kṛṣṇa replies.

1. Arjuna inquired: O my Lord, O Supreme Person, what is Brahman? What is the self? What are fruitive activities? What is this material manifestation? And what are the demigods? Please explain this to me.
2. Who is the Lord of sacrifice, and how does He live in the body, O Madhusūdana? And how can those engaged in devotional service know You at the time of death?
3. The Supreme Personality of Godhead said: The indestructible, transcendental living entity is called Brahman, and his eternal nature is called *adhyātma,* the self. Action pertaining to the development of the material bodies of the living entities is called *karma,* or fruitive activities.
4. O best of the embodied beings, the physical nature, which is constantly changing, is called *adhibhūta* [the material manifestation]. The universal form of the Lord, which includes all the demigods, like those of the sun and moon, is called *adhidaiva.* And I, the Supreme Lord, represented as the Supersoul in the heart of every embodied being, am called *adhiyajña* [the Lord of sacrifice].

Remember Me at the time of death.

5. And whoever, at the end of his life, quits his body, remembering Me alone, at once attains My nature. Of this there is no doubt.
6. Whatever state of being one remembers when he quits his body, O son of Kuntī, that state he will attain without fail.
7. Therefore, Arjuna, you should always think of Me in the form of Kṛṣṇa and at the same time carry out your prescribed duty of fighting. With your activities dedicated to Me and your mind and intelligence fixed on Me, you will attain Me without doubt.
8. He who meditates on Me as the Supreme Personality of Godhead, his mind constantly engaged in remembering Me, undeviated from the path, he, O Pārtha, is sure to reach Me.
9. One should meditate upon the Supreme Person as the one who knows everything, as He who is the oldest, who is the controller, who is smaller than the smallest, who is the maintainer of everything, who is beyond all material conception, who is inconceivable, and who is always a person. He is luminous like the sun, and He is transcendental, beyond this material nature.

10. One who, at the time of death, fixes his life air between the eyebrows and, by the strength of *yoga,* with an undeviating mind, engages himself in remembering the Supreme Lord in full devotion, will certainly attain to the Supreme Personality of Godhead.
11. Persons who are learned in the *Vedas,* who utter *oṁkāra* and who are great sages in the renounced order enter into Brahman. Desiring such perfection, one practices celibacy. I shall now briefly explain to you this process by which one may attain salvation.
12. The yogic situation is that of detachment from all sensual engagements. Closing all the doors of the senses and fixing the mind on the heart and the life air at the top of the head, one establishes himself in *yoga.*
13. After being situated in this *yoga* practice and vibrating the sacred syllable *oṁ,* the supreme combination of letters, if one thinks of the Supreme Personality of Godhead and quits his body, he will certainly reach the spiritual planets.
14. For one who always remembers Me without deviation, I am easy to obtain, O son of Pṛthā, because of his constant engagement in devotional service.
15. After attaining Me, the great souls, who are *yogīs* in devotion, never return to this temporary world, which is full of miseries, because they have attained the highest perfection.

The material world is miserable.

16. From the highest planet in the material world down to the lowest, all are places of misery wherein repeated birth and death take place. But one who attains to My abode, O son of Kuntī, never takes birth again.
17. By human calculation, a thousand ages taken together form the duration of Brahmā's one day. And such also is the duration of his night.
18. At the beginning of Brahmā's day, all living entities become manifest from the unmanifest state, and thereafter, when the night falls, they are merged into the unmanifest again.
19. Again and again, when Brahmā's day arrives, all living entities come into being, and with the arrival of Brahmā's night they are helplessly annihilated.

But Kṛṣṇa's abode is eternal.

20. Yet there is another unmanifest nature, which is eternal and is transcendental to this manifested and unmanifested matter. It is supreme and is never annihilated. When all in this world is annihilated, that part remains as it is.

21. That which the Vedāntists describe as unmanifest and infallible, that which is known as the supreme destination, that place from which, having attained it, one never returns—that is My supreme abode.

22. The Supreme Personality of Godhead, who is greater than all, is attainable by unalloyed devotion. Although He is present in His abode, He is all-pervading, and everything is situated within Him.

23. O best of the Bhāratas, I shall now explain to you the different times at which, passing away from this world, the *yogī* does or does not come back.

24. Those who know the Supreme Brahman attain that Supreme by passing away from the world during the influence of the fiery god, in the light, at an auspicious moment of the day, during the fortnight of the waxing moon, or during the six months when the sun travels in the north.

25. The mystic who passes away from this world during the smoke, the night, the fortnight of the waning moon, or the six months when the sun passes to the south reaches the moon planet but again comes back.

26. According to Vedic opinion, there are two ways of passing from this world—one in light and one in darkness. When one passes in light, he does not come back; but when one passes in darkness, he returns.

27. Although the devotees know these two paths, O Arjuna, they are never bewildered. Therefore be always fixed in devotion.

28. A person who accepts the path of devotional service is not bereft of the results derived from studying the *Vedas,* performing austere sacrifices, giving charity or pursuing philosophical and fruitive activities. Simply by performing devotional service, he attains all these, and at the end he reaches the supreme eternal abode.

9/ The Most Confidential Knowledge

Kṛṣṇa will now reveal the highest knowledge.

1. The Supreme Personality of Godhead said: My dear Arjuna, because you are never envious of Me, I shall impart to you this most

confidential knowledge and realization, knowing which you shall be relieved of the miseries of material existence.

2. This knowledge is the king of education, the most secret of all secrets. It is the purest knowledge, and because it gives direct perception of the self by realization, it is the perfection of religion. It is everlasting, and it is joyfully performed.

3. Those who are not faithful in this devotional service cannot attain Me, O conqueror of enemies. Therefore they return to the path of birth and death in this material world.

Everything is Kṛṣṇa, but He is still beyond everything.

4. By Me, in My unmanifested form, this entire universe is pervaded. All beings are in Me, but I am not in them.

5. And yet everything that is created does not rest in Me. Behold My mystic opulence! Although I am the maintainer of all living entities and although I am everywhere, I am not a part of this cosmic manifestation, for My Self is the very source of creation.

6. Understand that as the mighty wind, blowing everywhere, rests always in the sky, all created beings rest in Me.

7. O son of Kuntī, at the end of the millennium all material manifestations enter into My nature, and at the beginning of another millennium, by My potency, I create them again.

8. The whole cosmic order is under Me. Under My will it is automatically manifested again and again, and under My will it is annihilated at the end.

9. O Dhanañjaya, all this work cannot bind Me. I am ever detached from all these material activities, seated as though neutral.

10. This material nature, which is one of My energies, is working under My direction, O son of Kuntī, producing all moving and nonmoving beings. Under its rule this manifestation is created and annihilated again and again.

Fools deride Him.

11. Fools deride Me when I descend in the human form. They do not know My transcendental nature as the Supreme Lord of all that be.

12. Those who are thus bewildered are attracted by demonic and atheistic views. In that deluded condition, their hopes for liberation, their fruitive activities, and their culture of knowledge are all defeated.

Symptoms of a mahātmā.

13. O son of Pṛthā, those who are not deluded, the great souls, are under the protection of the divine nature. They are fully engaged in devotional service because they know Me as the Supreme Personality of Godhead, original and inexhaustible.
14. Always chanting My glories, endeavoring with great determination, bowing down before Me, these great souls perpetually worship Me with devotion.
15. Others, who engage in sacrifice by the cultivation of knowledge, worship the Supreme Lord as the one without a second, as diverse in many, and in the universal form.

Everything comes from Kṛṣṇa.

16. But it is I who am the ritual, I the sacrifice, the offering to the ancestors, the healing herb, the transcendental chant. I am the butter and the fire and the offering.
17. I am the father of this universe, the mother, the support and the grandsire. I am the object of knowledge, the purifier and the syllable *oṁ*. I am also the *Ṛg*, the *Sāma* and the *Yajur Vedas*.
18. I am the goal, the sustainer, the master, the witness, the abode, the refuge and the most dear friend. I am the creation and the annihilation, the basis of everything, the resting place and the eternal seed.
19. O Arjuna, I give heat, and I withhold and send forth the rain. I am immortality, and I am also death personified. Both spirit and matter are in Me.
20. Those who study the *Vedas* and drink the *soma* juice, seeking the heavenly planets, worship Me indirectly. Purified of sinful reactions, they take birth on the pious, heavenly planet of Indra, where they enjoy godly delights.
21. When they have thus enjoyed vast heavenly sense pleasure and the results of their pious activities are exhausted, they return to this mortal planet again. Thus those who seek sense enjoyment by adhering to the principles of the three *Vedas* achieve only repeated birth and death.
22. But those who always worship Me with exclusive devotion, meditating on My transcendental form—to them I carry what they lack, and I preserve what they have.
23. Those who are devotees of other gods and who worship them with faith actually worship only Me, O son of Kuntī, but they do so in a wrong way.

24. I am the only enjoyer and master of all sacrifices. Therefore, those who do not recognize My true transcendental nature fall down.
25. Those who worship the demigods will take birth among the demigods; those who worship the ancestors go to the ancestors; those who worship ghosts and spirits will take birth among such beings; and those who worship Me will live with Me.

Devotion to Kṛṣṇa is the highest truth.

26. If one offers Me with love and devotion a leaf, a flower, fruit or water, I will accept it.
27. Whatever you do, whatever you eat, whatever you offer or give away, and whatever austerities you perform—do that, O son of Kuntī, as an offering to Me.
28. In this way you will be freed from bondage to work and its auspicious and inauspicious results. With your mind fixed on Me in this principle of renunciation, you will be liberated and come to Me.
29. I envy no one, nor am I partial to anyone. I am equal to all. But whoever renders service unto Me in devotion is a friend, is in Me, and I am also a friend to him.
30. Even if one commits the most abominable action, if he is engaged in devotional service he is to be considered saintly because he is properly situated in his determination.
31. He quickly becomes righteous and attains lasting peace. O son of Kuntī, declare it boldly that My devotee never perishes.
32. O son of Pṛthā, those who take shelter in Me, though they be of lower birth—women, *vaiśyas* [merchants] and *śūdras* [workers]—can attain the supreme destination.
33. How much more this is so of the righteous *brāhmaṇas*, the devotees, and the saintly kings. Therefore, having come to this temporary, miserable world, engage in loving service unto Me.
34. Engage your mind always in thinking of Me, become My devotee, offer obeisances to Me and worship Me. Being completely absorbed in Me, surely you will come to Me.

10/ The Opulence of the Absolute

God is the Supreme Transcendence.

1. The Supreme Personality of Godhead said: Listen again, O mighty-armed Arjuna. Because you are My dear friend, for your benefit I shall speak to you further, giving knowledge that is better than what I have already explained.

2. Neither the hosts of demigods nor the great sages know My origin or opulences, for, in every respect, I am the source of the demigods and sages.

3. He who knows Me as the unborn, as the beginningless, as the Supreme Lord of all the worlds—he only, undeluded among men, is freed from all sins.

4–5. Intelligence, knowledge, freedom from doubt and delusion, forgiveness, truthfulness, control of the senses, control of the mind, happiness and distress, birth, death, fear, fearlessness, nonviolence, equanimity, satisfaction, austerity, charity, fame and infamy—all these various qualities of living beings are created by Me alone.

6. The seven great sages and before them the four other great sages and the Manus [progenitors of mankind] come from Me, born from My mind, and all the living beings populating the various planets descend from them.

7. One who is factually convinced of this opulence and mystic power of Mine engages in unalloyed devotional service; of this there is no doubt.

The four summary verses of the Gītā.

8. I am the source of all spiritual and material worlds. Everything emanates from Me. The wise who perfectly know this engage in My devotional service and worship Me with all their hearts.

9. The thoughts of My pure devotees dwell in Me, their lives are fully devoted to My service, and they derive great satisfaction and bliss from always enlightening one another and conversing about Me.

10. To those who are constantly devoted to serving Me with love, I give the understanding by which they can come to Me.

11. To show them special mercy, I, dwelling in their hearts, destroy with the shining lamp of knowledge the darkness born of ignorance.

Kṛṣṇa is the essence of all manifestations.

12–13. Arjuna said: You are the Supreme Personality of Godhead, the ultimate abode, the purest, the Absolute Truth. You are the eternal, transcendental, original person, the unborn, the greatest. All the great sages such as Nārada, Asita, Devala and Vyāsa confirm this truth about You, and now You Yourself are declaring it to me.

14. O Kṛṣṇa, I totally accept as truth all that You have told me.

Neither the demigods nor the demons, O Lord, can understand Your personality.
15. Indeed, You alone know Yourself by Your own internal potency, O Supreme Person, origin of all, Lord of all beings, God of gods, Lord of the universe!
16. Please tell me in detail of Your divine opulences by which You pervade all these worlds.
17. O Kṛṣṇa, O supreme mystic, how shall I constantly think of You, and how shall I know You? In what various forms are You to be remembered, O Supreme Personality of Godhead?
18. O Janārdana, again please describe in detail the mystic power of Your opulences. I am never satiated in hearing about You, for the more I hear the more I want to taste the nectar of Your words.
19. The Supreme Personality of Godhead said: Yes, I will tell you of My splendorous manifestations, but only of those which are prominent, O Arjuna, for My opulence is limitless.
20. I am the Supersoul, O Arjuna, seated in the hearts of all living entities. I am the beginning, the middle and the end of all beings.
21. Of the Ādityas I am Viṣṇu, of lights I am the radiant sun, of the Maruts I am Marīci, and among the stars I am the moon.
22. Of the *Vedas* I am the *Sāma Veda;* of the demigods I am Indra, the king of heaven; of the senses I am the mind; and in living beings I am the living force [consciousness].
23. Of all the Rudras I am Lord Śiva, of the Yakṣas and Rākṣasas I am the Lord of wealth [Kuvera], of the Vasus I am fire [Agni], and of mountains I am Meru.
24. Of priests, O Arjuna, know Me to be the chief, Bṛhaspati. Of generals I am Kārtikeya, and of bodies of water I am the ocean.
25. Of the great sages I am Bhṛgu; of vibrations I am the transcendental *oṁ.* Of sacrifices I am the chanting of the holy names [*japa*], and of immovable things I am the Himālayas.
26. Of all trees I am the banyan tree, and of the sages among the demigods I am Nārada. Of the Gandharvas I am Citraratha, and among perfected beings I am the sage Kapila.
27. Of horses know Me to be Uccaiḥśravā, produced during the churning of the ocean for nectar. Of lordly elephants I am Airāvata, and among men I am the monarch.
28. Of weapons I am the thunderbolt; among cows I am the *surabhi.* Of causes for procreation I am Kandarpa, the god of love, and of serpents I am Vāsuki.

29. Of the many-hooded Nāgas I am Ananta, and among the aquatics I am the demigod Varuṇa. Of departed ancestors I am Aryamā, and among the dispensers of law I am Yama, the lord of death.
30. Among the Daitya demons I am the devoted Prahlāda, among subduers I am time, among beasts I am the lion, and among birds I am Garuḍa.
31. Of purifiers I am the wind, of the wielders of weapons I am Rāma, of fishes I am the shark, and of flowing rivers I am the Ganges.
32. Of all creations I am the beginning and the end and also the middle, O Arjuna. Of all sciences I am the spiritual science of the self, and among logicians I am the conclusive truth.
33. Of letters I am the letter A, and among compound words I am the dual compound. I am also inexhaustible time, and of creators I am Brahmā.
34. I am all-devouring death, and I am the generating principle of all that is yet to be. Among women I am fame, fortune, fine speech, memory, intelligence, steadfastness and patience.
35. Of the hymns in the *Sāma Veda* I am the *Bṛhat-sāma,* and of poetry I am the Gāyatrī. Of months I am Mārgaśīrṣa [November–December], and of seasons I am flower-bearing spring.
36. I am also the gambling of cheats, and of the splendid I am the splendor. I am victory, I am adventure, and I am the strength of the strong.
37. Of the descendants of Vṛṣṇi I am Vāsudeva, and of the Pāṇḍavas I am Arjuna. Of the sages I am Vyāsa, and among great thinkers I am Uśanā.
38. Among all means of suppressing lawlessness I am punishment, and of those who seek victory I am morality. Of secret things I am silence, and of the wise I am the wisdom.
39. Furthermore, O Arjuna, I am the generating seed of all existences. There is no being—moving or nonmoving—that can exist without Me.
40. O mighty conqueror of enemies, there is no end to My divine manifestations. What I have spoken to you is but a mere indication of My infinite opulences.
41. Know that all opulent, beautiful and glorious creations spring from but a spark of My splendor.
42. But what need is there, Arjuna, for all this detailed knowledge? With a single fragment of Myself I pervade and support this entire universe.

11/ The Universal Form

Arjuna requests to see the Lord's cosmic form.

1. Arjuna said: By my hearing the instructions You have kindly given me about these most confidential spiritual subjects, my illusion has now been dispelled.
2. O lotus-eyed one, I have heard from You in detail about the appearance and disappearance of every living entity and have realized Your inexhaustible glories.
3. O greatest of all personalities, O supreme form, though I see You here before me in Your actual position, as You have described Yourself, I wish to see how You have entered into this cosmic manifestation. I want to see that form of Yours.
4. If You think that I am able to behold Your cosmic form, O my Lord, O master of all mystic power, then kindly show me that unlimited universal Self.
5. The Supreme Personality of Godhead said: My dear Arjuna, O son of Pṛthā, see now My opulences, hundreds of thousands of varied divine and multicolored forms.
6. O best of the Bhāratas, see here the different manifestations of Ādityas, Vasus, Rudras, Aśvinī-kumāras and all the other demigods. Behold the many wonderful things which no one has ever seen or heard of before.
7. O Arjuna, whatever you wish to see, behold at once in this body of Mine! This universal form can show you whatever you now desire to see and whatever you may want to see in the future. Everything moving and nonmoving—is here completely, in one place.
8. But you cannot see Me with your present eyes. Therefore I give you divine eyes. Behold My mystic opulence!

Revelation of the universal form.

9. Sañjaya said: O King, having spoken thus, the Supreme Lord of all mystic power, the Personality of Godhead, displayed His universal form to Arjuna.
10–11. Arjuna saw in that universal form unlimited mouths, unlimited eyes, unlimited wonderful visions. The form was decorated with many celestial ornaments and bore many divine upraised weapons. He wore celestial garlands and garments, and many divine scents

were smeared over His body. All was wondrous, brilliant, unlimited, all-expanding.

12. If hundreds of thousands of suns were to rise at once into the sky, their radiance might resemble the effulgence of the Supreme Person in that universal form.

13. At that time Arjuna could see in the universal form of the Lord the unlimited expansions of the universe situated in one place although divided into many, many thousands.

14. Then, bewildered and astonished, his hair standing on end, Arjuna bowed his head to offer obeisances and with folded hands began to pray to the Supreme Lord.

15. Arjuna said: My dear Lord Kṛṣṇa, I see assembled in Your body all the demigods and various other living entities. I see Brahmā sitting on the lotus flower, as well as Lord Śiva and all the sages and divine serpents.

16. O Lord of the universe, O universal form, I see in Your body many, many arms, bellies, mouths and eyes, expanded everywhere, without limit. I see in You no end, no middle and no beginning.

17. Your form is difficult to see because of its glaring effulgence, spreading on all sides, like blazing fire or the immeasurable radiance of the sun. Yet I see this glowing form everywhere, adorned with various crowns, clubs and discs.

18. You are the supreme primal objective. You are the ultimate resting place of all this universe. You are inexhaustible, and You are the oldest. You are the maintainer of the eternal religion, the Personality of Godhead. This is my opinion.

19. You are without origin, middle or end. Your glory is unlimited. You have numberless arms, and the sun and moon are Your eyes. I see You with blazing fire coming forth from Your mouth, burning this entire universe by Your own radiance.

20. Although You are one, You spread throughout the sky and the planets and all space between. O great one, seeing this wondrous and terrible form, all the planetary systems are perturbed.

21. All the hosts of demigods are surrendering before You and entering into You. Some of them, very much afraid, are offering prayers with folded hands. Hosts of great sages and perfected beings, crying "All peace!" are praying to You by singing the Vedic hymns.

22. All the various manifestations of Lord Śiva, the Ādityas, the Vasus, the Sādhyas, the Viśvedevas, the two Aśvins, the Maruts, the forefathers, the Gandharvas, the Yakṣas, the Asuras and the perfected demigods are beholding You in wonder.

23. O mighty-armed one, all the planets with their demigods are disturbed at seeing Your great form, with its many faces, eyes, arms, thighs, legs, and bellies and Your many terrible teeth; and as they are disturbed, so am I.
24. O all-pervading Viṣṇu, seeing You with Your many radiant colors touching the sky, Your gaping mouths, and Your great glowing eyes, my mind is perturbed by fear. I can no longer maintain my steadiness or equilibrium of mind.
25. O Lord of lords, O refuge of the worlds, please be gracious to me. I cannot keep my balance seeing thus Your blazing deathlike faces and awful teeth. In all directions I am bewildered.
26–27. All the sons of Dhṛtarāṣṭra, along with their allied kings, and Bhīṣma, Droṇa, Karṇa—and our chief soldiers also—are rushing into Your fearful mouths. And some I see trapped with heads smashed between Your teeth.
28. As the many waves of the rivers flow into the ocean, so do all these great warriors enter blazing into Your mouths.
29. I see all people rushing full speed into Your mouths, as moths dash to destruction in a blazing fire.
30. O Viṣṇu, I see You devouring all people from all sides with Your flaming mouths. Covering all the universe with Your effulgence, You are manifest with terrible, scorching rays.
31. O Lord of lords, so fierce of form, please tell me who You are. I offer my obeisances unto You; please be gracious to me. You are the primal Lord. I want to know about You, for I do not know what Your mission is.
32. The Supreme Personality of Godhead said: Time I am, the great destroyer of the worlds, and I have come here to destroy all people. With the exception of you [the Pāṇḍavas], all the soldiers here on both sides will be slain.
33. Therefore get up. Prepare to fight and win glory. Conquer your enemies and enjoy a flourishing kingdom. They are already put to death by My arrangement, and you, O Savyasācī, can be but an instrument in the fight.
34. Droṇa, Bhīṣma, Jayadratha, Karṇa and the other great warriors have already been destroyed by Me. Therefore, kill them and do not be disturbed. Simply fight, and you will vanquish your enemies in battle.
35. Sañjaya said to Dhṛtarāṣṭra: O King, after hearing these words from the Supreme Personality of Godhead, the trembling Arjuna offered obeisances with folded hands again and again. He fearfully

spoke to Lord Kṛṣṇa in a faltering voice, as follows.

Arjuna offers prayers.

36. Arjuna said: O master of the senses, the world becomes joyful upon hearing Your name, and thus everyone becomes attached to You. Although the perfected beings offer You their respectful homage, the demons are afraid, and they flee here and there. All this is rightly done.

37. O great one, greater even than Brahmā, You are the original creator. Why then should they not offer their respectful obeisances unto You? O limitless one, God of gods, refuge of the universe! You are the invincible source, the cause of all causes, transcendental to this material manifestation.

38. You are the original Personality of Godhead, the oldest, the ultimate sanctuary of this manifested cosmic world. You are the knower of everything, and You are all that is knowable. You are the supreme refuge, above the material modes. O limitless form! This whole cosmic manifestation is pervaded by You!

39. You are air, and You are the supreme controller! You are fire, You are water, and You are the moon! You are Brahmā, the first living creature, and You are the great-grandfather. I therefore offer my respectful obeisances unto You a thousand times, and again and yet again!

40. Obeisances to You from the front, from behind and from all sides! O unbounded power, You are the master of limitless might! You are all-pervading, and thus You are everything!

41–42. Thinking of You as my friend, I have rashly addressed You "O Kṛṣṇa," "O Yādava," "O my friend," not knowing Your glories. Please forgive whatever I may have done in madness or in love. I have dishonored You many times, jesting as we relaxed, lay on the same bed, or sat or ate together, sometimes alone and sometimes in front of many friends. O infallible one, please excuse me for all those offenses.

43. You are the father of this complete cosmic manifestation, of the moving and the nonmoving. You are its worshipable chief, the supreme spiritual master. No one is equal to You, nor can anyone be one with You. How then could there be anyone greater than You within the three worlds, O Lord of immeasurable power?

44. You are the Supreme Lord, to be worshiped by every living being. Thus I fall down to offer You my respectful obeisances and ask Your mercy. As a father tolerates the impudence of his son, or a friend tolerates the impertinence of a friend, or a wife tolerates the familiarity of her partner, please tolerate the wrongs I may have done You.

Arjuna is frightened and requests the Lord to again reveal His original form.

45. After seeing this universal form, which I have never seen before, I am gladdened, but at the same time my mind is disturbed with fear. Therefore please bestow Your grace upon me and reveal again Your form as the Personality of Godhead, O Lord of lords, O abode of the universe.

46. O universal form, O thousand-armed Lord, I wish to see You in Your four-armed form, with helmeted head and with club, wheel, conch and lotus flower in Your hands. I long to see You in that form.

47. The Supreme Personality of Godhead said: My dear Arjuna, happily have I shown you, by My internal potency, this supreme universal form within the material world. No one before you has ever seen this primal form, unlimited and full of glaring effulgence.

48. O best of the Kuru warriors, no one before you has ever seen this universal form of Mine, for neither by studying the *Vedas,* nor by performing sacrifices, nor by charity, nor by pious activities, nor by severe penances can I be seen in this form in the material world.

49. You have been perturbed and bewildered by seeing this horrible feature of Mine. Now let it be finished. My devotee, be free again from all disturbances. With a peaceful mind you can now see the form you desire.

50. Sañjaya said to Dhṛtarāṣṭra: The Supreme Personality of Godhead, Kṛṣṇa, having spoken thus to Arjuna, displayed His real four-armed form and at last showed His two-armed form, thus encouraging the fearful Arjuna.

51. When Arjuna thus saw Kṛṣṇa in His original form, he said: O Janārdana, seeing this humanlike form, so very beautiful, I am now composed in mind, and I am restored to my original nature.

52. The Supreme Personality of Godhead said: My dear Arjuna, this form of Mine you are now seeing is very difficult to behold. Even the demigods are ever seeking the opportunity to see this form, which is so dear.

Only by devotional service can one know Kṛṣṇa.

53. The form you are seeing with your transcendental eyes cannot be understood simply by studying the *Vedas,* nor by undergoing serious penances, nor by charity, nor by worship. It is not by these means that one can see Me as I am.

54. My dear Arjuna, only by undivided devotional service can I be understood as I am, standing before you, and can thus be seen directly. Only in this way can you enter into the mysteries of My understanding.

55. My dear Arjuna, he who engages in My pure devotional service, free from the contaminations of fruitive activities and mental speculation, he who works for Me, who makes Me the supreme goal of his life, and who is friendly to every living being—he certainly comes to Me.

12/ Devotional Service

Personal worship is better than impersonal.

1. Arjuna inquired: Which are considered to be more perfect, those who are always properly engaged in Your devotional service or those who worship the impersonal Brahman, the unmanifested?

2. The Supreme Personality of Godhead said: Those who fix their minds on My personal form and are always engaged in worshiping Me with great and transcendental faith are considered by Me to be most perfect.

3–4. But those who fully worship the unmanifested, that which lies beyond the perception of the senses, the all-pervading, inconceivable, unchanging, fixed and immovable—the impersonal conception of the Absolute Truth—by controlling the various senses and being equally disposed to everyone, such persons, engaged in the welfare of all, at last achieve Me.

5. For those whose minds are attached to the unmanifested, impersonal feature of the Supreme, advancement is very troublesome. To make progress in that discipline is always difficult for those who are embodied.

Stages of devotional service.

6–7. But those who worship Me, giving up all their activities unto Me and being devoted to Me without deviation, engaged in devotional service and always meditating upon Me, having fixed their minds upon Me, O son of Pṛthā—for them I am the swift deliverer from the ocean of birth and death.

8. Just fix your mind upon Me, the Supreme Personality of Godhead, and engage all your intelligence in Me. Thus you will live in Me always, without a doubt.

9. My dear Arjuna, O winner of wealth, if you cannot fix your mind upon Me without deviation, then follow the regulative principles of *bhakti-yoga.* In this way develop a desire to attain Me.

10. If you cannot practice the regulations of *bhakti-yoga,* then just try to work for Me, because by working for Me you will come to the perfect stage.

11. If, however, you are unable to work in this consciousness of Me, then try to act giving up all results of your work and try to be self-situated.

12. If you cannot take to this practice, then engage yourself in the cultivation of knowledge. Better than knowledge, however, is meditation, and better than meditation is renunciation of the fruits of action, for by such renunciation one can attain peace of mind.

The characteristics of a pure devotee.

13-14. One who is not envious but is a kind friend to all living entities, who does not think himself a proprietor and is free from false ego, who is equal in both happiness and distress, who is tolerant, always satisfied, self-controlled, and engaged in devotional service with determination, his mind and intelligence fixed on Me—such a devotee of Mine is very dear to Me.

15. He for whom no one is put into difficulty and who is not disturbed by anyone, who is equipoised in happiness and distress, fear and anxiety, is very dear to Me.

16. My devotee who is not dependent on the ordinary course of activities, who is pure, expert, without cares, free from all pains, and not striving for some result, is very dear to Me.

17. One who neither rejoices nor grieves, who neither laments nor desires, and who renounces both auspicious and inauspicious things—such a devotee is very dear to Me.

18-19. One who is equal to friends and enemies, who is equipoised in honor and dishonor, heat and cold, happiness and distress, fame and infamy, who is always free from contaminating association, always silent and satisfied with anything, who doesn't care for any residence, who is fixed in knowledge and who is engaged in devotional service—such a person is very dear to Me.

20. Those who follow this imperishable path of devotional service and who completely engage themselves with faith, making Me the supreme goal, are very, very dear to Me.

13/ Nature, the Enjoyer, and Consciousness

The field and the knower of the field.

1–2. Arjuna said: O my dear Kṛṣṇa, I wish to know about *prakṛti* [nature], *puruṣa* [the enjoyer], and the field and the knower of the field, and of knowledge and the object of knowledge.

The Supreme Personality of Godhead said: This body, O son of Kuntī, is called the field, and one who knows this body is called the knower of the field.

3. O scion of Bharata, you should understand that I am also the knower in all bodies, and to understand this body and its knower is called knowledge. That is My opinion.

4. Now please hear My brief description of this field of activity and how it is constituted, what its changes are, whence it is produced, who that knower of the field of activities is, and what his influences are.

5. That knowledge of the field of activities and of the knower of activities is described by various sages in various Vedic writings. It is especially presented in *Vedānta-sūtra* with all reasoning as to cause and effect.

6–7. The five great elements, false ego, intelligence, the unmanifested, the ten senses and the mind, the five sense objects, desire, hatred, happiness, distress, the aggregate, the life symptoms, and convictions—all these are considered, in summary, to be the field of activities and its interactions.

The items of knowledge.

8–12. Humility; pridelessness; nonviolence; tolerance; simplicity; approaching a bona fide spiritual master; cleanliness; steadiness; self-control; renunciation of the objects of sense gratification; absence of false ego; the perception of the evil of birth, death, old age and disease; detachment; freedom from entanglement with children, wife, home and the rest; evenmindedness amid pleasant and unpleasant events; constant and unalloyed devotion to Me; aspiring to live in a solitary place; detachment from the general mass of people; accepting the importance of self-realization; and philosophical search for the Absolute Truth—all these I declare to be knowledge, and besides this whatever there may be is ignorance.

The soul and the Supersoul.

13. I shall now explain the knowable, knowing which you will taste the eternal. Brahman, the spirit, beginningless and subordinate to Me, lies beyond the cause and effect of this material world.
14. Everywhere are His hands and legs, His eyes, heads and faces, and He has ears everywhere. In this way the Supersoul exists, pervading everything.
15. The Supersoul is the original source of all senses, yet He is without senses. He is unattached, although He is the maintainer of all living beings. He transcends the modes of nature, and at the same time He is the master of all the modes of material nature.
16. The Supreme Truth exists outside and inside of all living beings, the moving and the nonmoving. Because He is subtle, He is beyond the power of the material senses to see or to know. Although far, far away, He is also near to all.
17. Although the Supersoul appears to be divided among all beings, He is never divided. He is situated as one. Although He is the maintainer of every living entity, it is to be understood that He devours and develops all.
18. He is the source of light in all luminous objects. He is beyond the darkness of matter and is unmanifested. He is knowledge, He is the object of knowledge, and He is the goal of knowledge. He is situated in everyone's heart.
19. Thus the field of activities [the body], knowledge and the knowable have been summarily described by Me. Only My devotees can understand this thoroughly and thus attain to My nature.

How the living entities transmigrate.

20. Material nature and the living entities should be understood to be beginningless. Their transformations and the modes of matter are products of material nature.
21. Nature is said to be the cause of all material causes and effects,

whereas the living entity is the cause of the various sufferings and enjoyments in this world.

22. The living entity in material nature thus follows the ways of life, enjoying the three modes of nature. This is due to his association with that material nature. Thus he meets with good and evil amongst various species.

23. Yet in this body there is another, a transcendental enjoyer, who is the Lord, the supreme proprietor, who exists as the overseer and permitter, and who is known as the Supersoul.

24. One who understands this philosophy concerning material nature, the living entity and the interaction of the modes of nature is sure to attain liberation. He will not take birth here again, regardless of his present position.

25. Some perceive the Supersoul within themselves through meditation, others through the cultivation of knowledge, and still others through working without fruitive desires.

26. Again there are those who, although not conversant in spiritual knowledge, begin to worship the Supreme Person upon hearing about Him from others. Because of their tendency to hear from authorities, they also transcend the path of birth and death.

27. O chief of the Bhāratas, know that whatever you see in existence, both the moving and the nonmoving, is only a combination of the field of activities and the knower of the field.

28. One who sees the Supersoul accompanying the individual soul in all bodies, and who understands that neither the soul nor the Supersoul within the destructible body is ever destroyed, actually sees.

29. One who sees the Supersoul equally present everywhere, in every living being, does not degrade himself by his mind. Thus he approaches the transcendental destination.

30. One who can see that all activities are performed by the body, which is created of material nature, and sees that the self does nothing, actually sees.

31. When a sensible man ceases to see different identities due to different material bodies and he sees how beings are expanded everywhere, he attains to the Brahman conception.

32. Those with the vision of eternity can see that the imperishable soul is transcendental, eternal, and beyond the modes of nature. Despite contact with the material body, O Arjuna, the soul neither does anything nor is entangled.

33. The sky, due to its subtle nature, does not mix with anything, although it is all-pervading. Similarly, the soul situated in Brahman vision does not mix with the body, though situated in that body.
34. O son of Bharata, as the sun alone illuminates all this universe, so does the living entity, one within the body, illuminate the entire body by consciousness.
35. Those who see with eyes of knowledge the difference between the body and the knower of the body, and can also understand the process of liberation from bondage in material nature, attain to the supreme goal.

14/ The Three Modes of Material Nature

Goodness, passion and ignorance.

1. The Supreme Personality of Godhead said: Again I shall declare to you this supreme wisdom, thc best of all knowledge, knowing which all the sages have attained the supreme perfection.
2. By becoming fixed in this knowledge, one can attain to the transcendental nature like My own. Thus established, one is not born at the time of creation or disturbed at the time of dissolution.
3. The total material substance, called Brahman, is the source of birth, and it is that Brahman that I impregnate, making possible the births of all living beings, O son of Bharata.
4. It should be understood that all species of life, O son of Kuntī, are made possible by birth in this material nature, and that I am the seed-giving father.
5. Material nature consists of three modes—goodness, passion and ignorance. When the eternal living entity comes in contact with nature, O mighty-armed Arjuna, he becomes conditioned by these modes.
6. O sinless one, the mode of goodness, being purer than the others, is illuminating, and it frees one from all sinful reactions. Those situated in that mode become conditioned by a sense of happiness and knowledge.
7. The mode of passion is born of unlimited desires and longings, O

son of Kuntī, and because of this the embodied living entity is bound to material fruitive actions.

8. O son of Bharata, know that the mode of darkness, born of ignorance, is the delusion of all embodied living entities. The results of this mode are madness, indolence and sleep, which bind the conditioned soul.

9. O son of Bharata, the mode of goodness conditions one to happiness; passion conditions one to fruitive action; and ignorance, covering one's knowledge, binds one to madness.

10. Sometimes the mode of goodness becomes prominent, defeating the modes of passion and ignorance, O son of Bharata. Sometimes the mode of passion defeats goodness and ignorance, and at other times ignorance defeats goodness and passion. In this way there is always competition for supremacy.

11. The manifestations of the mode of goodness can be experienced when all the gates of the body are illuminated by knowledge.

12. O chief of the Bhāratas, when there is an increase in the mode of passion the symptoms of great attachment, fruitive activity, intense endeavor, and uncontrollable desire and hankering develop.

13. When there is an increase in the mode of ignorance, O son of Kuru, darkness, inertia, madness and illusion are manifested.

14. When one dies in the mode of goodness, he attains to the pure higher planets of the great sages.

15. When one dies in the mode of passion, he takes birth among those engaged in fruitive activities; and when one dies in the mode of ignorance, he takes birth in the animal kingdom.

16. The result of pious action is pure and is said to be in the mode of goodness. But action done in the mode of passion results in misery, and action performed in the mode of ignorance results in foolishness.

17. From the mode of goodness, real knowledge develops; from the mode of passion, greed develops; and from the mode of ignorance develop foolishness, madness and illusion.

18. Those situated in the mode of goodness gradually go upward to the higher planets; those in the mode of passion live on the earthly planets; and those in the abominable mode of ignorance go down to the hellish worlds.

19. When one properly sees that in all activities no other performer is at work than these modes of nature and he knows the Supreme Lord, who is transcendental to all these modes, he attains My spiritual nature.

Transcending the three modes.

20. When the embodied being is able to transcend these three modes associated with the material body, he can become free from birth, death, old age and their distresses and can enjoy nectar even in this life.
21. Arjuna inquired: O my dear Lord, by which symptoms is one known who is transcendental to these three modes? What is his behavior? And how does he transcend the modes of nature?
22-25. The Supreme Personality of Godhead said: O son of Pāṇḍu, he who does not hate illumination, attachment and delusion when they are present or long for them when they disappear; who is unwavering and undisturbed through all these reactions of the material qualities, remaining neutral and transcendental, knowing that the modes alone are active; who is situated in the self and regards alike happiness and distress; who looks upon a lump of earth, a stone and a piece of gold with an equal eye; who is equal toward the desirable and the undesirable; who is steady, situated equally well in praise and blame, honor and dishonor; who treats alike both friend and enemy; and who has renounced all material activities—such a person is said to have transcended the modes of nature.
26. One who engages in full devotional service, unfailing in all circumstances, at once transcends the modes of material nature and thus comes to the level of Brahman.

The Supreme Brahman rests in Kṛṣṇa.

27. And I am the basis of the impersonal Brahman, which is immortal, imperishable and eternal and is the constitutional position of ultimate happiness.

15/ The Yoga of the Supreme Person

The banyan tree of the material world.

1. The Supreme Personality of Godhead said: It is said that there is an imperishable banyan tree that has its roots upward and its branches down and whose leaves are the Vedic hymns. One who knows this tree is the knower of the *Vedas*.

2. The branches of this tree extend downward and upward, nourished by the three modes of material nature. The twigs are the objects of the senses. This tree also has roots going down, and these are bound to the fruitive actions of human society.

3–4. The real form of this tree cannot be perceived in this world. No one can understand where it ends, where it begins, or where its foundation is. But with determination one must cut down this strongly rooted tree with the weapon of detachment. Thereafter, one must seek that place from which, having gone, one never returns, and there surrender to that Supreme Personality of Godhead from whom everything began and from whom everything has extended since time immemorial.

Kṛṣṇa's abode.

5. Those who are free from false prestige, illusion and false association, who understand the eternal, who are done with material lust, who are freed from the dualities of happiness and distress, and who, unbewildered, know how to surrender unto the Supreme Person attain to that eternal kingdom.

6. That supreme abode of Mine is not illumined by the sun or moon, nor by fire or electricity. Those who reach it never return to this material world.

The struggling jīvas.

7. The living entities in this conditioned world are My eternal fragmental parts. Due to conditioned life, they are struggling very hard with the six senses, which include the mind.

8. The living entity in the material world carries his different conceptions of life from one body to another as the air carries aromas. Thus he takes one kind of body and again quits it to take another.

9. The living entity, thus taking another gross body, obtains a certain type of ear, eye, tongue, nose and sense of touch, which are grouped about the mind. He thus enjoys a particular set of sense objects.

10. The foolish cannot understand how a living entity can quit his body, nor can they understand what sort of body he enjoys under the spell of the modes of nature. But one whose eyes are trained in knowledge can see all this.

11. The endeavoring transcendentalists, who are situated in self-realization, can see all this clearly. But those whose minds are not developed and who are not situated in self-realization cannot see what is taking place, though they may try to.

The Supreme Personality of Godhead.

12. The splendor of the sun, which dissipates the darkness of this whole world, comes from Me. And the splendor of the moon and the splendor of fire are also from Me.
13. I enter into each planet, and by My energy they stay in orbit. I become the moon and thereby supply the juice of life to all vegetables.
14. I am the fire of digestion in the bodies of all living entities, and I join with the air of life, outgoing and incoming, to digest the four kinds of foodstuff.
15. I am seated in everyone's heart, and from Me come remembrance, knowledge and forgetfulness. By all the *Vedas,* I am to be known. Indeed, I am the compiler of *Vedānta,* and I am the knower of the *Vedas.*
16. There are two classes of beings, the fallible and the infallible. In the material world every living entity is fallible, and in the spiritual world every living entity is called infallible.
17. Besides these two, there is the greatest living personality, the Supreme Soul, the imperishable Lord Himself, who has entered the three worlds and is maintaining them.
18. Because I am transcendental, beyond both the fallible and the infallible, and because I am the greatest, I am celebrated both in the world and in the *Vedas* as that Supreme Person.
19. Whoever knows Me as the Supreme Personality of Godhead, without doubting, is the knower of everything. He therefore engages himself in full devotional service to Me, O son of Bharata.
20. This is the most confidential part of the Vedic scriptures, O sinless one, and it is disclosed now by Me. Whoever understands this will become wise, and his endeavors will know perfection.

16/ The Divine and Demoniac Natures

The divine nature.

1–3. The Supreme Personality of Godhead said: Fearlessness; purification of one's existence; cultivation of spiritual knowledge; charity; self-control; performance of sacrifice; study of the *Vedas;*

austerity; simplicity; nonviolence; truthfulness; freedom from anger; renunciation; tranquility; aversion to faultfinding; compassion for all living entities; freedom from covetousness; gentleness; modesty; steady determination; vigor; forgiveness; fortitude; cleanliness; and freedom from envy and from the passion for honor—these transcendental qualities, O son of Bharata, belong to godly men endowed with divine nature.

The demoniac nature.

4. Pride, arrogance, conceit, anger, harshness and ignorance—these qualities belong to those of demoniac nature, O son of Pṛthā.
5. The transcendental qualities are conducive to liberation, whereas the demoniac qualities make for bondage. Do not worry, O son of Pāṇḍu, for you are born with the divine qualities.
6. O son of Pṛthā, in this world there are two kinds of created beings. One is called the divine and the other demoniac. I have already explained to you at length the divine qualities. Now hear from Me of the demoniac.
7. Those who are demoniac do not know what is to be done and what is not to be done. Neither cleanliness nor proper behavior nor truth is found in them.
8. They say that this world is unreal, with no foundation, no God in control. They say it is produced of sex desire and has no cause other than lust.
9. Following such conclusions, the demoniac, who are lost to themselves and who have no intelligence, engage in unbeneficial, horrible works meant to destroy the world.
10. Taking shelter of insatiable lust and absorbed in the conceit of pride and false prestige, the demoniac, thus illusioned, are always sworn to unclean work, attracted by the impermanent.
11–12. They believe that to gratify the senses is the prime necessity of human civilization. Thus until the end of life their anxiety is immeasurable. Bound by a network of hundreds of thousands of desires and absorbed in lust and anger, they secure money by illegal means for sense gratification.
13–15. The demoniac person thinks: "So much wealth do I have today, and I will gain more according to my schemes. So much is mine now, and it will increase in the future, more and more. He is my enemy, and I have killed him, and my other enemies will also be killed. I am the lord of everything. I am the enjoyer. I am perfect, powerful and happy. I am the richest man, surrounded by aristocratic

relatives. There is none so powerful and happy as I am. I shall perform sacrifices, I shall give some charity, and thus I shall rejoice." In this way, such persons are deluded by ignorance.

16. Thus perplexed by various anxieties and bound by a network of illusions, they become too strongly attached to sense enjoyment and fall down into hell.

17. Self-complacent and always impudent, deluded by wealth and false prestige, they sometimes proudly perform sacrifices in name only, without following any rules or regulations.

18. Bewildered by false ego, strength, pride, lust and anger, the demons become envious of the Supreme Personality of Godhead, who is situated in their own bodies and in the bodies of others, and blaspheme against the real religion.

19. Those who are envious and mischievous, who are the lowest among men, I perpetually cast into the ocean of material existence, into various demoniac species of life.

Three gates to hell.

20. Attaining repeated birth amongst the species of demoniac life, O son of Kuntī, such persons can never approach Me. Gradually they sink down to the most abominable type of existence.

21. There are three gates leading to this hell—lust, anger and greed. Every sane man should give these up, for they lead to the degradation of the soul.

22. The man who has escaped these three gates of hell, O son of Kuntī, performs acts conducive to self-realization and thus gradually attains the supreme destination.

23. He who discards scriptural injunctions and acts according to his own whims attains neither perfection, nor happiness, nor the supreme destination.

24. One should therefore understand what is duty and what is not duty by the regulations of the scriptures. Knowing such rules and regulations, one should act so that he may gradually be elevated.

17/ The Divisions of Faith

Faith according to the three modes.

1. Arjuna inquired: O Kṛṣṇa, what is the situation of those who do not follow the principles of scripture but worship according to their own imagination? Are they in goodness, in passion or in ignorance?

2. The Supreme Personality of Godhead said: According to the modes of nature acquired by the embodied soul, one's faith can be of three kinds—in goodness, in passion or in ignorance. Now hear about this.

3. O son of Bharata, according to one's existence under the various modes of nature, one evolves a particular kind of faith. The living being is said to be of a particular faith according to the modes he has acquired.

4. Men in the mode of goodness worship the demigods; those in the mode of passion worship the demons; and those in the mode of ignorance worship ghosts and spirits.

5–6. Those who undergo severe austerities and penances not recommended in the scriptures, performing them out of pride and egoism, who are impelled by lust and attachment, who are foolish and who torture the material elements of the body as well as the Supersoul dwelling within, are to be known as demons.

7. Even the food each person prefers is of three kinds, according to the three modes of material nature. The same is true of sacrifices, austerities and charity. Now hear of the distinctions between them.

Food, sacrifice, austerity and charity in the modes.

8. Foods dear to those in the mode of goodness increase the duration of life, purify one's existence and give strength, health, happiness and satisfaction. Such foods are juicy, fatty, wholesome, and pleasing to the heart.

9. Foods that are too bitter, too sour, salty, hot, pungent, dry and burning are dear to those in the mode of passion. Such foods cause distress, misery and disease.

10. Food prepared more than three hours before being eaten, food that is tasteless, decomposed and putrid, and food consisting of remnants and untouchable things is dear to those in the mode of darkness.

11. Of sacrifices, the sacrifice performed according to the directions of scripture, as a matter of duty, by those who desire no reward, is of the nature of goodness.

12. But the sacrifice performed for some material benefit, or for the sake of pride, O chief of the Bhāratas, you should know to be in the mode of passion.

13. Any sacrifice performed without regard for the directions of scripture, without distribution of *prasādam* [spiritual food], without chanting of Vedic hymns and remunerations to the priests, and without faith is considered to be in the mode of ignorance.
14. Austerity of the body consists in worship of the Supreme Lord, the *brāhmaṇas,* the spiritual master, and superiors like the father and mother, and in cleanliness, simplicity, celibacy and nonviolence.
15. Austerity of speech consists in speaking words that are truthful, pleasing, beneficial, and not agitating to others, and also in regularly reciting Vedic literature.
16. And satisfaction, simplicity, gravity, self-control and purification of one's existence are the austerities of the mind.
17. This threefold austerity, performed with transcendental faith by men not expecting material benefits but engaged only for the sake of the Supreme, is called austerity in goodness.
18. Penance performed out of pride and for the sake of gaining respect, honor and worship is said to be in the mode of passion. It is neither stable nor permanent.
19. Penance performed out of foolishness, with self-torture or to destroy or injure others is said to be in the mode of ignorance.
20. Charity given out of duty, without expectation of return, at the proper time and place, and to a worthy person is considered to be in the mode of goodness.
21. But charity performed with the expectation of some return, or with a desire for fruitive results, or in a grudging mood, is said to be charity in the mode of passion.
22. And charity performed at an impure place, at an improper time, to unworthy persons, or without proper attention and respect is said to be in the mode of ignorance.

Oṁ tat sat.

23. From the beginning of creation, the three words *oṁ tat sat* were used to indicate the Supreme Absolute Truth. These three symbolic representations were used by *brāhmaṇas* while chanting the hymns of the *Vedas* and during sacrifices for the satisfaction of the Supreme.
24. Therefore, transcendentalists undertaking performances of sacrifice, charity and penance in accordance with scriptural regulations begin always with *oṁ,* to attain the Supreme.
25. Without desiring fruitive results, one should perform various kinds of sacrifice, penance and charity with the word *tat.* The purpose

of such transcendental activities is to get free from material entanglement.

26–27. The Absolute Truth is the objective of devotional sacrifice, and it is indicated by the word *sat.* The performer of such sacrifice is also called *sat,* as are all works of sacrifice, penance and charity which, true to the absolute nature, are performed to please the Supreme Person, O son of Pṛthā.

28. Anything done as sacrifice, charity or penance without faith in the Supreme, O son of Pṛthā, is impermanent. It is called *asat* and is useless both in this life and in the next.

18/ Conclusion—The Perfection of Renunciation

The purpose of renunciation.

1. Arjuna said: O mighty-armed one, I wish to understand the purpose of renunciation [*tyāga*] and of the renounced order of life [*sannyāsa*], O killer of the Keśī demon, master of the senses.

2. The Supreme Personality of Godhead said: The giving up of activities that are based on material desire is what great learned men call the renounced order of life [*sannyāsa*]. And giving up the results of all activities is what the wise call renunciation [*tyāga*].

3. Some learned men declare that all kinds of fruitive activities should be given up as faulty, yet other sages maintain that acts of sacrifice, charity and penance should never be abandoned.

4. O best of the Bhāratas, now hear My judgment about renunciation. O tiger among men, renunciation is declared in the scriptures to be of three kinds.

5. Acts of sacrifice, charity and penance are not to be given up; they must be performed. Indeed, sacrifice, charity and penance purify even the great souls.

6. All these activities should be performed without attachment or any expectation of result. They should be performed as a matter of duty, O son of Pṛthā. That is My final opinion.

Prescribed duties should not be renounced.

7. Prescribed duties should never be renounced. If one gives up his prescribed duties because of illusion, such renunciation is said to be in the mode of ignorance.

8. Anyone who gives up prescribed duties as troublesome or out of fear of bodily discomfort is said to have renounced in the mode of passion. Such action never leads to the elevation of renunciation.

9. O Arjuna, when one performs his prescribed duty only because it ought to be done, and renounces all material association and all attachment to the fruit, his renunciation is said to be in the mode of goodness.

10. The intelligent renouncer situated in the mode of goodness, neither hateful of inauspicious work nor attached to auspicious work, has no doubts about work.

11. It is indeed impossible for an embodied being to give up all activities. But he who renounces the fruits of action is called one who has truly renounced.

12. For one who is not renounced, the threefold fruits of action—desirable, undesirable and mixed—accrue after death. But those who are in the renounced order of life have no such results to suffer or enjoy.

The five factors of action.

13. O mighty-armed Arjuna, according to the *Vedānta* there are five causes for the accomplishment of all action. Now learn of these from Me.

14. The place of action [the body], the performer, the various senses, the many different kinds of endeavor, and ultimately the Supersoul—these are the five factors of action.

15. Whatever right or wrong action a man performs by body, mind or speech is caused by these five factors.

16. Therefore one who thinks himself the only doer, not considering the five factors, is certainly not very intelligent and cannot see things as they are.

17. One who is not motivated by false ego, whose intelligence is not entangled, though he kills men in this world, does not kill. Nor is he bound by his actions.

Three kinds of knowledge, actions, and workers.

18. Knowledge, the object of knowledge, and the knower are the three factors that motivate action; the senses, the work and the doer are the three constituents of action.

19. According to the three different modes of material nature, there are three kinds of knowledge, action and performer of action. Now hear of them from Me.

20. That knowledge by which one undivided spiritual nature is seen in all living entities, though they are divided into innumerable forms, you should understand to be in the mode of goodness.

21. That knowledge by which one sees that in every different body there is a different type of living entity you should understand to be in the mode of passion.

22. And that knowledge by which one is attached to one kind of work as the all in all, without knowledge of the truth, and which is very meager, is said to be in the mode of darkness.

23. That action which is regulated and which is performed without attachment, without love or hatred, and without desire for fruitive results is said to be in the mode of goodness.

24. But action performed with great effort by one seeking to gratify his desires, and enacted from a sense of false ego, is called action in the mode of passion.

25. That action performed in illusion, in disregard of scriptural injunctions, and without concern for future bondage or for violence or distress caused to others is said to be in the mode of ignorance.

26. One who performs his duty without association with the modes of material nature, without false ego, with great determination and enthusiasm, and without wavering in success or failure is said to be a worker in the mode of goodness.

27. The worker who is attached to work and the fruits of work, desiring to enjoy those fruits, who is greedy, always envious, impure, and moved by joy and sorrow, is said to be in the mode of passion.

28. The worker who is always engaged in work against the injunctions of the scripture, who is materialistic, obstinate, cheating and expert in insulting others, and who is lazy, always morose and procrastinating is said to be a worker in the mode of ignorance.

Three kinds of understanding and determination.

29. O winner of wealth, now please listen as I tell you in detail of the different kinds of understanding and determination, according to the three modes of material nature.

30. O son of Pṛthā, that understanding by which one knows what ought to be done and what ought not to be done, what is to be feared and what is not to be feared, what is binding and what is liberating, is in the mode of goodness.

31. O son of Pṛthā, that understanding which cannot distinguish between religion and irreligion, between action that should be done and action that should not be done, is in the mode of passion.
32. That understanding which considers irreligion to be religion and religion to be irreligion, under the spell of illusion and darkness, and strives always in the wrong direction, O Pārtha, is in the mode of ignorance.
33. O son of Pṛthā, that determination which is unbreakable, which is sustained with steadfastness by *yoga* practice, and which thus controls the activities of the mind, life and senses is determination in the mode of goodness.
34. But that determination by which one holds fast to fruitive results in religion, economic development and sense gratification is of the nature of passion, O Arjuna.
35. And that determination which cannot go beyond dreaming, fearfulness, lamentation, moroseness and illusion—such unintelligent determination, O son of Pṛthā, is in the mode of darkness.

Three kinds of happiness.

36. O best of the Bhāratas, now please hear from Me about the three kinds of happiness by which the conditioned soul enjoys, and by which he sometimes comes to the end of all distress.
37. That which in the beginning may be just like poison but at the end is just like nectar and which awakens one to self-realization is said to be happiness in the mode of goodness.
38. That happiness which is derived from contact of the senses with their objects and which appears like nectar at first but poison at the end is said to be of the nature of passion.
39. And that happiness which is blind to self-realization, which is delusion from beginning to end and which arises from sleep, laziness and illusion is said to be of the nature of ignorance.
40. There is no being existing, either here or among the demigods in the higher planetary systems, which is freed from these three modes born of material nature.
41. *Brāhmaṇas, kṣatriyas, vaiśyas* and *śūdras* are distinguished by the qualities born of their own natures in accordance with the material modes, O chastiser of the enemy.

Duties of the four orders of life.

42. Peacefulness, self-control, austerity, purity, tolerance, honesty, knowledge, wisdom and religiousness—these are the natural qualities by which the *brāhmaṇas* work.

43. Heroism, power, determination, resourcefulness, courage in battle, generosity and leadership are the natural qualities of work for the *kṣatriyas.*

44. Farming, cow protection and business are the natural work for the *vaiśyas,* and for the *śūdras* there is labor and service to others.

45. By following his qualities of work, every man can become perfect. Now please hear from Me how this can be done.

46. By worship of the Lord, who is the source of all beings and who is all-pervading, a man can attain perfection through performing his own work.

47. It is better to engage in one's own occupation, even though one may perform it imperfectly, than to accept another's occupation and perform it perfectly. Duties prescribed according to one's nature are never affected by sinful reactions.

48. Every endeavor is covered by some fault, just as fire is covered by smoke. Therefore one should not give up the work born of his nature, O son of Kuntī, even if such work is full of fault.

49. One who is self-controlled and unattached and who disregards all material enjoyments can obtain, by practice of renunciation, the highest perfect stage of freedom from reaction.

Attaining perfection by devotion to the Supreme Person.

50. O son of Kuntī, learn from Me how one who has achieved this perfection can attain to the supreme perfectional stage, Brahman, the stage of highest knowledge, by acting in the way I shall now summarize.

51–53. Being purified by his intelligence and controlling the mind with determination, giving up the objects of sense gratification, being freed from attachment and hatred, one who lives in a secluded place, who eats little, who controls his body, mind and power of speech, who is always in trance and is detached, free from false ego, false strength, false pride, lust, anger, and acceptance of material things, who is free from false proprietorship, and who is peaceful—such a person is certainly elevated to the position of self-realization.

54. One who is thus transcendentally situated at once realizes the Supreme Brahman and becomes fully joyful. He never laments or desires to have anything. He is equally disposed toward every living entity. In that state he attains pure devotional service unto Me.

55. One can understand Me as I am, as the Supreme Personality of

Godhead, only by devotional service. And when one is in full consciousness of Me by such devotion, he can enter into the kingdom of God.

56. Though engaged in all kinds of activities, My pure devotee, under My protection, reaches the eternal and imperishable abode by My grace.

57. In all activities just depend upon Me and work always under My protection. In such devotional service, be fully conscious of Me.

58. If you become conscious of Me, you will pass over all the obstacles of conditioned life by My grace. If, however, you do not work in such consciousness but act through false ego, not hearing Me, you will be lost.

59. If you do not act according to My direction and do not fight, then you will be falsely directed. By your nature, you will have to be engaged in warfare.

60. Under illusion you are now declining to act according to My direction. But, compelled by the work born of your own nature, you will act all the same, O son of Kuntī.

61. The Supreme Lord is situated in everyone's heart, O Arjuna, and is directing the wanderings of all living entities, who are seated as on a machine, made of the material energy.

62. O scion of Bharata, surrender unto Him utterly. By His grace you will attain transcendental peace and the supreme and eternal abode.

63. Thus I have explained to you knowledge still more confidential. Deliberate on this fully, and then do what you wish to do.

64. Because you are My very dear friend, I am speaking to you My supreme instruction, the most confidential knowledge of all. Hear this from Me, for it is for your benefit.

65. Always think of Me, become My devotee, worship Me and offer your homage unto Me. Thus you will come to Me without fail. I promise you this because you are My very dear friend.

The conclusion of the Gītā.

66. Abandon all varieties of religion and just surrender unto Me. I shall deliver you from all sinful reactions. Do not fear.

67. This confidential knowledge may never be explained to those who are not austere, or devoted, or engaged in devotional service, nor to one who is envious of Me.

68. For one who explains this supreme secret to the devotees, pure devotional service is guaranteed, and at the end he will come back to Me.

69. There is no servant in this world more dear to Me than he, nor will there ever be one more dear.

70. And I declare that he who studies this sacred conversation of ours worships Me by his intelligence.

71. And one who listens with faith and without envy becomes free from sinful reactions and attains to the auspicious planets where the pious dwell.

72. O son of Pṛthā, O conqueror of wealth, have you heard this with an attentive mind? And are your ignorance and illusions now dispelled?

73. Arjuna said: My dear Kṛṣṇa, O infallible one, my illusion is now gone. I have regained my memory by Your mercy. I am now firm and free from doubt and am prepared to act according to Your instructions.

74. Sañjaya said: Thus have I heard the conversation of two great souls, Kṛṣṇa and Arjuna. And so wonderful is that message that my hair is standing on end.

75. By the mercy of Vyāsa, I have heard these most confidential talks directly from the master of all mysticism, Kṛṣṇa, who was speaking personally to Arjuna.

76. O King, as I repeatedly recall this wondrous and holy dialogue between Kṛṣṇa and Arjuna, I take pleasure, being thrilled at every moment.

77. O King, as I remember the wonderful form of Lord Kṛṣṇa, I am struck with wonder more and more, and I rejoice again and again.

78. Wherever there is Kṛṣṇa, the master of all mystics, and wherever there is Arjuna, the supreme archer, there will also certainly be opulence, victory, extraordinary power, and morality. That is my opinion.

BHĀGAVATA PURĀṆA
(Summary Study)

ADVENT OF LORD KṚṢṆA

Once the world was overburdened by the unnecessary defense force of different kings, who were actually demons but were posing themselves as the royal order. At that time, the whole world became perturbed, and the predominating deity of this earth, known as Bhūmi, went to see Lord Brahmā to tell of her calamities due to the demoniac kings. Bhūmi assumed the shape of a cow and presented herself before Lord Brahmā with tears in her eyes. She was bereaved and was weeping just to invoke the lord's compassion. She related the calamitous position of the earth, and after hearing this, Lord Brahmā became much aggrieved, and he at once started for the ocean of milk, where Lord Viṣṇu resides. Lord Brahmā was accompanied by all the demigods headed by Lord Śiva, and Bhūmi also followed. Arriving on the shore of the milk ocean, Lord Brahmā began to pacify Lord Viṣṇu, who formerly saved the earthly planet by assuming the transcendental form of a boar.

In the Vedic *mantras,* there is a particular type of prayer called *Puruṣa-sūkta*. Generally, the demigods offer their obeisances unto Viṣṇu, the Supreme Personality of Godhead, by chanting the *Puruṣa-sūkta.* It is understood herein that the predominating deity of every planet can see the supreme lord of this universe, Brahmā, whenever there is some disturbance in his planet. And Brahmā can approach the Supreme Lord Viṣṇu, not by seeing Him directly, but by standing on the shore of the ocean of milk. There is a planet within this universe called Śvetadvīpa, and on that planet there is an ocean of milk. It is understood from various Vedic literatures that just as there is the ocean of salt water within this planet, there are various kinds of oceans in other planets. Somewhere there is an ocean of milk, somewhere an ocean of oil, and somewhere there is an ocean of liquor and many other types of oceans. *Puruṣa-sūkta* is the standard prayer which the demigods recite to appease the Supreme Personality of Godhead, Kṣīrodakaśāyī Viṣṇu. Because He is lying on the ocean of milk, He is called Kṣīrodakaśāyī Viṣṇu.

He is the Supreme Personality of Godhead, through whom all the incarnations within this universe appear.

After all the demigods offered the *Puruṣa-sūkta* prayer to the Supreme Personality of Godhead, they apparently heard no response. Then Lord Brahmā personally sat in meditation, and there was a message-transmission from Lord Viṣṇu to Brahmā. Brahmā then broadcast the message to the demigods. That is the system of receiving Vedic knowledge. The Vedic knowledge is received first by Brahmā from the Supreme Personality of Godhead, through the medium of the heart. As stated in the beginning of *Śrīmad-Bhāgavatam, tene brahma hṛdā:* the transcendental knowledge of the *Vedas* was transmitted to Lord Brahmā through the heart. Here also, in the same way, only Brahmā could understand the message transmitted by Lord Viṣṇu, and he broadcast it to the demigods for their immediate action. The message was: the Supreme Personality of Godhead will appear on the earth very soon along with His supreme powerful potencies, and as long as He remains on the earth planet to execute His mission of annihilating the demons and establishing the devotees, the demigods should also remain there to assist Him. They should all immediately take birth in the family of the Yadu dynasty, wherein the Lord will also appear in due course of time.

The Supreme Personality of Godhead Himself, Kṛṣṇa, personally appeared as the son of Vasudeva. Before He appeared, all the demigods, along with their wives, appeared in different pious families in the world just to assist the Lord in executing His mission. The exact word used here is *tat-priyārtham,* which means the demigods should appear on the earth in order to please the Lord. In other words, any living entity who lives only to satisfy the Lord is a demigod. The demigods were further informed that the plenary portion of Lord Kṛṣṇa, Ananta, who is maintaining the universal planets by extending His millions of hoods, would also appear on earth before Lord Kṛṣṇa's appearance. They were also informed that the external potency of Viṣṇu (Māyā), with whom all the conditioned souls are enamored, would also appear just to execute the purpose of the Supreme Lord.

After instructing and pacifying all the demigods, as well as Bhūmi, with sweet words, Lord Brahmā, the father of all Prajāpatis, or progenitors of universal population, departed for his own abode, the highest material planet, called Brahmaloka.

The leader of the Yadu dynasty, King Śūrasena, was ruling over the country known as Mathurā (the district of Mathurā) as well as the district known as Śūrasena. On account of the rule of King Śūrasena, Mathurā became the capital city of all the kings of the Yadus. Mathurā was also made the capital of the kings of the Yadu dynasty because the Yadus were a very pious family and knew that Mathurā is the place where Lord Śrī Kṛṣṇa lives eternally, just as He also lives in Dvārakā.

The son of Śūrasena was Vasudeva, and Kṛṣṇa was to appear as the son of Vasudeva. Vasudeva married Devakī, whose father Devaka, contributed an opulent dowry. The newly married couple were being driven home in a chariot in a grand procession led by Kaṁsa, Devakī's brother. Suddenly Kaṁsa heard a voice from the sky which announced to him that the eighth child born of his sister and brother-in-law would kill him. Being of demoniac mentality, Kaṁsa immediately tried to kill his sister, but Vasudeva persuaded him to spare her, and promised they would surrender to him whatever children were born.

Later the sage Nārada visited Kaṁsa and informed him that in his past life he had been killed by Viṣṇu and that the prediction of the child who would kill him referred to Lord Viṣṇu, who was to take birth as the son of Devakī.

Kaṁsa then decided to imprison both Devakī and Vasudeva. Within the prison shackled in chains, Vasudeva and Devakī gave birth to a male child year after year, and Kaṁsa, thinking each of the babies to be the incarnation of Viṣṇu, killed them one after another.

When Devakī was pregnant for the seventh time, an expansion of Kṛṣṇa known as Ananta appeared within her womb. Kṛṣṇa, the Supreme Lord, then ordered His internal mystic potency, Yogamāyā, to transfer Ananta to the womb of Rohiṇī, another of Vasudeva's wives who was—due to the persecutions of Kaṁsa—residing in Vṛndāvana at the house of King Nanda and Yaśodā. He then informed Yogamāyā that she would be born as the daughter of Nanda and Yaśodā.

BIRTH OF LORD KṚṢṆA

When the time was mature for the appearance of the Lord, the constellations became very auspicious. The astrological influence of the star known as Rohiṇī was also predominant because this star is considered to be very auspicious. Rohiṇī is under the direct supervision of Brahmā. According to the astrological conclusion, besides the proper situation of the stars, there are auspicious and inauspicious moments due to the different situations of the different planetary systems. At the time of

Kṛṣṇa's birth, the planetary systems were automatically adjusted so that everything became auspicious.

At that time, in all directions, east, west, south, north, everywhere, there was an atmosphere of peace and prosperity. There were auspicious stars visible in the sky, and on the surface in all towns and villages or pasturing grounds and within the mind of everyone there were signs of good fortune. The rivers were flowing full of waters, and lakes were beautifully decorated with lotus flowers. The forests were full with beautiful birds and peacocks. All the birds within the forests began to sing with sweet voices, and the peacocks began to dance along with their consorts. The wind blew very pleasantly, carrying the aroma of different flowers, and the sensation of bodily touch was very pleasing. At home, the *brāhmaṇas,* who were accustomed to offer sacrifices in the fire, found their homes very pleasant for offerings. Due to disturbances created by the demoniac kings, the sacrificial fire altar had been almost stopped in the houses of *brāhmaṇas,* but now they could find the opportunity to start the fire peacefully. Being forbidden to offer sacrifices, the *brāhmaṇas* were very distressed in mind, intelligence and activities, but just on the point of Kṛṣṇa's appearance, automatically their minds became full of joy because they could hear loud vibrations in the sky of transcendental sounds proclaiming the appearance of the Supreme Personality of Godhead.

The denizens of the Gandharva and Kinnara planets began to sing, and the denizens of Siddhaloka and the planets of the Cāraṇas began to offer prayers in the service of the Personality of Godhead. In the heavenly planets, the angels along with their wives, accompanied by the Apsarās, began to dance.

The great sages and the demigods, being pleased, began to shower flowers. At the seashore, there was the sound of mild waves, and above the sea there were clouds in the sky which began to thunder very pleasingly.

When things were adjusted like this, Lord Viṣṇu, who is residing within the heart of every living entity, appeared in the darkness of night as the Supreme Personality of Godhead before Devakī, who also appeared as one of the demigoddesses. The appearance of Lord Viṣṇu at that time could be compared to the full moon in the sky as it rises on the eastern horizon. The objection may be raised that, since Lord Kṛṣṇa appeared on the eighth day of the waning moon, there could be no rising of the full moon. In answer to this it may be said that Lord Kṛṣṇa appeared in the dynasty which is in the hierarchy of the moon; therefore, although the moon was incomplete on that night, because of the Lord's appearance in the dynasty wherein the moon is himself the original person, the moon was in an overjoyous condition, so by the grace of Kṛṣṇa he could appear just as a full moon.

In an astronomical treatise by the name *Khamāṇikya,* the constellations at the time of the appearance of Lord Kṛṣṇa are very nicely described. It is confirmed that the child born at that auspicious moment was the Supreme Brahman or the Absolute Truth.

Vasudeva saw that wonderful child born as a baby with four hands, holding conchshell, club, disc and lotus flower, decorated with the mark of Śrīvatsa, wearing the jeweled necklace of *kaustubha* stone, dressed in yellow silk, appearing dazzling like a bright blackish cloud, wearing a helmet bedecked with the *vaidūrya* stone, valuable bracelets, earrings and similar other ornaments all over His body and an abundance of hair on His head. Due to the extraordinary features of the child, Vasudeva was struck with wonder. How could a newly born child be so decorated? He could therefore understand that Lord Kṛṣṇa had now appeared, and he became overpowered by the occasion. Vasudeva very humbly wondered that although he was an ordinary living entity conditioned by material nature and was externally imprisoned by Kaṁsa, the all-pervading Personality of Godhead, Viṣṇu or Kṛṣṇa, was appearing as a child in his home, exactly in His original position. No earthly child is born with four hands and decorated with ornaments and nice clothing, fully equipped with all the signs of the Supreme Personality of Godhead. Over and over again, Vasudeva glanced at his child, and he considered how to celebrate this auspicious moment: "Generally, when a male child is born," he thought, "people observe the occasion with jubilant celebrations, and in my home, although I am imprisoned, the Supreme Personality of Godhead has taken birth. How many millions and millions of times should I be prepared to observe this auspicious ceremony!"

When Vasudeva, who is also called Ānakadundubhi, was looking at his newborn baby, he was so happy that he wanted to give many thousands of cows in charity to the *brāhmaṇas.* According to the Vedic system, whenever there is an auspicious ceremony in the *kṣatriya* king's palace, the king gives many things in charity. Cows decorated with golden ornaments are delivered to the *brāhmaṇas* and sages. Vasudeva wanted to perform a charitable ceremony to celebrate Kṛṣṇa's appearance, but because he was shackled within the walls of Kaṁsa's prison, this was not possible. Instead, within his mind he gave thousands of cows to the *brāhmaṇas.*

When Vasudeva was convinced that the newborn child was the Supreme Personality of Godhead Himself, he bowed down with folded hands and began to offer Him prayers. At that time Vasudeva was in the transcendental position, and he became completely free from all fear of Kaṁsa. The newborn baby was also flashing His effulgence within the room in which He appeared.

Vasudeva then began to offer his prayers: "My dear Lord, I can understand who You are. You are the Supreme Personality of Godhead, the Supersoul of all living entities and the Absolute Truth. You have appeared in Your own eternal form, which is directly perceived by us. I understand that because I am afraid of Kaṁsa, You have appeared just to deliver me from that fear. You do not belong to this material world; You are the same person who brings about the cosmic manifestation simply by glancing over material nature."

The Lord spoke to Devakī and Vasudeva: "I appeared in this Viṣṇu form just to convince you that I am the same Supreme Personality of Godhead again taken birth. I could have appeared just like an ordinary child, but in that way you would not believe that I, the Supreme Personality of Godhead, have taken birth in your womb. My dear father and mother, you have therefore raised Me many times as your child, with great affection and love, and I am therefore very pleased and obliged to you. And I assure you that this time you shall go back home, back to Godhead, on account of your perfection in your mission. I know you are very concerned about Me and afraid of Kaṁsa. Therefore I order you to take Me immediately to Gokula and replace Me with the daughter who has just been born to Yaśodā."

Having spoken thus in the presence of His father and mother, the Lord turned Himself into an ordinary child and remained silent.

Being ordered by the Supreme Personality of Godhead, Vasudeva attempted to take his son from the delivery room, and exactly at that time, a daughter was born of Nanda and Yaśodā. She was Yogamāyā, the internal potency of the Lord. By the influence of this internal potency, Yogamāyā, all the residents of Kaṁsa's palace, especially the doorkeepers, were overwhelmed with deep sleep, and all the palace doors opened, although they were barred and shackled with iron chains. The night was very dark, but as soon as Vasudeva took Kṛṣṇa on his lap and went out, he could see everything just as in the sunlight.

In the *Caitanya-caritāmṛta* it is said that Kṛṣṇa is just like sunlight, and wherever there is Kṛṣṇa, the illusory energy, which is compared to darkness, cannot remain. When Vasudeva was carrying Kṛṣṇa, the darkness of the night disappeared. All the prison doors automatically opened. At the same time there was thunder in the sky and severe rainfall. While Vasudeva was carrying his son Kṛṣṇa in the falling rain, Lord Śeṣa in the shape of a serpent spread His hood over the head of Vasudeva so that he would not be hampered by the rainfall. Vasudeva came onto the bank of the Yamunā and saw that the water of the Yamunā was roaring with waves and that the whole span was full of foam. Still, in that furious feature, the river gave passage to Vasudeva to cross, just as the great Indian Ocean gave a path to Lord Rāma when He was bridging over the gulf. In this way Vasudeva crossed the River Yamunā. On the other side, he went to the place of Nanda Mahārāja situated in Gokula, where he saw that all the cowherd men were fast asleep. He took the opportunity of silently entering into the house of Yaśodā, and without difficulty he exchanged his son for the baby girl newly born in the house of Yaśodā. Then, after entering the house very silently and exchanging the boy with the girl, he again returned to the prison of Kaṁsa and silently put the girl on the lap of Devakī. He again clamped the shackles on himself so that Kaṁsa could not recognize that so many things had happened.

Mother Yaśodā understood that a child was born of her, but because she was very tired from the labor of childbirth, she was fast asleep. When she awoke, she could not remember whether she had given birth to a male or female child.

KAṀSA BEGINS HIS PERSECUTIONS

After Vasudeva adjusted all the doors and gates, the gatekeepers awoke and heard the newborn child crying. Kaṁsa was waiting to hear the news of the child's birth, and the gatekeepers immediately approached him and informed him that the child was born. At that time, Kaṁsa got up from his bed very quickly and exclaimed, "Now the cruel death of my life is born!" Kaṁsa became perplexed now that his death was approaching, and his hair stood on end. Immediately he proceeded toward the place where the child was born.

Devakī, on seeing her brother approaching, prayed in a very meek attitude to Kaṁsa: "My dear brother, please do not kill this female child. I promise that this child will be the wife of your son; therefore don't kill her. You are not to be killed by any female child. That was the omen. You are to be killed by a male child, so please do not kill her. My dear brother, you have killed so many of my children who were just born, shining as the sun. That is not your fault. You have been advised by demoniac friends to kill my children. But now I beg you to excuse this girl. Let her live as my daughter."

Kaṁsa was so cruel that he did not listen to the beautiful prayers of his sister Devakī. He forcibly grabbed the newborn child to rebuke his sister and attempted to dash her on the stone mercilessly. This is a graphic example of a cruel brother who could sacrifice all relationships for the sake of personal gratification. But immediately the child slipped out of his hands, went up in the sky and appeared with eight arms as the younger sister of Viṣṇu. She was decorated with a nice dress and flower garlands and ornaments; in her eight hands she held a bow, lance, arrows, bell, conchshell, disc, club and shield.

Seeing the appearance of the child (who was actually the goddess Durgā), all the demigods from different planets like Siddhaloka, Cāraṇaloka, Gandharvaloka, Apsaroloka, Kinnaraloka and Uragaloka presented her articles and began to offer their respective prayers. From above, the goddess addressed Kaṁsa: "You rascal, how can you kill me? The child who will kill you is already born before me somewhere within this world. Don't be so cruel to your poor sister." After this appearance, the goddess Durgā became known by various names in various parts of the world.

Kaṁsa became very fearful and released Vasudeva and Devakī from prison. But the next day his demoniac ministers convinced him that he should try to remove the danger to his life by killing all children who had been born within ten days and to persecute the *brāhmaṇas* and Vaiṣṇavas. Baby Kṛṣṇa, however, was living incognito in Vṛndāvana as the son of Nanda, and He thus escaped the persecutions of Kaṁsa. He began to perform miraculous pastimes, even as an infant. Thus giant demons such as Pūtanā and Tṛṇāvarta, sent to kill infants, were killed by Kṛṣṇa in displays of His supreme power. Meanwhile Vasudeva did not reveal that he was the father of Kṛṣṇa, but he encouraged Nanda to raise the child with all care.

VISION OF THE UNIVERSAL FORM

After this incident, Vasudeva asked his family priest Gargamuni to visit the place of Nanda Mahārāja in order to astrologically calculate the future life of Kṛṣṇa. Gargamuni was a great saintly sage who underwent many austerities and penances and was appointed priest of the Yadu dynasty. When Gargamuni arrived at the home of Nanda Mahārāja, Nanda Mahārāja was very pleased to see him and immediately stood up with folded hands and offered his respectful obeisances. He received Gargamuni with the feeling of one who is worshiping God or the Supreme Personality of Godhead. He offered him a nice sitting place, and when he sat down, Nanda Mahārāja offered him a warm reception. Addressing him very politely, he said: "My dear *brāhmaṇa,* your appearance in a householder's place is only to enlighten. We are always engaged in household duties and are forgetting our real duty of self-realization. Your coming to our house is to give us some enlightenment about spiritual life. You have no other purpose to visit householders." Actually a saintly person or a *brāhmaṇa* has no business visiting householders, who are always busy in the matter of dollars and cents. If it is asked, "Why don't the householders go to a saintly person or a *brāhmaṇa* for enlightenment?" the answer is that householders are very poor-hearted. Generally householders think that their engagement in family affairs is their prime duty and that self-realization or enlightenment in spiritual knowledge is secondary. Out of compassion only, saintly persons and *brāhmaṇas* go to householders' homes.

Nanda Mahārāja addressed Gargamuni as one of the great authorities in astrological science. The foretellings of astrological science, such as the occurrence of solar or lunar eclipses, are wonderful calculations, and by this particular science, a person can understand the future very clearly. Gargamuni was proficient in this knowledge. By this knowledge one can understand what his previous activities were, and by the result of such activities one may enjoy or suffer in this life.

Upon this request, Gargamuni replied, "Vasudeva has sent me to see to the reformatory performances of these boys, especially Kṛṣṇa's. I am their family priest, and incidentally, it appears to me that Kṛṣṇa is the son of Devakī." By his astrological calculation, Gargamuni could understand that Kṛṣṇa was the son of Devakī but that He was being kept under the care of Nanda Mahārāja, which Nanda did not know. Indirectly he said that Kṛṣṇa and Balarāma were both sons of Vasudeva. Balarāma was known as the son of Vasudeva because His mother, Rohiṇī, was present there, but Nanda Mahārāja did not know about Kṛṣṇa. Gargamuni indirectly disclosed the fact that Kṛṣṇa was the son of Devakī. Gargamuni also warned Nanda Mahārāja that if he would perform the reformatory ceremony, then Kaṁsa, who was naturally very sinful, would understand that Kṛṣṇa was the son of Devakī and Vasudeva. According to astrological calculation, Devakī could not have a female child, although everyone thought that the eighth child of Devakī was female. In this way Gargamuni intimated to Nanda Mahārāja that the female child was born of Yaśodā and that Kṛṣṇa was born of Devakī, and they were exchanged. The female child, or Durgā, also informed Kaṁsa that the child who would kill him was already born somewhere else. Gargamuni stated, "If I give your child a name and if He fulfills the prophecy of the female child to Kaṁsa, then it may be that the sinful demon will come and kill this child also after the name-giving ceremony. But I do not want to become responsible for all these future calamities."

On hearing the words of Gargamuni, Nanda Mahārāja said, "If there is such danger, then it is better not to plan any gorgeous name-giving ceremony. It would be better for you to simply chant the Vedic hymns and perform the purificatory process. We belong to the twice-born caste, and I am taking this opportunity of your presence. So please perform the name-giving ceremony without external pomp." Nanda Mahārāja wanted to keep the name-giving ceremony a secret and yet take advantage of Gargamuni's performing the ceremony.

When Gargamuni was so eagerly requested by Nanda Mahārāja, he performed the name-giving ceremony as secretly as possible in the cowshed of Nanda Mahārāja. He informed Nanda Mahārāja that Balarāma, the son of Rohiṇī, would be very pleasing to His family members and relatives and therefore would be called Rāma. In the future He would be extraordinarily strong and therefore would be called Balarāma. Gargamuni said further, "Because your family and the family of the Yadus are so intimately connected and attracted, His name will also be Saṅkarṣaṇa." This means that Gargamuni awarded three names to the son of Rohiṇī—namely Balarāma, Saṅkarṣaṇa, and Baladeva. But he carefully did not disclose the fact that Balarāma also appeared in the womb of Devakī and was subsequently transferred to the womb of Rohiṇī. Kṛṣṇa and Balarāma are real brothers, being originally sons of Devakī.

Gargamuni then informed Nanda Mahārāja, "As far as the other boy is concerned, this child has taken different bodily complexions in different *yugas* (millennia). First of all He assumed the color white, then He assumed the color red, then the color yellow, and now He has assumed the color black. Besides that, He was formerly the son of Vasudeva; therefore His name should be Vāsudeva as well as Kṛṣṇa. Some people will call Him Kṛṣṇa, and some will call Him Vāsudeva. But one thing you must know: This son has had many, many other names and activities due to His different pastimes."

Gargamuni gave Nanda Mahārāja a further hint that his son would also be called Giridhārī because of His uncommon pastimes of lifting Govardhana Hill. Since he could understand everything past and future, he said, "I know everything about His activities and name, but others do not know. This child will be very pleasing to all the cowherd men and cows. Being very popular in Vṛndāvana, He will be the cause of all good fortune for you. Because of His presence, you will overcome all kinds of material calamities, despite opposing elements."

Gargamuni continued to say, "My dear King of Vraja, in His previous births, this child many times protected righteous persons from the hands of rogues and thieves whenever there was a political disruption. Your child is so powerful that anyone who will become a devotee of your boy will never be troubled by enemies. Just as demigods are always protected by Lord Viṣṇu, the devotees of your child will always be protected by Nārāyaṇa, the Supreme Personality of Godhead. This child will grow in power, beauty, opulence—in everything—on the level of Nārāyaṇa, the Supreme Personality of Godhead. Therefore I would advise that you protect Him very carefully so that He may grow without disturbance."

Gargamuni further informed Nanda Mahārāja that because he was a great devotee of Nārāyaṇa, Lord Nārāyaṇa gave a son who is equal to Him. At the same time he indicated, "Your son will be disturbed by so many demons, so be careful and protect Him." In this way, Gargamuni convinced Nanda Mahārāja that Nārāyaṇa Himself had become his son. In various ways he described the transcendental qualities of his son. After giving this information, Gargamuni returned to his home. Nanda Mahārāja began to think of himself as the most fortunate person, and he was very satisfied to be benedicted in this way.

A short time after this incident, both Balarāma and Kṛṣṇa began to crawl on Their hands and knees. When They were crawling like that, They pleased Their mothers. The bells tied to Their waist and ankles sounded fascinating, and They would move around very pleasingly. Sometimes, just like ordinary children, They would be frightened by others and would immediately hurry to Their mothers for protection. Sometimes They would fall into the clay and mud of Vṛndāvana and would approach Their mothers smeared with clay and saffron. They were actually smeared with saffron and sandalwood pulp by Their mothers, but due to crawling over muddy clay, They would simultaneously smear Their bodies with clay. As soon as They would come crawling to Their mothers, Yaśodā and Rohiṇī would take Them on their laps and, covering the lower portion of their saris, allow Them to suck their breasts. When the babies were sucking their breasts, the mothers would see small teeth coming in. Thus their joy would be intensified to see their children grow. Sometimes the naughty babies would crawl up to the cowshed, catch the tail of a calf and stand up. The calves, being disturbed, would immediately begin running here and there, and the children would be dragged over clay and cow dung. To see this fun, Yaśodā and Rohiṇī would call all their neighboring friends, the *gopīs.* Upon seeing these childhood pastimes of Lord Kṛṣṇa, the *gopīs* would be merged in transcendental bliss. In their enjoyment they would laugh very loudly.

Both Kṛṣṇa and Balarāma were so restless that Their mothers Yaśodā and Rohiṇī would try to protect Them from cows, bulls, monkeys, water, fire and birds while they were executing their household duties. Always being anxious to protect the children and to execute their duties, they were not very tranquil. In a very short time, both Kṛṣṇa and Balarāma began to stand up and slightly move on Their legs. When Kṛṣṇa and Balarāma began to walk, other friends of the same age joined Them, and together they began to give the highest transcendental pleasure to the *gopīs,* specifically to mother Yaśodā and Rohiṇī.

All the *gopī* friends of Yaśodā and Rohiṇī enjoyed the naughty childish activities of Kṛṣṇa and Balarāma in Vṛndāvana. In order to enjoy further transcendental bliss, they all assembled and went to mother Yaśodā to lodge complaints against the restless boys. When Kṛṣṇa was sitting before mother Yaśodā, all the elderly *gopīs* began to lodge complaints against Him so that Kṛṣṇa could hear. They said, "Dear Yaśodā, why don't you restrict your naughty Kṛṣṇa. He comes to our houses along with Balarāma every morning and evening, and before the milking of the cows They let loose the calves, and the calves drink all the milk of the cows. So when we go to milk the cows, we find no milk, and we have to return with empty pots. If we warn Kṛṣṇa and Balarāma about doing this, They simply smile charmingly. We cannot do anything. Also, your Kṛṣṇa and Balarāma find great pleasure in stealing our stock of yogurt and butter from wherever we keep it. When Kṛṣṇa and Balarāma are caught stealing the yogurt and butter, They say, 'Why do you charge Us with stealing? Do you think that butter and yogurt are in scarcity in our house?' Sometimes They steal butter, yogurt and milk and distribute them to the monkeys. When the monkeys are well fed and do not take any more, then your boys chide, 'This milk and butter and yogurt are useless—even the monkeys won't take it.' And They break the pots and throw them hither and thither. If we keep our stock of yogurt, butter and milk in a solitary dark place, your Kṛṣṇa and Balarāma find it in the darkness by the glaring effulgence of the ornaments and jewels on Their bodies. If by chance They cannot find the hidden butter and yogurt, They go to our little babies and pinch their bodies so that they cry, and then They go away. If we keep our stock of butter and yogurt high on the ceiling, hanging on a swing, although it is beyond Their reach, They arrange to reach it by piling all kinds of wooden crates over the grinding machine. And if They cannot reach, They make a hole in the pot. We think therefore that you'd better take all the jeweled ornaments from the bodies of your children."

On hearing this, Yaśodā would say, "All right, I will take all the jewels from Kṛṣṇa so that He cannot see the butter hidden in the darkness." Then the *gopīs* would say, "No, no don't do this. What good will you do by taking away the jewels? We do not know what kind of boys these are, but even without ornaments They spread some kind of effulgence so that even in darkness They can see everything." Then mother Yaśodā would inform them, "All right, keep your butter and yogurt carefully so that They may not reach it." In reply to this, the *gopīs* said, "Yes, actually we do so, but because we are sometimes engaged in our household duties, these naughty boys enter our house somehow or other and spoil everything. Sometimes being unable to steal our butter and yogurt, out of anger They pass urine on the clean floor and sometimes spit on it. Just see your boy now—He is hearing this complaint. All day They simply make arrangements to steal our butter and yogurt, and now They are sitting just like very silent good boys. Just see His face." When mother Yaśodā thought to chastise her boy after hearing all the complaints, she saw His pitiable face, and smiling, she did not chastise Him.

Another day, when Kṛṣṇa and Balarāma were playing with Their friends, all the boys joined Balarāma and told mother Yaśodā that Kṛṣṇa had eaten clay. On hearing this, mother Yaśodā caught hold of Kṛṣṇa's hand and said, "My dear Kṛṣṇa, why have You eaten earth in a solitary place? Just see, all Your friends, including Balarāma, are complaining about You." Being afraid of His mother, Kṛṣṇa replied, "My dear mother, all these boys, including My elder brother Balarāma, are speaking lies against Me. I have never eaten clay. My elder brother Balarāma, while playing with Me today, became angry, and therefore He has joined with the other boys to complain against Me. They have all combined together to complain so you will be angry and chastise Me. If you think they are truthful, then you can look within My mouth to see whether I have taken clay or not." His mother replied, "All right, if You have actually not taken any clay, then just open Your mouth. I shall see."

When the Supreme Personality of Godhead Kṛṣṇa was so ordered by His mother, He immediately opened His mouth just like an ordinary boy. Then mother Yaśodā saw within that mouth the complete opulence of creation. She saw the entire outer space in all directions, mountains, islands, oceans, seas, planets, air, fire, moon and stars. Along with the moon and the stars she also saw the entire elements, water, sky, the extensive ethereal existence along with the total ego and the products of the senses and the controller of the senses, all the demigods, the objects of the senses like sound and smell, and the three qualities of material nature. She also could perceive that within His mouth were all living entities, eternal time, material nature, spiritual nature, activity, consciousness and different forms of the whole creation. Yaśodā could find within the mouth of her child everything necessary for cosmic manifestation. She also saw, within His mouth, herself taking Kṛṣṇa on her lap and having Him sucking her breast. Upon seeing all this, she became struck with awe and began to wonder whether she were dreaming or actually seeing something extraordinary. She concluded that she was either dreaming or seeing the play of the illusory energy of the Supreme Personality of Godhead. She thought that she had become mad, mentally deranged, to see all those wonderful things. Then she thought, "It may be cosmic mystic power attained by my child, and therefore I am perplexed by such visions within His mouth. Let me offer my respectful obeisances unto the Supreme Personality of Godhead, under whose energy bodily self and bodily possessions are conceived." She then said, "Let me offer my respectful obeisances unto Him, under whose illusory energy I am thinking that Nanda Mahārāja is my husband and Kṛṣṇa is my son, that all the properties of Nanda Mahārāja belong to me and that all the cowherd men and women are my subjects. All this misconception is due to the illusory energy of the Supreme Lord. So let me pray to Him that He may protect me always."

While mother Yaśodā was thinking in this high philosophical way, Lord Kṛṣṇa again expanded His internal energy just to bewilder her with maternal affection. Immediately mother Yaśodā forgot all philosophical speculation and accepted Kṛṣṇa as her own child. She took Him on her lap and became overwhelmed with maternal affection. She thus began to think, "Kṛṣṇa is not understandable to the masses through the gross process of knowledge, but He can be received through the *Upaniṣads* and the *Vedānta* or mystic *yoga* system and Sāṅkhya philosophy." Then she began to think of the Supreme Personality of Godhead as her own begotten child.

THE KILLING OF THE AGHĀSURA DEMON

Once the Lord desired to go early in the morning with all His cowherd boy friends to the forest, where they were to assemble together and take lunch. As soon as He got up from bed, He blew a buffalo horn and called all His friends together. Keeping the calves before them, they started for the forest. In this way, Lord Kṛṣṇa assembled thousands of His boy friends. They were each equipped with a stick, flute and horn as well as lunch bag, and each of them was taking care of thousands of calves. All the boys appeared very jolly and happy in that excursion. Each and every one of them was attentive for his personal calves. The boys were fully decorated with various kinds of golden ornaments, and out of sporting propensities they began to pick up flowers, leaves, twigs, peacock feathers and red clay from different places in the forest, and they began to dress themselves in different ways. While passing through the forest, one boy stole another boy's lunch package and passed it to a third. And when the boy whose lunch package was stolen came to know of it, he tried to take it back. But one threw it to another boy. This sportive playing went on amongst the boys as childhood pastimes.

When Lord Kṛṣṇa went ahead to a distant place in order to see some specific scenery, the boys behind Him tried to run to catch up and be the first to touch Him. So there was a great competition. One would say, "I will go there and touch Kṛṣṇa," and another would say, "Oh, you cannot go. I'll touch Kṛṣṇa first." Some of them played on their flutes or vibrated bugles made of buffalo horn. Some of them gladly followed the peacocks and imitated the onomatopoetic sounds of the cuckoo. While the birds were flying in the sky, the boys ran after the birds' shadows along the ground and tried to follow their exact courses. Some of them went to the monkeys and silently sat down by them, and some of them imitated the dancing of the peacocks. Some of them caught the tails of the monkeys and played with them, and when the monkeys jumped in a tree, the boys also followed. When a monkey showed its face and teeth, a boy imitated and showed his teeth to the monkey. Some of the boys played with the frogs on the bank of the Yamunā, and when, out of fear, the frogs jumped in the water, the boys immediately dove in after them, and they would come out of the water when they saw their own shadows and stand imitating, making caricatures and laughing. They would also go to an empty well and make loud sounds, and when the echo came back, they would call it ill names and laugh.

As stated personally by the Supreme Personality of Godhead in the *Bhagavad-gītā,* He is realized proportionately by transcendentalists as Brahman, Paramātmā and the Supreme Personality of Godhead. Here, in confirmation of the same statement, Lord Kṛṣṇa, who awards the impersonalist Brahman realization by His bodily effulgence, also gives pleasure to the devotees as the Supreme Personality of Godhead. Those who are under the spell of external energy, *māyā,* take Him only as a beautiful child. Yet He gave full transcendental pleasure to the cowherd boys who played with Him. Only after accumulating heaps of pious activities, those boys were promoted to personally associate with the Supreme Personality of Godhead. Who can estimate the transcendental fortune of the residents of Vṛndāvana? They were personally visualizing the Supreme Personality of Godhead face to face, He whom many *yogīs* cannot find even after undergoing severe austerities, although He is sitting within the heart. This is also confirmed in the *Brahma-saṁhitā.* One may search for Kṛṣṇa, the Supreme Personality of Godhead, through the pages of the *Vedas* and *Upaniṣads,* but if one is fortunate enough to associate with a devotee, he can see the Supreme Personality of Godhead face to face. After accumulating pious activities in many, many previous lives, the cowherd boys were seeing Kṛṣṇa face to face and playing with Him as friends. They could not understand that Kṛṣṇa is the Supreme Personality of Godhead, but they were playing as intimate friends with intense love for Him.

When Lord Kṛṣṇa was enjoying His childhood pastimes with His boy friends, one Aghāsura demon became very impatient. He was unable to see Kṛṣṇa playing, so he appeared before the boys intending to kill them all. This Aghāsura was so dangerous that even the denizens of heaven were afraid of him. Although the denizens of heaven drank nectar daily to prolong their lives, they were afraid of this Aghāsura and were wondering, "When will the demon be killed?" The denizens used to drink nectar to become immortal, but actually they were not confident of their immortality. On the other hand, the boys who were playing with Kṛṣṇa had no fear of the demons. They were free of fear. Any material arrangement for protecting oneself from death is always unsure, but if one is in Kṛṣṇa consciousness, then immortality is confidently assured.

The demon Aghāsura appeared before Kṛṣṇa and His friends.

Aghāsura happened to be the younger brother of Pūtanā and Bakāsura, and he thought, "Kṛṣṇa has killed my brother and sister. Now I shall kill Him along with all His friends and calves." Aghāsura was instigated by Kaṁsa, so he had come with determination. Aghāsura also began to think that when he would offer grains and water in memory of his brother and kill Kṛṣṇa and all the cowherd boys, then automatically all the inhabitants of Vṛndāvana would die. Generally, for the householders, the children are the life and breath force. When all the children die, then naturally the parents also die on account of strong affection for them.

Aghāsura, thus deciding to kill all the inhabitants of Vṛndāvana, expanded himself by the yogic *siddhi* called *mahimā.* The demons are generally expert in achieving almost all kinds of mystic powers. In the *yoga* system, by the perfection called *mahimā-siddhi,* one can expand himself as he desires. The demon Aghāsura expanded himself up to eight miles and assumed the shape of a very fat serpent. Having attained this wonderful body, he stretched his mouth open just like a mountain cave. Desiring to swallow all the boys at once, including Kṛṣṇa and Balarāma, he sat on the path.

The demon in the shape of a big fat serpent expanded his lips from land to sky; his lower lip was touching the ground, and his upper lip was touching the clouds. His jaws appeared like a big mountain cave, without limitation, and his teeth appeared just like mountain summits. His tongue appeared to be a broad traffic way, and he was breathing just like a hurricane. The fire of his eyes was blazing. At first the boys thought that the demon was a statue, but after examining it, they saw that it was more like a big serpent lying down in the road and widening his mouth. The boys began to talk among themselves: "This figure appears to be a great animal, and he is sitting in such a posture just to swallow us all. Just see—is it not a big snake that has widened his mouth to eat all of us?"

One of them said, "Yes, what you say is true. This animal's upper lip appears to be just like the sunshine, and its lower lip is just like the reflection of red sunshine on the ground. Dear friends, just look to the right and left hand side of the mouth of the animal. Its mouth appears to be like a big mountain cave, and its height cannot be estimated. The chin is also raised just like a mountain summit. That long highway appears to be its tongue, and inside the mouth it is as dark as a mountain cave. The hot wind that is blowing like a hurricane is his breathing, and the fishy bad smell coming out from his mouth is the smell of his intestines."

Then they further consulted among themselves: "If we all at one time entered into the mouth of this great serpent, how could it possibly swallow all of us? And even if it were to swallow all of us at once, it could not swallow Kṛṣṇa. Kṛṣṇa will immediately kill him, as He did Bakāsura." Talking in this way, all the boys looked at the beautiful lotus-like face of Kṛṣṇa, and they began to clap and smile. And so they marched forward and entered the mouth of the gigantic serpent.

Meanwhile, Kṛṣṇa, who is the Supersoul within everyone's heart, could understand that the big statuesque figure was a demon. While He was planning how to stop the destruction of His intimate friends, all the boys along with their cows and calves entered the mouth of the serpent. But Kṛṣṇa did not enter. The demon was awaiting Kṛṣṇa's entrance, and he was thinking, "Everyone has entered except Kṛṣṇa, who has killed my brothers and sisters."

Kṛṣṇa is the assurance of safety to everyone. But when He saw that His friends were already out of His hands and were lying within the belly of a great serpent, He became momentarily aggrieved. He was also struck with wonder how the external energy works so wonderfully. He then began to consider how the demon should be killed and how He could save the boys and calves. Although there was no factual concern on Kṛṣṇa's part, He was thinking like that. Finally, after some deliberation, He also entered the mouth of the demon. When Kṛṣṇa entered, all the demigods, who had gathered to see the fun and who were hiding within the clouds, began to express their feelings with the words, "Alas! Alas!" At the same time, all the friends of Aghāsura, especially Kaṁsa, who were all accustomed to eating flesh and blood, began to express their jubilation, understanding that Kṛṣṇa had also entered the mouth of the demon.

While the demon was trying to smash Kṛṣṇa and His companions, Kṛṣṇa heard the demigods crying, "Alas, alas," and He immediately began to expand Himself within the throat of the demon. Although he had a gigantic body, the demon choked by the expanding of Kṛṣṇa. His big eyes moved violently, and he quickly suffocated. His life-air could not come out from any source, and ultimately it burst out of a hole in the upper part of his skull. Thus his life-air passed off. After the demon dropped dead, Kṛṣṇa, with His transcendental glance alone, brought all the boys and calves back to consciousness and came with them out of the mouth of the demon. While Kṛṣṇa was within the mouth of Aghāsura, the demon's spirit soul came out like a dazzling light, illuminating all directions, and waited in the sky. As soon as Kṛṣṇa with His calves and friends came out of the mouth of the demon, that glittering effulgent light immediately merged into the body of Kṛṣṇa within the vision of all the demigods.

The demigods became overwhelmed with joy and began to shower flowers on the Supreme Personality of Godhead, Kṛṣṇa, and thus they worshiped Him. The denizens of heaven began to dance in jubilation, and the denizens in Gandharvaloka began to offer various kinds of prayers. Drummers began to beat drums in jubilation, the *brāhmaṇas* began to recite Vedic hymns, and all the devotees of the Lord began to chant the words, "*Jaya! Jaya!* All glories to the Supreme Personality of Godhead."

When Lord Brahmā heard those auspicious vibrations, which sounded throughout the higher planetary system, he immediately came down to see what had happened. He saw that the demon was killed, and he was struck with wonder at the uncommon, glorious pastimes of the Personality of Godhead. The gigantic mouth of the demon remained in an open position for many days and gradually dried up; it remained a spot of pleasure pastimes for all the cowherd boys.

The killing of Aghāsura took place when Kṛṣṇa and all His boy friends were under five years old. Children under five years old are called *kaumāra.* After five years up to the tenth year they are called *paugaṇḍa,* and after the tenth year up to the fifteenth year they are called *kaiśora.* After the fifteenth year, boys are called youths. So for one year there was no discussion of the incident of the Aghāsura demon in the village of Vraja. But when they attained their sixth year, they informed their parents of the incident with great wonder. The reason for this will be clear in the next chapter.

For Śrī Kṛṣṇa, the Supreme Personality of Godhead, who is far greater than such demigods as Lord Brahmā, it is not at all difficult to award one the opportunity of merging with His eternal body. This He awarded to Aghāsura. Aghāsura was certainly the most sinful living entity, and it is not possible for the sinful to merge into the existence of the Absolute Truth. But in this particular case, because Kṛṣṇa entered into Aghāsura's body, the demon became fully cleansed of all sinful reaction. Persons constantly thinking of the eternal form of the Lord in the shape of the Deity or in the shape of a mental form are awarded the transcendental goal of entering into the kingdom of God and associating with the Supreme Personality of Godhead. So we can just imagine the elevated position of someone like Aghāsura, into whose body the Supreme Personality of Godhead, Kṛṣṇa, personally entered. Great sages, meditators and devotees constantly keep the form of the Lord within the heart, or they see the Deity form of the Lord in the temples; in that way, they become liberated from all material contamination and at the end of the body enter into the kingdom of God. This perfection is possible simply by keeping the form of the Lord within the mind. But in the case of Aghāsura, the Supreme Personality of Godhead personally entered. Aghāsura's position was therefore greater than the ordinary devotee's or the greatest *yogī's*.

Mahārāja Parīkṣit, who was engaged in hearing the transcendental pastimes of Lord Kṛṣṇa (who saved the life of Mahārāja Parīkṣit while he was in the womb of his mother), became more and more interested to hear about Him. And thus he questioned the sage Śukadeva Gosvāmī, who was reciting *Śrīmad-Bhāgavatam* before the King.

King Parīkṣit was a bit astonished to understand that the killing of the Aghāsura demon was not discussed for one year, until after the boys attained the *paugaṇḍa* age. Mahārāja Parīkṣit was very inquisitive to learn about this, for he was sure that such an incident was due to the working of Kṛṣṇa's different energies.

Generally, the *kṣatriyas* or the administrative class are always busy with their political affairs, and they have very little chance to hear about the transcendental pastimes of Lord Kṛṣṇa. But while Parīkṣit Mahārāja was hearing these transcendental pastimes, he considered himself to be very fortunate because he was hearing from Śukadeva Gosvāmī, the greatest authority on the *Śrīmad-Bhāgavatam.* Thus being requested by Mahārāja Parīkṣit, Śukadeva Gosvāmī continued to speak about the transcendental pastimes of Lord Kṛṣṇa in the matter of His form, quality, fame and paraphernalia.

THE STEALING OF THE BOYS AND CALVES BY BRAHMĀ

Lord Kṛṣṇa brought His friends to the bank of Yamunā and addressed them as follows: "My dear friends, just see how this spot is very nice for taking lunch and playing on the soft sandy Yamunā bank. You can see how the lotus flowers in the water are beautifully blown and how they distribute their flavor all around. The chirping of the birds along with the cooing of the peacocks, surrounded by the whispering of the leaves in the trees, combine and present sound vibrations that echo one another. And this just enriches the beautiful scenery created by the trees here. Let us have our lunch in this spot because it is already late and we are feeling hungry. Let the calves remain near us, and let them drink water from the Yamunā. While we are engaged in our lunch-taking, the calves may engage in eating the soft grasses that are in this spot."

On hearing this proposal from Kṛṣṇa, all the boys became very glad and said, "Certainly let us all sit down here to take our lunch." They then let loose the calves to eat the soft grass. Sitting down on the ground and keeping Kṛṣṇa in the center, they began to open their different boxes brought from home. Lord Śrī Kṛṣṇa was seated in the center of the circle, and all the boys kept their faces toward Him. They ate and constantly enjoyed seeing the Lord face to face. Kṛṣṇa appeared to be the whorl of a lotus flower, and the boys surrounding Him appeared to be its different petals. The boys collected flowers, leaves of flowers and the bark of trees and placed them under their different boxes, and thus they began to eat their lunch, keeping company with Kṛṣṇa. While taking lunch, each boy began to manifest different kinds of relations with Kṛṣṇa, and they enjoyed each other's company with joking words. While Lord Kṛṣṇa was thus enjoying lunch with His friends, His flute was pushed within the belt of His cloth, and His bugle and cane were pushed in on the left-hand side of His cloth. He was holding a lump of foodstuff prepared with yogurt, butter, rice and pieces of fruit salad in His left palm, which could be seen through His petallike finger joints. The Supreme Personality of Godhead, who accepts the results of all great sacrifices, was laughing and joking, enjoying lunch with His friends in Vṛndāvana. And thus the scene was being observed by the demigods in heaven. As for the boys, they were simply enjoying transcendental bliss in the company of the Supreme Personality of Godhead.

At that time, the calves that were pasturing nearby entered into the deep forest, allured by new grasses, and gradually went out of sight. When the boys saw that the calves were not nearby, they became afraid for their safety, and they immediately cried out, "Kṛṣṇa!" Kṛṣṇa is the killer of fear personified. Everyone is afraid of fear personified, but fear personified is afraid of Kṛṣṇa. By crying out the word "Kṛṣṇa," the boys at once transcended the fearful situation. Out of His great affection, Kṛṣṇa did not want His friends to give up their pleasing lunch engagement and go searching for the calves. He therefore said, "My dear friends, you need not interrupt your lunch. Go on enjoying. I am going personally where the calves are." Thus the Lord immediately started to search out the calves in the caves and bushes. He searched in the mountain holes and in the forests, but nowhere could He find them.

At the time when Aghāsura was killed and the demigods were looking on the incident with great surprise, Brahmā, who was born of the lotus flower growing out of the navel of Viṣṇu, also came to see. He was surprised how a little boy like Kṛṣṇa could act so wonderfully. Although he was informed that the little cowherd boy was the Supreme Personality of Godhead, he wanted to see more glorified pastimes of the Lord, and thus he stole all the calves and cowherd boys and took them to a different place. Lord Kṛṣṇa, therefore, in spite of searching for the calves, could not find them, and He even lost His boy friends on the bank of the Yamunā where they had been taking their lunch. In the form of a cowherd boy, Lord Kṛṣṇa was very little in comparison to Brahmā, but because He is the Supreme Personality of Godhead, He could immediately understand that all the calves and boys had been stolen by Brahmā. Kṛṣṇa thought, "Brahmā has taken away all the boys and calves. How can I alone return to Vṛndāvana? The mothers will be aggrieved!"

Therefore in order to satisfy the mothers of His friends as well as to convince Brahmā of the supremacy of the Personality of Godhead, He immediately expanded Himself as the cowherd boys and calves. In the *Vedas* it is said that the Supreme Personality of Godhead expands Himself in so many living entities by His energy. Therefore it is not very difficult for Him to expand Himself again into so many boys and calves. He expanded Himself to become exactly like the boys, who were of all different features, facial and bodily construction, and who were different in their clothing and ornaments and in their behavior and personal activities. In other words, everyone has different tastes; being an individual soul, each person has entirely different activities and behavior. Yet Kṛṣṇa exactly expanded Himself into all the different positions of the individual boys. He also became the calves, who were also of different sizes, colors, activities, etc. This was possible because everything is an expansion of Kṛṣṇa's energy. In the *Viṣṇu Purāṇa* it is said, *parasya brahmaṇaḥ śaktiḥ:* Whatever we actually see in the cosmic manifestation—be it matter or the activities of the living entities—is simply an expansion of the energies of the Lord, as heat and light are the different expansions of fire.

Thus expanding Himself as the boys and calves in their individual capacities, and surrounded by such expansions of Himself, Kṛṣṇa entered the village of Vṛndāvana. The residents had no knowledge of what had happened. After entering the village, Vṛndāvana, all the calves entered their respective cowsheds, and the boys also went to their respective mothers and homes.

The mothers of the boys heard the vibration of their flutes before their entrance, and to receive them, they came out of their homes and embraced them. And out of maternal affection, milk was flowing from their breasts, and they allowed the boys to drink it. However, their offering was not exactly to their boys but to the Supreme Personality of Godhead who had expanded Himself into such boys. This was another chance for all the mothers of Vṛndāvana to feed the Supreme Personality of Godhead with their own milk. Therefore not only did Lord Kṛṣṇa give Yaśodā the chance to feed Him, but this time He gave the chancc to all the elderly *gopīs.*

All the boys began to deal with their mothers as usual, and the mothers also, on the approach of evening, began to bathe their respective children, decorate them with *tilaka* and ornaments and give them necessary food after the day's labor. The cows also, who were away in the pasturing ground, returned in the evening and began to call their respective calves. The calves immediately came to their mothers, and the mothers began to lick the bodies of the calves. These relations between the cows and the *gopīs* with their calves and boys remained unchanged, although actually the original calves and boys were not there. Actually the cows' affection for their calves and the elderly *gopīs'* affection for the boys causelessly incrcased. Their affection increased naturally, even though the calves and boys were not their offspring. Although the cows and elderly *gopīs* of Vṛndāvana had greater affection for Kṛṣṇa than for their own offspring, after this incident their affection for their offspring increased exactly as it did for Kṛṣṇa. For one year continually, Kṛṣṇa Himself expanded as the calves and cowherd boys and was present in the pasturing ground.

As it is stated in the *Bhagavad-gītā,* Kṛṣṇa's expansion is situated in everyone's heart as the Supersoul. Similarly, instead of expanding Himself as the Supersoul, He expanded Himself as a portion of calves and cowherd boys for one continuous year.

One day, when Kṛṣṇa, along with Balarāma, was maintaining the calves in the forest, They saw some cows grazing on the top of Govardhana Hill. The cows could see down into the valley where the calves were being taken care of by the boys. Suddenly, on sighting their calves, the cows began to run towards them. They leaped downhill with joined front and rear legs. The cows were so melted with affection for their calves that they did not care about the rough path from the top of Govardhana Hill down to the pasturing ground. They began to approach the calves with their milk bags full of milk, and they raised their tails upwards. When they were coming down the hill, their milk bags were pouring milk on the ground out of intense maternal affection for the calves, although they were not their own calves. These cows had their own calves, and the calves that were grazing beneath Govardhana Hill were larger; they were not expected to drink milk directly from the milk bag but were satisfied with the grass. Yet all the cows came immediately and began to lick their bodies, and the calves also began to suck milk from the milk bags. There appeared to be a great bondage of affection between the cows and calves.

When the cows were running down from the top of Govardhana Hill, the men who were taking care of them tried to stop them. Elderly cows are taken care of by the men, and the calves are taken care of by the boys; and as far as possible, the calves are kept separate from the cows, so that the calves do not drink all the available milk. Therefore the men who were taking care of the cows on the top of Govardhana Hill tried to stop them, but they failed. Baffled by their failure, they were feeling ashamed and angry. They were very unhappy, but when they came down and saw their children taking care of the calves, they all of a sudden became very affectionate toward the children. It was very astonishing. Although the men came down disappointed, baffled and angry, as soon as they saw their own children, their hearts melted with great affection. At once their anger, dissatisfaction and unhappiness disappeared. They began to show paternal love for the children, and with great affection they lifted them in their arms and embraced them. They began to smell their children's heads and enjoy their company with great happiness. After embracing their children, the men again took the cows back to the top of Govardhana Hill. Along the way they began to think of their children, and affectionate tears fell from their eyes.

When Balarāma saw this extraordinary exchange of affection between the cows and their calves and between the fathers and their children—when neither the calves nor the children needed so much care—He began to wonder why this extraordinary thing happened. He was astonished to see all the residents of Vṛndāvana so affectionate for their own children, exactly as they had been for Kṛṣṇa. Similarly, the cows had grown affectionate for their calves—as much as for Kṛṣṇa. Balarāma therefore concluded that the extraordinary show of affection was something mystical, either performed by the demigods or by some powerful man. Otherwise, how could this wonderful change take place? He concluded that this mystical change must have been caused by Kṛṣṇa, whom Balarāma considered His worshipable Personality of Godhead. He thought, "It was arranged by Kṛṣṇa, and even I could not check its mystic power." Thus Balarāma understood that all those boys and calves were only expansions of Kṛṣṇa.

Balarāma inquired from Kṛṣṇa about the actual situation. He said, "My dear Kṛṣṇa, in the beginning I thought that all these cows, calves and cowherd boys were either great sages and saintly persons or demigods, but at the present it appears that they are actually Your expansions. They are all You; You Yourself are playing as the calves and cows and boys. What is the mystery of this situation? Where have those other calves and cows and boys gone? And why are You expanding Yourself as the cows, calves, and boys? Will You kindly tell Me what is the cause?" At the request of Balarāma, Kṛṣṇa briefly explained the whole situation: how the calves and boys were stolen by Brahmā and how He was concealing the incident by expanding Himself so people would not know that the original cows, calves, and boys were missing.

While Kṛṣṇa and Balarāma were talking, Brahmā returned after a moment's interval (according to the duration of his life). We have information of Lord Brahmā's duration of life from the *Bhagavad-gītā:* 1,000 times the duration of the four ages, or 4,300,000 X 1,000 years, comprise Brahmā's twelve hours. Similarly, one moment of Brahmā is equal to one year of our solar calculation. After one moment of Brahmā's calculation, Brahmā came back to see the fun caused by his stealing the boys and calves. But he was also afraid that he was playing with fire. Kṛṣṇa was his master, and he had played mischief for fun by taking away His calves and boys. He was really anxious, so he did not stay away very long; he came back after a moment (of his calculation). He saw that all the boys, calves and cows were playing with Kṛṣṇa in the same way as when he had come upon them, although he was confident that He had taken them and made them lie down asleep under the spell of his mystic power. Brahmā began to think, "All the boys, calves and cows were taken away by me, and I know they are still sleeping. How is it that a similar batch of cows, boys and calves is playing with Kṛṣṇa? Is it that they are not influenced by my mystic power? Have they been playing continually for one year with Kṛṣṇa?" Brahmā tried to understand who they were and how they were uninfluenced by his mystic power, but he could not ascertain it. In other words, he himself came under the spell of his own mystic power. The influence of his mystic power appeared like snow in darkness or the glow worm in daytime. During the night's darkness, the glowworm can show some glittering power, and the snow piled up on the top of a hill or on the ground can shine during the daytime. But at night the snow has no silver glitter; nor does the glowworm have any illuminating power during the daytime. Similarly, when the small mystic power exhibited by Brahmā was before the mystic power of Kṛṣṇa, it was just like snow or the glowworm. When a man of small mystic power wants to show potency in the presence of greater mystic power, he diminishes his own influence; he does not increase it. Even such a great personality as Brahmā, when he wanted to show his mystic power before Kṛṣṇa, became ludicrous. Brahmā was thus confused about his own mystic power.

In order to convince Brahmā that all those cows, calves and boys were not the original ones, the cows, calves and boys who were playing with Kṛṣṇa transformed into Viṣṇu forms. Actually, the original ones were sleeping under the spell of Brahmā's mystic power, but the present ones, seen by Brahmā, were all immediate expansions of Kṛṣṇa, or Viṣṇu. Viṣṇu is the expansion of Kṛṣṇa, so the Viṣṇu forms appeared before Brahmā. All the Viṣṇu forms were of bluish color and dressed in yellow garments; all of Them had four hands decorated with club, disc, lotus flower and conchshell. On Their heads were glittering golden jeweled helmets; They were bedecked with pearls and earrings, and garlanded with beautiful flowers. On Their chests was the mark of Śrīvatsa; Their arms were decorated with armlets and other jewelry. Their necks were smooth just like conchshell, Their legs were decorated with bells, Their waists decorated with golden bells, and Their fingers decorated with jeweled rings. Brahmā also saw that upon the whole body of Lord Viṣṇu, fresh *tulasī* buds were thrown, beginning from His lotus feet up to the top of the head. Another significant feature of the Viṣṇu forms was that all of Them were looking transcendentally beautiful. Their smiling resembled the moonshine, and Their glancing resembled the early rising of the sun. Just by Their glancing They appeared as the creators and maintainers of the modes of passion and ignorance. Viṣṇu represents the mode of goodness, Brahmā represents the mode of passion, and Lord Śiva represents the mode of ignorance. Therefore as maintainer of everything in the cosmic manifestation, Viṣṇu is also creator and maintainer of Brahmā and Lord Śiva.

After this manifestation of Lord Viṣṇu, Brahmā saw that many other Brahmās and Śivas and demigods and even insignificant living entities down to the ants and very small straws—movable and immovable living entities—were dancing, surrounding Lord Viṣṇu. Their dancing was accompanied by various kinds of music, and all of Them were worshiping Lord Viṣṇu. Brahmā realized that all those Viṣṇu forms were complete, beginning from the *aṇimā* perfection of becoming small like an atom, up to becoming infinite like the cosmic manifestation. All the mystic powers of Brahmā, Śiva, all the demigods and the twenty-four elements of cosmic manifestation were fully represented in the person of Viṣṇu. By the influence of Lord Viṣṇu, all subordinate mystic powers were engaged in His worship. He was being worshiped by time, space, cosmic manifestation, reformation, desire, activity and the three qualities of material nature. Lord Viṣṇu, Brahmā also realized, is the reservoir of all truth, knowledge and bliss, and He is the object of worship by the followers of the *Upaniṣads*. Brahmā realized that all the different forms of cows, boys and calves transformed into Viṣṇu forms were not transformed by a mysticism of the type that a *yogī* or a demigod can display by specific powers invested in him. The cows, calves and boys transformed into *viṣṇu-mūrtis,* or Viṣṇu forms, were not displays of *viṣṇu-māyā* or Viṣṇu energy, but were Viṣṇu Himself. The respective qualifications of Viṣṇu and *viṣṇu-māyā* are just like fire and heat. In the heat there is the qualification of fire, namely warmth; and yet heat is not fire. The manifestation of the Viṣṇu forms of the boys, cows and calves was not like the heat, but rather the fire—they were all actually Viṣṇu. Factually, the qualification of Viṣṇu is full truth, full knowledge and full bliss. Another example can be given with material objects, which are reflected in many, many forms. For example, the sun is reflected in many waterpots, but the reflections of the sun in many pots are not actually the sun. There is no actual heat and light from the sun in the pot, although it appears as the sun. But the forms which Kṛṣṇa assumed were each and every one full Viṣṇu. *Satya* means truth; *jñāna,* full knowledge; and *ānanda,* full bliss.

Transcendental forms of the Supreme Personality of Godhead in His person are so great that the impersonal followers of the *Upaniṣads* cannot reach the platform of knowledge to understand them. Particularly, the transcendental forms of the Lord are beyond the reach of the impersonalist who can only understand, through the study of *Upaniṣads,* that the Absolute Truth is not matter and that the Absolute Truth is not materially limited potency. Lord Brahmā understood Kṛṣṇa and His expansion into Viṣṇu forms and could understand that, due to expansion of energy of the Supreme Lord, everything movable and immovable within the cosmic manifestation is existing.

When Brahmā was thus standing baffled in his limited power and conscious of his limited activities within the eleven senses, he could at least realize that he was also a creation of the material energy, just like a puppet. As a puppet has no independent power to dance but dances according to the direction of the puppet master, so the demigods and living entities are all subordinate to the Supreme Personality of Godhead. As it is stated in the *Caitanya-caritāmṛta,* the only master is Kṛṣṇa, and all others are servants. The whole world is under the waves of the material spell, and beings are floating like straws in water. So their struggle for existence is continuing. But as soon as one becomes conscious that he is the eternal servant of the Supreme Personality of Godhead, this *māyā,* or illusory struggle for existence, is stopped.

Lord Brahmā, who has full control over the goddess of learning and who is considered to be the best authority in Vedic knowledge, was thus perplexed, being unable to understand the extraordinary power manifested in the Supreme Personality of Godhead. In the mundane world, even a personality like Brahmā is unable to understand the potential mystic power of the Supreme Lord. Not only did Brahmā fail to understand, but he was perplexed even to see the display being manifested by Kṛṣṇa before him.

Kṛṣṇa took compassion upon Brahmā's inability to see even how He was displaying the force of Viṣṇu in transferring Himself into cows and cowherd boys, and thus, while fully manifesting the Viṣṇu expansion, He suddenly pulled His curtain of *yogamāyā* over the scene. In the *Bhagavad-gītā* it is said that the Supreme Personality of Godhead is not visible due to the curtain spread by *yogamāyā.* That which covers the reality is *mahāmāyā,* or the external energy, which does not allow a conditioned soul to understand the Supreme Personality of Godhead beyond the cosmic manifestation. But the energy that partially manifests the Supreme Personality of Godhead and partially does not allow one to see is called *yogamāyā.* Brahmā is not an ordinary conditioned soul. He is far, far superior to all the demigods, and yet he could not comprehend the display of the Supreme Personality of Godhead; therefore Kṛṣṇa willingly stopped manifesting any further potency. The conditioned soul not only becomes bewildered, but is completely unable to understand. The curtain of *yogamāyā* was drawn so that Brahmā would not become more and more perplexed.

When Brahmā was relieved from his perplexity, he appeared to be awakened from an almost dead state, and he began to open his eyes with great difficulty. Thus he could see the eternal cosmic manifestation with common eyes. He saw all around him the superexcellent view of Vṛndāvana—full with trees—which is the source of life for all living entities. He could appreciate the transcendental land of Vṛndāvana, where all the living entities are transcendental to ordinary nature. In the forest of Vṛndāvana, even ferocious animals like tigers and others live peacefully along with the deer and human being. He could understand that, because of the presence of the Supreme Personality of Godhead in Vṛndāvana, that place is transcendental to all other places and that there is no lust and greed there. Brahmā thus found Śrī Kṛṣṇa, the Supreme Personality of Godhead, playing the part of a small cowherd boy; he saw that little child with a lump of food in His left hand, searching out His friends, cows and calves, just as He was actually doing one year before, after their disappearance.

Immediately Brahmā descended from his great swan carrier and fell down before the Lord just like a golden stick. The word used among the Vaiṣṇavas for offering respect is *daṇḍavat.* This word means falling down like a stick; one should offer respect to the superior Vaiṣṇava by falling down straight, with his body just like a stick. So Brahmā fell down before the Lord just like a stick to offer respect; and because the complexion of Brahmā is golden, he appeared to be like a golden stick lying down before Lord Kṛṣṇa. All the four helmets on the four heads of Brahmā touched the lotus feet of Kṛṣṇa. Brahmā, being very joyful, began to shed tears, and he washed the lotus feet of Kṛṣṇa with his tears. Repeatedly he fell and rose as he recalled the wonderful activities of the Lord. After repeating obeisances for a long time, Brahmā stood up and smeared his hands over his eyes. Seeing the Lord before him, he, trembling, began to offer prayers with great respect, humility and attention.

Brahmā said, "My dear Lord, You are the only worshipful Supreme Lord, Personality of Godhead; therefore I am offering my humble obeisances and prayers just to please You. Your bodily features are of the color of clouds filled with water. You are glittering with a silver electric aura emanating from Your yellow garments.

"Let me offer my respectful repeated obeisances unto the son of Mahārāja Nanda, who is standing before me with conchshell, earrings and peacock feather on His head. His face is beautiful; He is wearing a helmet, garlanded by forest flowers, and He stands with a morsel of food in His hand. He is decorated with cane and bugle, and He carries a buffalo horn and flute. He stands before me with small lotus feet.

"My dear Lord, people may say that I am the master of all Vedic knowledge, and I am supposed to be the creator of this universe, but it has been proved now that I cannot understand Your personality, even though You are present before me just like a child. You are playing with Your boy friends, calves and cows, which might imply that You do not even have sufficient education. You are appearing just like a village boy, carrying Your food in Your hand and searching for Your calves. And yet there is so much difference between Your body and mine that I cannot estimate the potency of Your body. As I have already stated in the *Brahma-saṁhitā,* Your body is not material."

In the *Brahma-saṁhitā* it is stated that the body of the Lord is all spiritual; there is no difference between the Lord's body and His self. Each limb of His body can perform the actions of all the others. The Lord can see with His hands, He can hear with His eyes, He can accept offerings with His legs and He can create with His mouth.

Brahmā continued: "Your appearance as a cowherd child is for the benefit of the devotees, and although I have committed offenses at Your lotus feet by stealing away Your cows, boys and calves, I can understand that You have mercy upon me. That is Your transcendental quality; You are very affectionate toward Your devotees. In spite of Your affection for me, I cannot estimate the potency of Your bodily activities. It is to be understood that when I, Lord Brahmā, the supreme personality of this universe, cannot estimate the childlike body of the Supreme Personality of Godhead, then what to speak of others? Therefore, as it is said in the *Bhagavad-gītā,* anyone who can understand a little of the transcendental pastimes, appearance and disappearance of the Lord becomes immediately eligible to enter into the kingdom of God after quitting this material body. This statement is confirmed in the *Vedas,* and it is stated simply: by understanding the Supreme Personality of Godhead, one can overcome the chain of repeated birth and death. I therefore recommend that people should not try to understand You by their speculative knowledge.

"The best process of understanding You is to submissively give up the speculative process and try to hear about You, either from Yourself as You have given statements in the *Bhagavad-gītā* and many similar Vedic literatures, or from a realized devotee who has taken shelter at Your lotus feet. One has to hear from a devotee without speculation. One does not even need to change his worldly position; he simply has to hear Your message. Although You are not understandable by the material senses, simply by hearing about You, one can gradually conquer the nescience of misunderstanding. By Your grace only, You become revealed to a devotee. You are unconquerable by any other means. Speculative knowledge without any trace of devotional service is simply a useless waste of time in the search for You. Devotional service is so important that even a little attempt can raise one to the highest perfectional platform. One should not, therefore, neglect this auspicious process of devotional service and take to the speculative method. By the speculative method one may gain partial knowledge of Your cosmic manifestation, but it is not possible to understand You, the origin of everything. The attempt of persons who are interested only in speculative knowledge is simply wasted labor, like the labor of a person who attempts to gain something by beating the empty husk of a rice paddy. A little quantity of paddy can be husked by the grinding wheel, and one can gain some grains of rice, but if the skin of the paddy is already beaten by the grinding wheel, there is no further gain in beating the husk. It is simply useless labor.

"My dear Lord, there are many instances in the history of human society where a person, after failing to achieve the transcendental platform, engaged himself in devotional service with his body, mind and words and thus attained the highest perfectional stage of entering into Your abode. The processes of understanding You by speculation or mystic meditation are all useless without devotional service. One should therefore engage himself in Your devotional service even in his worldly activities, and one should always keep himself near You by the process of hearing and chanting Your transcendental glories. Simply by being attached to hearing and chanting Your glories, one can attain the highest perfectional stage and enter into Your kingdom. If a person, therefore, always keeps in touch with You by hearing and chanting Your glories and offers the results of his work for Your satisfaction only, he very easily and happily attains entrance into Your supreme abode. You are realizable by persons who have cleansed their hearts of all contamination. This cleansing of the heart is made possible by chanting and hearing the glories of Your Lordship."

Appendixes

The First Indologists

The first Westerners to investigate the Vedic literatures were the British, in the last half of the eighteenth century. It is best to understand their work in the larger historical context[1] of the British rule of India.

A Brief History of the British in India

Early invaders of India included the Persians (600 B.C.) and the Greeks under Alexander the Great (300 B.C.). India's first great Hindu empire, the Maurya Empire founded by Candragupta (300 B.C.), expanded under Emperor Aśoka to embrace the whole subcontinent, and it also fostered Buddhism. After Aśoka, assorted northern tribes invaded India, until the reign of another Gupta dynasty, which united a section of the country for centuries. In the seventh century the Arab Muslims began conquering India, and various Muslim leaders developed empires up until the Mogul Empire, whose chief ruler was Akbar. During the reign of Akbar's son Jahangir (1605–1627), the British established their first trading station in India. The Portuguese had been the first Europeans to arrive, and they competed with the French and English for commercial control of port cities. Through treaties with local rulers, the trading companies became more powerful than the Mogul Empire. The companies received official monopolies from their governments and held huge armies of mercenaries. By defeating an Indian army at the Battle of Plassey, in 1757, the British East India Company finally gained supremacy. Through the eighteenth century, the company made treaties or annexed areas by military campaigns; at last in full control of India, it ceded the country to the British government.

At first, the British government was careful not to force any change in religion upon the Indian people. This policy had always seemed most judicious for ruling the several hundred million Indian citizens without precipitating rebellion. Thus, under Lord Cornwallis (1786–1793, 1805) *laissez-faire* had dominated the East India Company's attitude toward the Indian way of life.[2] Through the East India Company's regulations of 1793, the governor general had promised to "preserve the laws of the Shaster and the Koran, and to protect the natives of India in the free exercise of their religion."[3] However, a year before these regulations went into effect, Charles Grant had written, "The company manifested a laudable zeal for extending, as far as its means went, the knowledge of the Gospel to the pagan tribes among whom its factories were placed."[4] In 1808, the same author described openings of Christian schools and translations of the Bible into Indian dialects as "principal efforts made under the patronage of the British government in India, to impart to the natives a knowledge of Christianity."[5]

Historian Vincent Smith describes three broad tendencies in Britain's policy at the start of the 1800's.[6] The conservatives were interested in improving the Indian way of life, but recommended extreme caution for fear of violent reaction; they saw no easy overthrow of Indian tradition. The liberals felt the need to introduce Western ideas and values, but they hoped to integrate gradually. The rationalists, led by George Berkeley and David Hume, had a more radical approach. They trusted that reason could abolish all human ignorance. And since the West was the champion of reason, the East could only profit by the acquaintance.

To most eighteenth-century Englishmen (whether at home or abroad), religion meant Christianity. Naturally, racism played its part also. "This attitude of Europeans toward Indians was due to a sense of racial superiority—a cherished conviction which was shared by every Englishman in India, from the highest to the lowest."[7] Thus, upon arriving in India in 1813, the governor general marquis of Hastings wrote, "The Hindoo appears a being merely limited to mere animal functions, and even in them indifferent . . . with no higher intellect than a dog."[8]

Without governmental sanction or license, the Christian evangelists came to India and proselytized to undermine the "superstitions of the country."[9] Alexander Duff (1806–1878) founded Scots College, in Calcutta, which he envisioned as a "headquarters for a great campaign against Hinduism."[10] Duff sought to convert the natives by enrolling them in English-run schools and colleges, and he placed emphasis on learning Christianity through the English language. Another leading missionary, a Baptist, William Carey (1761–1834), smuggled himself into India and propagandized against the Vedic culture so zealously that the British government in Bengal curbed him as a political danger. On confiscating a batch of Bengali-language pamphlets produced by Carey, India's Governor General Lord Minto described them as "scurrilous invective. . . . Without arguments of any kind, they were filled with hell fire and still hotter fire, denounced against a whole race of men merely for believing in the religion they were taught by their fathers."[11] Duff, Carey, and other missionaries gradually gained strength and became more aggressive; finally, they gained permission to conduct their campaigns without governmental license. The missionaries actively opposed the British government's attempt to take a neutral stand toward Indian culture and worked with optimism for the complete conversion of the natives. They did not hesitate to denounce the Vedic literatures as "absurdities" meant "for the amusement of children."[12]

Historian Arthur D. Innes writes, "The educators had hardly concealed their expectations that with Western knowledge the sacred fairy tales of the East would be dissolved and the basis of popularly cherished creeds would be swept away."[13] The suspicion of religious coercion disrupted British-Indian relations and in 1857 helped touch off the Sepoy Rebellion (of Indian mercenaries).[14]

The First Scholars

Such was the setting in which the first Indologists appeared. These first Vedic scholars did not form a unified political or academic party; they were variously conservative, liberal, and radical. Sir William Jones, the first Britisher to master Sanskrit and study the *Vedas,* drew fire from the eminent British historian James Mill for his "hypothesis of a high state of civilization."[15] Typically, Mill believed that the people of India never had been advanced and that therefore their claim to a glorious past (which some of the early Indologists supported) was historical fantasy. At any rate, by translating the *Vedas* for the Western reader and thus evincing the ancient Vedic genius, the scholars increased India's prestige in the West. On the other hand, as Aubrey Menen has said, "It should be remembered that they [the English of the seventeenth century] were not the almost pagan English of today. Every man was a Christian, and it was a Christian's duty to wash the heathen in the blood of the lamb."[16]

Nonetheless, some of the early scholars rather admired the Vedic culture they were investigating, even though they initially conceived of themselves as bearers of Christian light to the sacred darkness of the heathens.

Sir William Jones (1746–1794), Charles Wilkins (1749–1836), and Thomas Colebrooke (1765–1837) are considered the fathers of Indology.[17] Jones was educated at Oxford and there began his studies in Oriental and other languages; he is said to have mastered a total of sixteen. In addition, he wrote a Persian grammar, translated various Oriental literatures, and also practiced law. After his appointment as judge of the Supreme Court, Sir William went to Calcutta, in 1783. There he founded the Asiatic Society of Bengal and was its president throughout his life. He translated a number of Sanskrit works into English, and his investigations into languages mark him as one of the most brilliant minds of the eighteenth century. Sir William was not prone to invective against another's religion, particularly the Vedic, which he admired. In his view the narratives of the East, like those of Greece and Rome, could enrich both the English tradition and the human mind. Notwithstanding, Sir William's stance was that of "a devout and convinced Christian."[18] Thus, he described the *Bhāgavata Purāṇa* as "a motley story,"[19] and he speculated that the *Bhāgavata* came from the Christian gospels, which had been brought to India and "repeated to the Hindus, who ingrafted them on the old fable of Ce'sava [Keśava, a name for Kṛṣṇa], the Apollo of Greece."[20] Of course, this theory has been discredited since records of Kṛṣṇa worship predate Christ by centuries.[21]

H. H. Wilson (1786–1860), described as "the greatest Sanskrit scholar of his time,"[22] received his education in London and journeyed to India in the East India Company's medical service. He became secretary of the Asiatic Society of Bengal (1811–1833), and medical duties notwithstanding, he published a Sanskrit-English dictionary. He became Boden Professor of Sanskrit at Oxford in 1833, librarian of the India House in 1836, and director of the Royal Asiatic Society in 1837. Titles credited to his name include *Viṣṇu Purāṇa, Lectures on the Religious and Philosophical Systems of the Hindus,* and *Ṛg Veda,* among others. Also, he helped Mill's *History of India* and edited several other translations of Eastern literatures. He also proposed that Britain restrain herself from forcing the Hindus to give up their religious traditions. Compared to the evangelists, he appears to have been a champion of the preservation of Vedic ideas. Yet we may be a little startled by his stated motives:

> From the survey which has been submitted to you, you will perceive that the practical religion of the Hindus is by no means a concentrated and compact system, but a heterogeneous compound made up of various and not infrequently incompatible ingredients, and that to a few ancient fragments it has made large and unauthorized additions, most of which are of an exceedingly mischievous and disgraceful nature. It is, however, of little avail yet to attempt to undeceive the multitude; their superstition is based upon ignorance, and until the foundation is taken away, the superstructure, however crazy and rotten, will hold together.[23]

Ultimately, Wilson felt that the Christian culture should simply replace the Vedic culture, and he believed that full knowledge of the Indian tradition would help effect that conversion. In his modulated conservatism he seemed to echo the East India Company. Aware that the people of India would not easily give up their tradition, he made this shrewd commentary:

> The whole tendency of brahminical education is to enforce dependence upon authority—in the first instance upon the *guru,* in the next upon the books. A learned *brāhmaṇa* trusts solely to his learning; he never ventures upon independent thought; he appeals to memory; he quotes texts without measure and in unquestioning trust. It will be difficult to persuade him that the *Vedas* are human and very ordinary writings, that the *Purāṇas* are modern and unauthentic, or even that the *tantras* are not entitled to respect. As long as he opposes authority to reason, and stifles the workings of conviction by the dicta of a reputed sage, little impression can be made upon his understanding. Certain it is, therefore, that he will have recourse to his authorities, and it is therefore important to show that his authorities are worthless.[24]

Wilson also warned that the Vedic adherents were likely to show "tenacious obstinacy" about their "speculative tenets . . . particularly those regarding the nature and condition of the soul."[25] But he was hopeful that by inspired, diligent effort the "specious" system of Vedic thought would be "shown to be fallacious and false by the Ithuriel spear of Christian truth."[26] As the first holder of Oxford's Boden Chair for Sanskrit, H. H. Wilson delivered public lectures to promote his cause. He intended that the lectures "help candidates for a prize of two hundred pounds . . . for the best refutation of the Hindu religious system."[27] Wilson's writings are full of similar passages, including a detailed method for exploiting the native Vedic psychology by use of a counterfeit *guru*-disciple relationship. Now, in Wilson's case, the charge of bias has become aggravated by charges of invalid scholarship. Recently, Natalie P. R. Sirkin presented documented evidence that betrays Wilson as a plagiarist: his most important publications were collected manuscripts by deceased authors whose works he credited to himself, as well as works done without research. "He wrote an analysis of the *Purāṇas* without reading them."[28]

Another renowned pioneer Indologist was F. Max Müller (1823–1900), born at Dessau and educated in Leipzig. He learned Sanskrit and translated the ancient *Hitopadeśa* before coming to England, in 1846.

Comissioned by the East India Company to translate the *Ṛg Veda*, he lived at Oxford and wrote many books on mythology and comparative religion. Müller is best known for his series *Sacred Books of the East*, a fifty-volume work which he devoted himself to editing in 1875.

In 1876, Müller wrote to a friend, "India is much riper for Christianity than Rome or Greece were at the time of Saint Paul."[29] He added that he would not like to go to India as a missionary, because that would make him dependent on the government. His preference was this: "I should like to live for ten years quite quietly and learn the language, try to make friends, and then see whether I was fit to take part in a work, by means of which the old mischief of Indian priestcraft could be overthrown and the way opened for the entrance of simple Christian teaching."[30] Müller regarded Vedic philosophy as "Āryan legend" and "myth," and he believed that Āryan civilizations had simply helped bring about the evolution of Christianity. "History seems to think that the whole human race required gradual education before, in the fullness of time, it could be admitted to the truths of Christianity."[31] Müller added, "The ancient religions of the world may have but served to prepare the way of Christ by helping through its very errors."[32]

H. H. Wilson's successor in Oxford's Boden Chair was Sir Monier Monier-Williams (1819–1899). Born in Bombay, Monier-Williams attended the East India Company's college and later taught there. After his appointment as a professor of Sanskrit at Oxford, in 1870, he delivered an inaugural lecture entitled "The Study of Sanskrit in Relation to Missionary Work in India." Monier-Williams also wrote a book called *Hinduism* (1894), which was published and distributed by the Society for Promoting Christian Knowledge. He is best known to twentieth-century Indology students for his *Sanskrit-English Dictionary*. Also, he dedicated twenty-five years to founding an institution at Oxford for disseminating information about Indian literature and culture. He succeeded, and the Indian Institute formally opened in 1896. Monier-Williams disapproved of Müller's evolution-to-Christianity view of the Vedic *śāstra:*

> There can be no doubt of a greater mistake than to force these non-Christian bibles into conformity with some scientific theory of development and then point to the Christian's *Holy Bible* as the crowning product of religious evolution. So far from this, these non-Christian bibles are all developments in the wrong direction. They all begin with some flashes of true light and end in utter darkness.[33]

Monier-Williams further wrote, "It seems to me that our missionaries are already sufficiently convinced of the necessity of studying these works, and of making themselves conversant with the false creeds they have to fight against. How could an army of invaders have any chance of success in an enemy's country without a knowledge of the position and strength of its fortresses, and without knowing how to turn the batteries they may capture against the foe?"[34]

Another early Indologist was Theodore Goldstücker (1821–1872), born at Königsberg and educated there and at Bonn, where he studied Sanskrit, philosophy, and Oriental languages. After settling in England, in 1850, he received appointment as a professor of Sanskrit at London's University College; he held this post until his death. Goldstücker wrote a number of books on Sanskrit literature and founded the Society for the Publication of Sanskrit Texts. He also participated in many writing and research projects concerning India. The *Dictionary of Indian Biography* describes him as an authority on ancient Hindu literature.[35] Goldstücker regarded the people of India as being burdened by Vedic religion, which had only brought them worldwide "contempt and ridicule." Thus, he proposed to reeducate them with European values. Goldstücker wrote, "The means for combating that enemy is as simple as it is irresistible: a proper instruction of the growing generation in its ancient literature."[36] In his book *Inspired Writings of Hinduism,* Goldstücker assailed the validity of Vedic literature. His aim was to demonstrate to the new generation of Vedic followers that he had scholastically annihilated their scripture and that they should show their appreciation by adopting European values and improving their character.

It is lamentable that this sectarian *raison d'être* clouded the early study of Vedic literature. At any rate, when reading the theories or analyses of these early Indologists, the student would do well to bear in mind the bias behind the brilliant scholarship.

Their Influence on Modern Scholarship

Of course, college Sanskrit departments no longer award prizes for "the best refutation of Hinduism." In fact, when one samples the current selection of books by Vedic scholars, he finds the authors describing themselves as "sympathetic outsiders," "friends of India," and "admirers of the tradition of tolerance in Indian religion."

Nonetheless, some of the missionary Indologists' main theses still crop up as time-honored facts. Simply by being the pioneers, Wilson,

Monier-Williams, Müller, and others have left a lasting impression of how one should go about studying the *śāstras*. "The foundations for the recovery of India's past were laid by certain eminent classical scholars, including Sir William Jones, James Prinsep, H. T. Colebrooke, and H. H. Wilson. . . . the debt owed these men is great."[37]

Modern Vedic scholars are hardly missionaries; still, largely out of academic habit, they give tacit approval to many of the first Indologists' conclusions. For instance, the early researchers portrayed Vedic literature as a hodgepodge of disharmonious texts. Sir Monier Monier-Williams wrote, "Yes, after a lifelong study of the religious books of the Hindus, I feel compelled to publicly express my opinion of them. They begin with much promise amid scintillations of truth and light and occasional sublime thoughts from the source of all truth and light, but end in sad corruptions and lamentable impurities."[38] Like their predecessors, today's scholars discredit the *Purāṇas,* although the Vedic *ācāryas* themselves have accepted the *Purāṇas* on a par with the other Vedic *śāstras.* Recently, one scholar has commented that Müller attempted to change Hinduism to a "new and purer form" and failed, but that "his conception of the history of Hinduism, which presented an antithesis between its Vedic form and the so-called Purāṇic form . . . still survives in a modified version."[39] In addition, many of today's scholars still teach that the *Vedas* are essentially mythological and that the *Purāṇas* are not even consonant with the Vedic mythology. In other words, the scholars disavow what the *ācāryas* affirm—namely, that the Vedic literatures form a coherent whole, and that the *Purāṇas* are the culmination. But since it is the *Purāṇas* that substantiate monotheism, if we dismiss them we miss part of the Vedic picture of the Absolute Truth.

As we would expect, many of today's students are coming to think of the Vedic literature as lacking clarity and conclusiveness. More often than not, as one begins his Indological studies he hears that Vedic authority is dubious, that eternal existence is simply a wish for self-perpetuation, and that God and the demigods are *ipso facto* myths. In fact, the *Vedas'* compiler, Vyāsadeva, often receives no mention. Moriz Winternitz writes that the names of the authors of Vedic literature are unknown to us and that sometimes "a mythical seer of primitive times is named as author."[40] Yet Vedic evidence confirms Vyāsadeva as the literature's actual compiler: "Thereafter, in the seventeenth incarnation of Godhead, Śrī Vyāsadeva appeared in the womb of Satyavatī, wife of Parāśara Muni, and he divided the one *Veda* into several branches and subbranches."[41] Still, Winternitz makes this comment: "The orthodox . . . believe the same Vyāsa who compiled the *Vedas* and composed the Mahābhārata, who also in the beginning of Kali-yuga, the present age of the world, was the author of the eighteen *Purāṇas.* But this Vyāsadeva is a form of the exalted God Viṣṇu Himself."[42] And thus, without further word, Winternitz rejects the possibility of Vyāsadeva's authorship and goes on to discuss other possible authors: since the *Purāṇas* present Vyāsadeva as an *avatāra,* he obviously could never have existed. In this way, Vedic personalities and statements become suspect, even "mythological," simply because they are supramundane. The student of the *Vedas* should understand plainly that the *Vedas* do describe the supramundane, and that to reject their statements on this basis is really self-defeating. One should approach the *Vedas* with an open mind and let them speak for themselves. Otherwise, they will remain a hodgepodge of "sad corruptions and lamentable impurities."

Today many scholars continue to minimize the existential and transcendental validity of the *Vedas,* often without so much as an explanation why empiric knowledge should take precedence over *śabda,* knowledge from authority. Thus, subtly but surely, the Indological scholars of the present day have inherited the pioneers' bias, and though today's bias is not "evangelist" but "empiricist," it slants just the same. With all deference to the laudable efforts of the empiricists, we suggest that the student try to take a fresh look at Vedic literature, through the eyes of the *Vedas* themselves. Momentarily setting aside the legacy of the British Indological pioneers, the new student of Vedic literature will benefit by returning to the primary sources—the original *śāstras* and the commentaries of the *ācāryas.* In this way, without preconceived notions, the student may better appreciate the coherent and many-faceted knowledge that the *Vedas* offer.

Notes

Chapter One

1. Moriz Winternitz says the *Purāṇas* are sacred books of a second grade. F. Max Müller theorizes that they are the antithesis of the *Vedas* and are savage and degraded. Horace H. Wilson attributes the *Bhāgavata Purāṇa's* composition to the grammarian Vopadeva. These are examples of how Vedic literatures other than the four *Vedas* are seen as less genuine or later productions.
2. A.C. Bhaktivedanta Swami Prabhupāda, *Śrīmad-Bhāgavatam, First Canto,* vol. 1, p. 210 (also known as *Bhāgavata Purāṇa*. Hereafter cited as *Bhāgavatam.*).
3. Karl H. Potter, *Presuppositions of India's Philosophies,* p. *vii.*
4. Sarvepalli Radhakrishnan and Charles A. Moore, p. *xxiii.*
5. Heinrich Zimmer, *Philosophies of India,* p. 4.
6. A.C. Bhaktivedanta Swami Prabhupāda, *Bhagavad-gītā As It Is,* p. 630 (13.8–12) (hereafter cited as *Gītā*. The chapter and verse numbers, e.g., "13.8–12," are given to facilitate using the complete *Bhagavad-gītā* in the Anthology).
7. *Indian Thought and Its Development,* trans. Mrs. Charles E.B. Russell, p. 1.
8. Bhakti Śrī Rūpa Siddhāntī Gosvāmī et al., trans. *Vedānta-sūtra* (of Kṛṣṇa Dvaipāyana-Vyāsa), p. 45.
9. Bhaktivinoda Ṭhākura, "Aruṇodaya-kīrtana," *Songs of the Vaiṣṇava Ācāryas,* comp. Acyutānanda Svāmī, p. 29.
10. *Gītā,* p. 80.
11. Rai Bahadur Srisa Chandra Vasu Vidyarnava, trans. *The Bṛhad-āraṇyaka Upaniṣad (of the White Yajur Veda)*, p. 217.
12. Hiriyanna, Mysore, *Popular Essays in Indian Philosophy,* p. 14.
13. Ananda K. Coomerswamy, ed., *Am I My Brother's Keeper?,* p. 55.
14. Bhakti Śrī Rūpa Siddhāntī Gosvāmī et al., trans., *Muṇḍaka Upaniṣad (of the Atharva Veda)*, p. 89.
15. Hiriyanna, *Popular Essays,* p. 13.
16. A.C. Bhaktivedanta Swami Prabhupāda, *The Nectar of Instruction,* p. 1.
17. A.C. Bhaktivedanta Swami Prabhupāda, *Śrī Caitanya-caritāmṛta, Ādi-līlā,* vol. 1, p. 255.
18. Narottama dāsa Ṭhākura, "Nāma-saṅkīrtana," *Songs,* comp. Acyutānanda, pp. 60–61.
19. Bhakti Śrī Rūpa Siddhāntī Gosvāmī, trans., *Śvetāśvatara Upaniṣad (of the Black Yajur Veda)*, p. 388.
20. A.C. Bhaktivedanta Swami Prabhupāda, *Kṛṣṇa, the Supreme Personality of Godhead,* vol. 3, pp. 75–76.
21. Ibid., p. 76.
22. Troy Wilson Organ, *Hinduism,* p. 57.
23. Hemchandra Raychaudhuri, *Studies in Indian Antiquity,* p. 174.
24. Radhakrishnan and Moore, *A Sourcebook in Indian Philosophy,* p. 66.

25. Sarvepalli Radhakrishnan, *Indian Philosophy,* pp. 57–59.
26. A.C. Bhaktivedanta Swami Prabhupāda, *Teachings of Lord Caitanya,* p. 30.

Chapter Two

1. p. 1.
2. Sarvepalli Radhakrishnan and Charles A. Moore, *A Sourcebook in Indian Philosophy,* p. 355.
3. Sten Konow and Paul Tuxen, "The Indus Civilization," *Traditional India,* ed. O.L. Chavarria-Aguilar, p. 28.
4. *A History of Ancient Sanskrit Literature As It Illustrates the Primitive Religion of the Brahmins,* p. 63.
5. Sarvepalli Radhakrishnan, *Indian Philosophy,* pp. 57–58.
6. Moriz Winternitz, *A History of Indian Literature,* vol. 1, trans. S. Ketkar, p. 24.
7. Ibid.
8. Ibid.
9. Ibid.
10. Kendrick Frazier, "Human Evolution," *Science News,* July, 1975.
11. Chavarria-Aguilar, *Traditional India,* p. 24.
12. Sir Mortimer Wheeler, Civilizations of the Indus Valley and Beyond, p. 78.
13. Chavarria-Aguilar, *Traditional India,* p. 11.
14. Ibid.
15. Patty Jo Watson, *Explanation in Archaeology,* pp. 22–23.
16. *Encyclopedia Brittanica,* s.v. "Prehistoric Religion."
17. *Encyclopedia Brittanica,* s.v. "Linguistics."
18. Stuart Piggot, *Prehistoric India to 1000 B.C.,* p. 249.
19. Ibid., p. 248.
20. S.M. Natarajan, "Vedic Society and Religion," *An Outline of the Cultural History of India,* ed. Syad Latif, p. 14.
21. George Cardona, ed., *Indo-European and Indo-Europeans: Papers Presented at the Third International Indo-European Conference at the University of Pennsylvania,* p. 253.
22. Piggot, *Prehistoric India,* p. 248.
23. Cardona, *Indo-European and Indo-Europeans,* pp. 1–2.
24. Charles F. Hockett, *A Course in Modern Linguistics,* p. 531.
25. Ibid.
26. Richard Garbe, *India and Christendom: The Historical Connection Between Their Religions,* trans. Lydia J. Robinson, pp. 214–217.

Chapter Three

1. A.C. Bhaktivedanta Swami Prabhupāda, *Śrīmad-Bhāgavatam, First Canto,* vol. 1, p. 98 (also known as *Bhāgavata Purāṇa.*) (Hereafter cited as *Bhagavatam*).
2. Bhakti Śrī Rūpa Siddhāntī Gosvāmī et al., *Vedānta-sūtra* (of Kṛṣṇa Dvaipāyana-Vyāsa), p. 63.
3. *The Thirteen Principal Upaniṣads,* trans. Robert Ernest Hume, p. 373.

4. Sarvepalli Radhakrishnan and Charles A. Moore, *A Sourcebook in Indian Philosophy,* p. 38.
5. Thomas Hopkins, *The Hindu Religious Tradition,* p. 39.
6. Ibid., p. 37.
7. A.C. Bhaktivedanta Swami Prabhupāda, *Bhagavad-gītā As It Is,* pp. 86, 98 (2.12; 2.20) (hereafter cited as *Gītā*. Chapter and verse numbers, within parentheses, refer also to Anthology.).
8. Ibid., p. 100.
9. Ibid., p. 651 (13.25).
10. Ibid., p. 330 (6.20–23).
11. Ibid., p. 712 (15.15).
12. *Bhāgavatam,* p. 131 (1.2.33).
13. *Gītā,* p. 292 (5.18).
14. Ibid., pp. 316, 341 (6.8; 6.32).
15. Bhaktisiddhānta Sarasvatī Gosvāmī Ṭhākura, trans., *Śrī Brahma-saṁhitā,* ed. Bhaktivilāsa Tīrtha Gosvāmī, p. 124 (hereafter cited as *Brahma-saṁhitā*).
16. Ibid., p. 128.
17. *Gītā,* p. 371 (7.7).
18. *Brahma-saṁhitā,* p. 1.
19. *Bhāgavatam,* pp. 166–167.
20. A.C. Bhaktivedanta Swami Prabhupāda, *Śrī Caitanya-caritāmṛta, Ādi-līlā,* vol. 1, p. 159.
21. *Brahma-saṁhitā,* p. 65.
22. *Gītā,* pp. 430–431 (8.20–21).
23. Ibid., p. 94 (2.17).
24. Ibid., p. 95.
25. Radhakrishnan and Moore, *Sourcebook,* p. 508.
26. Troy Wilson Organ, *Hinduism,* p. 115.
27. Ruth Reyna, *Introduction to Indian Philosophy,* p. 61.
28. *Gītā,* p. 380 (7.14).
29. Ibid., p. 380.
30. Ibid., pp. 381–382 (7.15).
31. Radhakrishnan and Moore, *Sourcebook,* p. 45.
32. *Gītā,* p. 380 (7.14).
33. Ibid., p. 263 (4.37).
34. Ibid., p. 789 (18.11).
35. Ibid., p. 670 (14.7).
36. Ibid., p. 671 (14.8).
37. Ibid., p. 677 (14.14–15).
38. Satischandra Chatterjee, *The Fundamentals of Hinduism,* p. 40.
39. *Gītā,* p. 129 (2.45).
40. Swami Nikhilananda, trans., *The Upaniṣads: A Second Selection,* p. 133.
41. *Gītā,* p. 370 (7.6).
42. Ibid., pp. 369–370.
43. Ibid., pp. 367, 369 (7.4–5).
44. as *Webster's New World Dictionary of the English Language,* p. 175.

45. Baron John S. Teignmouth, *Memoirs of the Life, Writings and Correspondence of Sir William Jones,* p. 362.
46. *Gītā,* pp. 427, 429 (8.17–18).
47. *Brahma-saṁhitā,* p. 139.
48. A.C. Bhaktivedanta Swami Prabhupāda, *The Nectar of Devotion,* p. 103.
49. Louis Renou, *Hinduism,* p. 20.

Chapter Four

1. Śrīdhara Svāmī, *Subodhinī-ṭikā,* trans. Nārāyaṇa dāsa Bhakti-sudhākāra, p. 2.
2. Thomas Hopkins, *The Hindu Religious Tradition,* p. 91.
3. A.C. Bhaktivedanta Swami Prabhupāda, *Bhagavad-gītā As It Is,* p. 28 (hereafter cited as *Gītā.* Chapter and verse numbers, within parentheses, in some following notes, refer also to Anthology.).
4. *Hinduism,* p. 33.
5. *Hinduism and Buddhism,* p. 5.
6. *Gītā,* pp. 718–719 (15.19–20).
7. Ibid., p. 835 (18.66).
8. Hopkins, *Hindu Religious Tradition,* p. 94.
9. V.D. Mahajan, *Ancient India,* p. 72.
10. Ruth Reyna, *Introduction to Indian Philosophy,* p. 16.
11. Sarvepalli Radhakrishnan and Charles A. Moore, *A Sourcebook in Indian Philosophy,* p. 355.
12. A.C. Bhaktivedanta Swami Prabhupāda, *Śrīmad-Bhāgavatam, First Canto,* vol. 1, p. 44 (also known as *Bhāgavata Purāṇa.* Hereafter cited as *Bhāgavatam.*).
13. Ibid., pp. 207–214.
14. Ainslee T. Embree, *The Hindu Tradition,* p. 5.
15. Sayana Acarya, trans., *Ṛg Veda,* p. 32.
16. *Gītā,* p. 772 (17.23).
17. Ibid., p. 394 (7.22).
18. Ibid., p. 127 (2.42–43).
19. A.C. Bhaktivedanta Swami Prabhupāda, *Śrī Īśopaniṣad,* pp. 72–73.
20. Bhaktivinoda Ṭhākura, and Bhakti Śrī Rūpa Siddhāntī Gosvāmī, trans., *Śrīmad Bhagavad-gītā with the Gītā-bhūṣaṇa Commentary of Śrīla Baladeva Vidyābhūṣaṇa,* p. 769.
21. Ibid., p. 770.
22. *Gītā,* p. 504.
23. Ibid., p. 129 (2.45).
24. Hopkins, *Hindu Religious Tradition,* p. 39.
25. *Encyclopedia of Religion and Ethics,* s.v. "Vedic Religion."
26. Nalinimohan M. Sastri, *A Study of Śaṅkara,* p. 22.
27. Swami Nikhilananda, trans., *The Upaniṣads: A Second Selection,* p. 99.
28. Swami Gambhirananda, trans., *Eight Upaniṣads,* p. 22.
29. Major B.D. Basu, I.M.S., ed., *The Sacred Books of the Hindus,* vol. 1, p. 128.
30. *Gītā,* p. 102.

31. A.C. Bhaktivedanta Swami Prabhupāda, *Śrī Caitanya-caritāmṛta, Ādi-līlā,* vol. 2, p. 88.
32. Ibid., p. 89.
33. Ibid.
34. Dr. Nisikanta Sanyal, Bh.S., comp, *Śruti-ratna-mālā,* p. 195.
35. Embree, *Hindu Tradition,* pp. 214–215.
36. Mahajan, *Ancient India,* p. 13.
37. *Bhāgavatam,* pp. 43–44.
38. Ibid., p. 90.
39. Ibid., p. 100.
40. George L. Hart III, *A Rapid Sanskrit Method,* p. *iv.*
41. *Gītā,* p. 227–228 (4.9).
42. *Bhāgavatam,* pp. 166–167.

Chapter Five

1. Troy Wilson Organ, *Hinduism,* p. 7.
2. A.C. Bhaktivedanta Swami Prabhupāda, *Śrī Caitanya-caritāmṛta, Madhya-līlā,* vol. 7, p. 272.

Chapter Six

1. A.C. Bhaktivedanta Swami Prabhupāda, *Śrī Īśopaniṣad,* p. 1.
2. A.C. Bhaktivedanta Swami Prabhupāda, *Bhagavad-gītā As It Is,* pp. 503, 690 (10.8; 14.27) (hereafter cited as *Gītā.* Chapter and verse numbers, within parentheses, refer also to Anthology.).
3. Mahārṣi Kṛṣṇa Dvaipāyana Veda-vyāsa, *Śrīmad-Bhāgavata Mahā-purāṇa,* p. 482.
4. Bhakti Śrī Rūpa Siddhāntī Gosvāmī et al., trans., *Kaṭha Upaniṣad* (*of the Black Yajur Veda*), p. 347.
5. *Gītā,* p. 86 (2.12).
6. *The Speaking Tree: A Study of Indian Culture and Society,* p. 362.
7. Bhaktivedanta, *Śrī Īśopaniṣad,* pp. 62, 68 (or see Anthology).
8. Ibid., p. 1 (or see Anthology).
9. A.C. Bhaktivedanta Swami Prabhupāda, *Śrī Caitanya-caritāmṛta, Ādi-līlā,* vol. 2, pp. 95–96.
10. Ibid., p. 95.
11. Dinkar Vishnu Gokhale, ed., *The Bhagavad-gītā with the Commentary of Śrī Śaṅkarācārya,* p. 6.
12. Ibid.
13. Ibid.

Chapter 7

1. *The Hindu Tradition,* p. 8.
2. A.C. Bhaktivedanta Swami Prabhupāda, *Śrī Īśopaniṣad,* p. 4 (or see Anthology).
3. Finley P. Dunne, Jr., *The World Religions Speak on the Relevance of Religion in the Modern World,* p. 10.

4. A.C. Bhaktivedanta Swami Prabhupāda, *Śrīmad-Bhāgavatam, Fourth Canto,* vol. 3, p. 931.
5. Ibid., p. 932.
6. A.C. Bhaktivedanta Swami Prabhupāda, *Bhagavad-gītā As It Is,* p. 235 (4.13) (hereafter cited as *Gītā.* Chapter and verse numbers, within parentheses, refer also to Anthology.).
7. Munilala Gupta, trans., *Viṣṇu Purāṇa,* p. 228.
8. A.C. Bhaktivedanta Swami Prabhupāda, *Śrīmad-Bhāgavatam, First Canto,* vol. 1, p. 102.
9. Max Weber, *The Religion of India: The Sociology of Hinduism and Buddhism,* trans. Hans Garth et al., p. 61.
10. Ibid., *passim.*
11. Richard Lannoy, *The Speaking Tree: A Study of Indian Culture and Society,* p. 353.
12. *Gītā,* p. 813 (18.43).
13. Ibid., (18.44).
14. Ibid., p. 486 (9.32).
15. Ibid., pp. 838–839 (18.68–69).

"The First Indologists"

1. W.H. Moreland et. al., *A Shorter History of India, passim.*
2. J. Allan et al., *The Cambridge Shorter History of India,* p. 557.
3. H.H. Dodwell, ed., *The Cambridge History of the British Empire,* vol. 5, p. 122.
4. House of Commons, ed., *Observations on the State of Society,* p. 1.
5. Robert Chatfield, *The Rise and Progress of Christianity in the East,* p. 367.
6. Vincent A. Smith, *The Oxford History of India,* p. 579.
7. R.C. Majumdar et al., eds., *History and Culture of the Indian People,* vol. 10, p. 348.
8. Ibid., p. 337.
9. George Smith, *Dictionary of National Biography,* vol. 6, p. 126.
10. Ibid.
11. H.G. Rawlinson, *The British Achievement in India,* p. 53.
12. Christian Literature Society for India, *Hindu Series: Epic Poems and Puranas,* pp. 140, 142.
13. Arthur D. Innes, *Shorter History of the British in India,* p. 303.
14. T. Walter Wallbank, *India: A Survey of the Heritage and Growth of Indian Nationalism,* p. 27.
15. Majumdar, *History and Culture,* p. 338.
16. Aubrey Menen, *The Mystics,* p. 118.
17. A.L. Basham, *The Wonder That Was India,* p. 5.
18. "Jones Tradition in British Orientalism," *Indian Arts and Letters* 20 (1946): 10.
19. Sir William Jones, *The Works of Sir William Jones,* p. 395.
20. Ibid.
21. Richard Garbe, *India and Christendom: The Historical Connection Between Their Religions,* trans. Lydia J. Robinson, pp. 214–217.

22. C.E. Buckland, *Dictionary of Indian Biography,* p. 455.
23. H.H. Wilson, *Works,* vol. 2, pp. 79–80.
24. Ibid., pp. 80–81.
25. Ibid., p. 114.
26. Ibid., p. 115.
27. "Horace Hayman Wilson," *Emminent Orientalists,* pp. 71–72.
28. "H.H. Wilson and Gamesmanship in Indology," *Asian Studies* 3 (1965): 303.
29. Nirad C. Chaudhuri, *Scholar Extraordinary,* p. 325.
30. Ibid.
31. Vivekenanda Rock Memorial Committee, *India's Contribution to World Thought and Culture,* pp. 167–168.
32. Ibid.
33. Sir Monier Monier-Williams, *Religious Thought and Life in India,* p. 10.
34. Ibid.
35. Buckland, *Dictionary,* p. 169.
36. Theodore Goldstucker, *Inspired Writings of Hinduism,* p. 115.
37. Wm. Theodore de Bary et al., eds., *Approaches to Asian Civilizations,* p. 29.
38. Monier-Williams, *Religious Thought,* pp. 34–35.
39. Chaudhuri, *Scholar Extraordinary,* p. 327.
40. Moriz Winternitz, *A History of Indian Literatures,* vol. 1, trans. S. Ketkar, p. 26.
41. A.C. Bhaktivedanta Swami Prabhupāda, *Śrīmad-Bhāgavatam, First Canto,* vol. 3, p. 57.
42. Winternitz, *History,* p. 527.

Bibliography

ACYUTĀNANDA SVĀMĪ, comp. *Songs of the Vaiṣṇava Ācāryas.* New York: Bhaktivedanta Book Trust, 1974.

ALLAN, J. et al. *The Cambridge Shorter History of India.* Delhi: S. Chand and Co., 1964.

BASHAM, A.L. *The Wonder that Was India.* London: Sidgwick and Jackson, 1954.

BASU, MAJOR B.D., I.M.S., ed. *The Sacred Book of the Hindus,* vol. 1. Allahabad: Panini Office, n.d.

BHAKTISIDDHĀNTA SARASVATĪ GOSVĀMĪ ṬHĀKURA. *Śrī Brahma-saṁhitā.* Madras: Tridaṇḍī Śrī Bhaktiprajña Yati, 1973.

BHAKTIVEDANTA SWAMI PRABHUPĀDA, A.C. *Bhagavad-gītā As It Is.* New York: Macmillan Co., 1972.

BHAKTIVEDANTA SWAMI PRABHUPĀDA, A.C. *Kṛṣṇa, the Supreme Personality of Godhead,* vol. 3. New York: Bhaktivedanta Book Trust, 1974.

BHAKTIVEDANTA SWAMI PRABHUPĀDA, A.C. *The Nectar of Devotion* (a summary study of Śrīla Rūpa Gosvāmī's *Bhakti-rasāmṛta-sindhu*). New York: Bhaktivedanta Book Trust, 1970.

BHAKTIVEDANTA SWAMI PRABHUPĀDA, A.C. *The Nectar of Instruction* (a summary study of Śrīla Rūpa Gosvāmī's *Śrī Upadeśāmṛta*). New York: Bhaktivedanta Book Trust, 1975.

BHAKTIVEDANTA SWAMI PRABHUPĀDA, A.C. *Śrī Caitanya-caritāmṛta, Ādi-līlā,* vols. 1, 2; *Madhya-līlā,* vol. 8. New York: Bhaktivedanta Book Trust, 1974–1975.

BHAKTIVEDANTA SWAMI PRABHUPĀDA, A.C. *Śrī Īśopaniṣad.* New York: Bhaktivedanta Book Trust, 1974.

BHAKTIVEDANTA SWAMI PRABHUPĀDA, A.C. *Śrīmad-Bhāgavatam, First Canto,* vol. 1; *Fourth Canto,* vol. 3. New York: Bhaktivedanta Book Trust, 1974.

BHAKTIVEDANTA SWAMI PRABHUPĀDA, A.C. *Teachings of Lord Caitanya.* New York: Bhaktivedanta Book Trust, 1974.

BUCKLAND, C.E. *Dictionary of Indian Biography.* London: Swan Sonnerschein and Co., 1906.

CARDONA, GEORGE et al., ed. *Indo-European and Indo-Europeans: Papers Presented at the Third International Indo-European Conference at the University of Pennsylvania.* Philadelphia: University of Pennsylvania, 1971.

CHATFIELD, ROBERT. *The Rise and Progress of Christianity in the East.* London, 1808.

CHATTERJEE, SATISCHANDRA. *The Fundamentals of Hinduism.* Calcutta: University of Calcutta Press, 1970.

CHAUDHURI, NIRAD C. *Scholar Extraordinary.* London, 1974.

CHAVARRIA-AGUILAR, O.L., ed. *Traditional India.* Englewood Cliffs, N.J.: Prentice-Hall, 1964.

CHRISTIAN LITERATURE SOCIETY FOR INDIA. *Hindu Series: Epic Poems and Puranas.* London and Madras, 1898.

Coomerswamy, Ananda K., ed. *Am I My Brother's Keeper?* New York: John Day Co., 1974.
Coomerswamy, Ananda K., *Hinduism and Buddhism.* New York: Philosophic Library, n.d.
de Bary, William Theodore et al., ed. *Approaches to Asian Civilization.* New York: Columbia University Press, 1964.
Dodwell, H.H., ed. *The Cambridge History of the British Empire.* Cambridge: University Press, 1964.
Dunne, Finley P. Jr., ed. *The World Religions Speak on the Relevance of Religion in the Modern World.* The Hague: Dr. W. Junk N.V. Publishers, 1970.
Embree, Ainslee T. *The Hindu Tradition.* New York: Vintage, 1972.
Eminent Orientalists. Madras: G.A. Natesan and Co., 1922.
Encyclopedia Brittanica. 30 vols. Chicago, 1974.
Encyclopedia of Religion and Ethics. 12 vols. New York, 1922.
Frazier, Kendrick. "Human Evolution," *Science News* July, 1975.
Gambhirananda, Swami, trans. *Eight Upaniṣads,* II. Calcutta: Advaita Ashrama, 1966.
Garbe, Richard. *India and Christendom: The Historical Connection Between Their Religions.* Translated by Lydia J. Robinson. La Salle, Illinois: Open Court Publishing Co., 1959.
Gokhale, Dinkar Vishnu, ed. *The Bhagavad-gītā with the Commentary of Śrī Śaṅkarācārya.* Poona, India: Oriental Book Agency, 1931.
Gupta, Munilala, trans. *Viṣṇu Purāṇa.* Gorakha Pura, India: Gita Press, n.d.
Goldstücker, Theodore. *Inspired Writings of Hinduism.* Calcutta: Susil Gupta, 1952.
Hart, George L. III. *A Rapid Sanskrit Method.* Madison: University of Wisconsin Department of Indian Studies, 1972.
"H.H. Wilson and Gamemanship in Indology." *Asian Studies* 3 (1965): 303.
Hiriyanna, Mysore. *Popular Essays in Indian Philosophy.* Mysore, India: Kevalaya Publishers, 1952.
Hockett, Charles F. *A Course in Modern Linguistics.* New York: Macmillan Co., 1958.
Hopkins, Thomas. *The Hindu Religious Tradition.* Encino, Calif.: Dickenson Publishing Company, 1971.
House of Commons, ed. *Observations on the State of Society.* London, 1823.
Hume, Robert Ernest, trans. *The Thirteen Principal Upaniṣads.* London: Oxford University Press, 1934.
Innes, Arthur D. *Shorter History of the British in India.* London, 1902.
Jones, Sir William. *The Works of Sir William Jones.* London, 1807.
"Jones Tradition in British Orientalism." *Indian Arts and Letters* 20 (1946): 10.
Lannoy, Richard. *The Speaking Tree: A Study of Indian Culture and Society.* London: Oxford University Press, 1971.
Latif, Syad, ed. *An Outline of the Cultural History of India.* Hyderabad: Institute of Indo-Middle East Cultural Studies, 1958.
Mahajan, V.D. *Ancient India.* New Delhi: S. Chand and Co., 1974.

MAJUMDAR, R.C. et al., ed. *History and Culture of the Indian People.* Bombay: Bharatiya Vidya Bhavan, 1965.
MENEN, AUBREY. *The Mystics.* New York: Dial, 1974.
MONIER-WILLIAMS, SIR MONIER. *Religious Thought and Life in India.* Oxford: Oxford University Press, 1885.
MORELAND, W.H. et al. *A Shorter History of India.* London: Longmans Green and Co., 1957.
MÜLLER, F. MAX. *A History of Ancient Sanskrit Literature as It Illustrates the Primitive Religion of the Brahmins.* Varanasi: Chowkhambha Sanskrit Series Office, 1968.
NIKHILANANDA, SWAMI, trans. *The Upaniṣads: A Second Selection.* London: Phoenix House, 1954.
ORGAN, TROY WILSON. *Hinduism.* Woodbury, New York: Barron's Educational Series, 1974.
PIGGOT, STUART. *Prehistoric India to 1000 B.C.* London: Cassell and Co., 1962.
POTTER, KARL H. *Presuppositions of India's Philosophies.* Englewood Cliffs, N.J.: Prentice-Hall, 1963.
RADHAKRISHNAN, SARVEPALLI and MOORE, CHARLES A. *A Sourcebook in Indian Philosophy.* Princeton, N.J.: Princeton University Press, 1957.
RADHAKRISHNAN, SARVEPALLI. *Indian Philosophy.* New York: Macmillan Co., 1923.
RAWLINSON, H.G. *The British Achievement in India.* London: Hodge, 1948.
RAYCHARIDHURI, HEMCHANDRA. *Studies in Indian Antiquity.* Calcutta: Calcutta University Press, 1958.
RENOU, LOUIS. *Hinduism.* New York: Washington Square Press, 1969.
REYNA, RUTH. *Introduction to Indian Philosophy.* New Delhi: Tata McGraw-Hill Publishing Co., 1964.
ŚAṄKARĀCĀRYA. *Viveka-cuḍāmaṇi.* Mayavati, India: Advaita Ashrama, 1926.
SANYAL, DR. NISIKANTA, BH. S., comp. *Śruti-ratna-mālā.* Nadia, West Bengal: Sundara Vidyāvinoda, 1941.
SASTRI, NALINIMOHAN S. *A Study of Śaṅkara.* Calcutta: University of Calcutta, 1942.
SAYANA, ACARYA, trans. *Ṛg Veda.* Mathura, India: Vedanurgi Acarya Gopala Prasada, 1868.
SCHWEITZER, ALBERT. *Indian Thought and Its Development.* Boston: Beacon Press, 1936.
SIDDHĀNTĪ GOSVĀMĪ, BHAKTI ŚRĪ RŪPA et al., trans. *Kaṭha Upaniṣad.* Calcutta: Sārasvata Gauḍīya Mission, 1971.
SIDDHĀNTĪ GOSVĀMĪ, BHAKTI ŚRĪ RŪPA et al., *Muṇḍaka Upaniṣad.* Calcutta: Sārasvata Gauḍīya Mission, 1971.
SIDDHĀNTĪ GOSVĀMĪ, BHAKTI ŚRĪ RŪPA, ed. *Śrīmad Bhagavad-gītā with the Gītā-bhūṣaṇa Commentary of Śrīla Baladeva Vidyābhūṣaṇa.* Calcutta: Sārasvata Gauḍīya Mission, 1967.
SIDDHĀNTĪ GOSVĀMĪ, BHAKTI ŚRĪ RŪPA et al., trans. *Śvetāśvatara Upaniṣad.* Calcutta: Sarasvata Gauḍiya Mission, 1971.

SIDDHĀNTĪ GOSVĀMĪ, BHAKTI ŚRĪ RŪPA et al., trans. *Vedānta-sūtra.* Nadia, West Bengal: Sārasvata Gauḍīya Mission, 1968.

SIRKIN, NATALIE P.R. "H.H. Wilson and Gamesmanship in Indology," *Asian Studies* 3 (1965).

SMITH, VINCENT A. *The Oxford History of India.* Oxford: Oxford University Press, 1958.

SMITH, GEORGE. *Dictionary of National Biography* (21 vols.). Oxford: Oxford University Press, 1950.

ŚRĪDHARA SVĀMĪ, *Subodhinī-ṭikā* (on *Bhagavad-gītā*). Calcutta: Gauḍīya Mission, 1946.

TEIGNMOUTH, BARON JOHN S. *Memoirs of the Life, Writings and Correspondence of Sir William Jones.* London: J. Hatchard, 1804.

VEDA-VYĀSA, KṚṢṆA DVAIPĀYANA. *Śrīmad-Bhāgavata Mahā-Purāṇa.* Gorakha Pura, India: Gita Press, n.d.

VIDYARNAVA, RAI B.S.C. VASU, trans. *Bṛhad-āraṇyaka Upaniṣad.* Allahabad: The Painini Office, 1933.

VIVEKENANDA ROCK MEMORIAL COMMITTEE. *India's Contribution to World Thought and Culture.* Madras, 1970.

WALLBANK, T. WALTER. *India: A Survey of the Heritage and Growth of Indian Nationalism.* New York: Henry Holt and Co., 1948.

WATSON, PATTY JO. *Explanation in Archaeology.* New York: Columbia University Press, 1971.

WEBER, MAX. *The Religion of India: The Sociology of Hinduism and Buddhism.* Translated by Hans Garth et al. Glencoe, Illinois: The Free Press, 1958.

WEBSTER'S NEW WORLD DICTIONARY OF THE AMERICAN LANGUAGE. Cleveland: The World Publishing Co., 1964.

WHEELER, SIR MORTIMER. *Civilizations of the Indus Valley and Beyond.* London: Thames and Hudson, 1966.

WILSON, H.H. *Works.* London: Trubner and Co., 1862.

WINTERNITZ, MORIZ. *A History of Indian Literature,* vol. 1. Calcutta: University of Calcutta, 1927.

ZIMMER, HEINRICH. *Philosophies of India.* New York: Pantheon Books, 1951.

Glossary

Ācārya—one who teaches by personal example; a spiritual preceptor learned in scripture; *guru.*

Acintya—inconceivable, i.e. beyond material conception, beyond the perceptual and cognitive limits of the material senses, mind and intellect; understandable only through spiritual cognition.

Agni—the demigod who controls fire.

Akarma—action performed selflessly for God and therefore not incurring a reaction under the law of *karma.*

Anumāna—in Vedic epistemology, the path of acquiring knowledge through inductive reasoning.

Arjuna—the fabled bowman to whom Kṛṣṇa reveals perfect wisdom in the classic spiritual text *Bhagavad-gītā.*

Artha—economic development. Follows *dharma* (religiosity) and precedes *kāma* (sense gratification) in the progressive path toward *mokṣa* (liberation).

Āśramas—the four developmental divisions of the human life-cycle (meant to elevate one to spiritual perfection). These begin with *brahmacarya* (celibacy and study), proceed to *gṛhastha* (householder life) and *vānaprastha* (retirement) and culminate in *sannyāsa* (the renounced order).

Ātmā—the self. Although the word *ātmā* can refer, in different contexts, to the body, mind or intellect, it generally indicates the eternal, individual soul or spirit.

Avatāra—(literally, "one who descends") A plenary or partial incarnation of God who appears in the mundane realm to execute a particular divine mission.

Bhagavad-gītā—the paramount scripture of the Vedic tradition, embodying the teachings of Kṛṣṇa to Arjuna and expounding devotion to God as the principal means and end of spiritual attainment.

Bhagavān—(*bhaga*—opulence & *vān*—possessing) God, the Absolute Truth realized as the Supreme Person who possesses all opulences (viz. beauty, strength, fame, wealth, knowledge and renunciation).

Bhakti—selfless, spiritual devotion (to God).

Bhārata-varṣa—the traditional, scriptural name for India (literally, "the land of Bharata." Bharata was a king of ancient India).

Brahmā—the first created living being of the universe, supervisor of the material mode of passion (*rajo-guṇa*). Brahmā creates the multiplicity of life forms in the universe, under the direction of Viṣṇu.

Brahmacārī—a celibate student of the *Vedas* living under the supervision of a spiritual mentor.

Brahmacarya—the first of the four *āśramas* (spiritual divisions of the human life-cycle). During *brahmacarya,* the young student (ages 5–25) practices celibacy and studies the *Vedas* under the guidance of a *guru.*

Brahman—1. spirit; 2. the impersonal, all-pervasive aspect of the Supreme; 3. the Supreme Being.

Brāhmaṇa—a member of the highest of the four *varṇas* (occupational and social divisions of Vedic society); a spiritually trained person qualified to act as a teacher or priest.

Brāhmaṇas—the portions of the *Vedas* that provide elaborate instructions for the performance of ritualistic sacrifices.

Cit-śakti—the spiritual energy of the Absolute Truth that manifests the spiritual world (Vaikuṇṭha).

Dharma—duty or religion. *Sva-dharma* refers to one's worldly or occupational duty, whereas *sanātana-dharma* refers to one's eternal nature, i.e. love of and service to God.

Gopīs—cowherd women; the maidens of Vṛndāvana whose pure devotional love for Kṛṣṇa is depicted in the *Bhāgavata Purāṇa* and later devotional works.

Gṛhastha—1. the second of the four *āśramas* (spiritual divisions of the human life-cycle). As a *gṛhastha* one enters household family life and pursues an occupation. 2. one situated in that station of life.

Guṇas—(literally, "ropes") The three qualities or modes of material nature—goodness (*sattva*), passion (*rajas*) and ignorance (*tamas*)—which condition the illusioned souls and bind them to the material world.

Guṇa-avatāras—the three deities who preside over the three modes of nature (*guṇas*). Lord Viṣṇu presides over the mode of goodness (*sattva*), Lord Brahmā controls the mode of passion (*rajas*), and Lord Śiva controls the mode of ignorance (*tamas*).

Guru—spiritual master or preceptor.

Indra—the chief sovereign of the heavenly kingdom and the presiding deity of rain.

Indraloka—the heavenly planet where Indra resides.

Īśvara—controller; specifically the supreme controller (*parameśvara*), Bhagavān.

Jīva—the eternal, individual soul or spirit.

Kali-yuga—the present historical age (fourth and last in a perpetually repeating cycle of four progressively degenerate ages). Kali-yuga is characterized by a progressive decline in spiritual knowledge and, consequently, the degeneration of human civilization. Some 5,000 of a total of 432,000 years of Kali-yuga have already passed, according to Vedic eschatology.

Kāma—gratification of the senses. Follows *dharma* (religiosity) and *artha* (economic development) in the progressive path toward *mokṣa* (liberation).

Karma—1. fruitive material actions or work, performed according to scriptural regulation; 2. the material reactions of one's work; 3. the law governing work (action) and its reactions.

Karma-kāṇḍa—the division of the *Vedas* dealing with fruitive activities performed by materialists for gradual purification and elevation to the spiritual platform.

Karma-yoga—the path of spiritual elevation through selfless, nonfruitive actions dedicated to the Supreme.

Kṛṣṇa—the original form of Bhagavān, the speaker of *Bhagavad-gītā;* the Supreme Person (Puruṣottama).

Kṣatriya—a member of the second of the four *varṇas* (occupational and social divisions of Vedic society); a warrior, statesman or public administrator.

Mahābhārata—the great epic history of ancient India, attributed to Vyāsadeva and including the text of the *Bhagavad-gītā.*

Mahātmā—(literally, "great soul") A broad-minded or broad-visioned person.

Mantra—a syllable, word or verse chanted or meditated upon to invoke spiritual understanding or realization.

Māyā—illusion; the energy of the Supreme that deludes the living entity into forgetfulness of his real, spiritual nature.

Mokṣa—liberation from the cycle of birth and death in the material world.

Nārāyaṇa—a name for the personal form of the Absolute Truth; the four-armed expansion of Śrī Kṛṣṇa.

Parabrahman—the Supreme Spirit; the Supreme Lord; Bhagavān.

Paramātmā—the Supersoul or Oversoul; the four-armed form of Lord Viṣṇu that accompanies every living entity bound in the cycle of birth and death in the material world.

Prakṛti—(literally, "that which is predominated") The predominated energies of the Supreme, of which there are two: *parā* (superior) *prakṛti* (the living entities) and *aparā* (inferior) *prakṛti* (material nature or dead matter).

Pratyakṣa—in Vedic epistemology, the path of acquiring knowledge through the material senses; empiricism.

Purāṇas—the eighteen epic texts expounding the teachings of the *Vedas* through historical and allegorical narrations.

Puruṣa—(literally, "the enjoyer") 1. The supreme predominator or enjoyer (of *prakṛti,* nature), i.e. Bhagavān. 2. The individual *jīva* (living being) as the predominator and enjoyer of the material body.

Rajo-guṇa—(*rajas*—passion & *guṇa*—mode) The material mode of passion, characterized by fruitive activity and desire for sense gratification.

Ṛṣi—sage, holyman.

Śabda—(literally, "sound") In Vedic epistemology, the path of acquiring knowledge through scriptural revelation.

Sac-cid-ānanda—eternity, knowledge and bliss, the spiritual qualities of the Supreme Lord (Bhagavān) and of the minute, eternal living entities (*jīvas*).

Sādhu—saint, holyman.

Saṁhitās—sections of the *Vedas* containing prayers and hymns recited to propitiate or glorify various demigods.

Sampradāya—a disciplic succession of *gurus* through which Vedic teachings are preserved and transmitted from generation to generation.

Saṁsāra—the "wheel" of repeated birth and death in the material world, from which a living being can free himself through various spiritual disciplines.

Sāṅkhya—the analytical study of the elements of the material world, culminating in the realization that the soul is transcendental to material nature.

Sannyāsa—the fourth and last of the four *āśramas* (spiritual divisions of the human life-cycle). In *sannyāsa* one renounces all family and social ties and dedicates oneself fully to spiritual advancement.

Sannyāsī—one in the order of *sannyāsa;* a renunciant or monk.

Śāstras—revealed scriptures (the *Vedas* and Vedic literature).

Sattva-guṇa—(*sattva*—goodness & *guṇa*—mode) The material mode of goodness, characterized by self-purification and the development of spiritual knowledge.

Siddhānta—(literally, "conclusion") A philosophical conclusion (as of Vedic literature).

Siddhis—special powers or abilities achieved through the practice of mystic *yoga,* such as the ability to fly, walk on water, etc.

Śiṣya—a student or disciple of a *guru.*

Śiva—the demigod who supervises the material mode of ignorance (*tamo-guṇa*) and who annihilates the material cosmos at the end of Brahmā's lifetime.

Smṛti—literatures supplementary to the *Vedas,* viz. the *Purāṇas, Bhagavad-gītā* and *Mahābhārata.*

Soma-rasa—a special beverage imbibed by the demigods in the heavenly planets to increase lifespan and the capacity for sensual pleasure.

Śrīmad-Bhāgavatam (Bhāgavata Purāṇa)—the most popular of the eighteen *Purāṇas.* Promulgates the path of *bhakti* (devotion) to Śrī Kṛṣṇa. Famed for its celebrated Tenth Canto, describing the pastimes of Śrī Kṛṣṇa.

Śruti—(literally, "that which is heard" [from Nārāyaṇa, God]); the four *Vedas: Ṛg, Sāma, Yajur* and *Atharva.*

Śūdra—a member of the fourth of the four *varṇas* (occupational and social divisions of Vedic society); a laborer or craftsman.

Svāmī—(literally, "master of the senses") A title given to *sannyāsīs* (renounced monks and teachers).

Tamo-guṇa—(*tamas*—ignorance & *guṇa*—mode) The material mode of ignorance, characterized by ignorance, lethargy and madness.

Upaniṣad—a division of Vedic literature (*śruti*) consisting of 108 metaphysical texts.

Upāsanā-kāṇḍa—the division of the *Vedas* prescribing worship of demigods for material fruitive results.

Vaikuṇṭha—(literally, "without anxiety") The eternal spiritual world beyond the material cosmos.

Vaiṣṇava—a devotee or worshiper of Viṣṇu, Kṛṣṇa or another form of Bhagavān.

Vaiśya—a member of the third of the four *varṇas* (occupational and social divisions of Vedic society); a farmer or merchant.

Vānaprastha—the third of the four *āśramas* (spiritual divisions of the human life-cycle); the stage following *gṛhastha* (householder life). In *vānaprastha* life one retires from active family and social life and travels to holy places of pilgrimage to prepare for the last stage, *sannyāsa* (the renounced order).

Varṇas—the four social and occupational divisions of Vedic society, viz. *brāhmaṇas* (priests and teachers), *kṣatriyas* (warriors and public administrators), *vaiśyas* (farmers and merchants) and *śūdras* (laborers and craftsmen).

Varṇāśrama-dharma—the ancient Vedic system of arranging society into four social-occupational divisions (*varṇas*) and four spiritual divisions (*āśramas*) to promote social, economic and political stability and the spiritual welfare of all members of society.

Vedānta-sūtra—the philosophical treatise written by Vyāsadeva, comprised of succinct aphorisms explaining the essential meaning of the *Upaniṣads*.

Vedas—the four original revealed Vedic scriptures (*Ṛg, Sāma, Yajur* and *Atharva*), said to have originally emanated from the Supreme and later to have been compiled by the sage Vyāsadeva.

Viṣṇu—an expansion of Bhagavān Śrī Kṛṣṇa. Viṣṇu, usually depicted with four arms, maintains the material mode of goodness (*sattva-guṇa*) and is the source of Brahmā and Śiva. There are many Viṣṇu expansions, all of whom are the one same Supreme Person, Bhagavān.

Vyāsadeva (Kṛṣṇa Dvaipāyana Vyāsa)—the "literary incarnation of God," who, according to orthodox Vedic historiography, compiled the *Vedas* and *Upaniṣads* and wrote the *Vedānta-sūtras, Purāṇas* and *Mahābhārata.*

Yajña—a sacrifice or sacrificial performance.

Yoga—a system of spiritual discipline (e.g. *karma-yoga, aṣṭāṅga-yoga, jñāna-yoga, bhakti-yoga*) for approaching the Supreme.

Yogī—one who practices a system of *yoga*.

Indexes

This book includes two indexes. The first index, beginning below, pertains to Chapters 1–7 and *The First Indologists*. The second index, which begins on page 222, pertains to the readings themselves.

Brāhmaṇas (saintly intellectuals)
defined, 65
qualities of, 11, 66, 67
smārta-, 11
in social body, 67
Wilson quoted on, 177
See also: Varṇāśrama-dharma
Brāhmaṇās tena vedāś ca
verse quoted, 41–42
Brāhmaṇa Vedas, 46
Brahmaṇyo devakī-putraḥ
quoted, 43
Brahma-saṁhitā
cited on Brahmā, 33
quoted on Bhagavān, 24
quoted on Kṛṣṇa, 25
Brahma-sampradāya, 7
Brahma satyaṁ jagan mithyā
quoted, 59
Brahma-sūtra. See: Vedānta-sūtra
Brahmin. *See:* Brāhmaṇa
Bṛhad-āraṇyaka Upaniṣad, quotations from
on body & soul, 57
on Brahman, 43
on Brahman philosophers, 22
on miserly man, 3
on *Vedas'* origin, 3–4
on whole, 44
Britain
India taken over by, 173–174
See also: Englishmen
Buddha
death of, as Indian history's "beginning," 14
Vedic literature rejected by, 49
Buddhism
in India, 49
Māyāvāda philosophy as, 60
as non-Vedic, 2
Śaṅkara vs., 50, 60

Caitanya
historical accounts on, 52–53
as Rūpa Gosvāmī's spiritual master, 8
taught by example, 9
Vedānta commentary of, 59
Caitanya-caritāmṛta, Śrī, as Caitanya's biography, 52–53
Cāṇakya Paṇḍita, cited on educated man, 68–69
Candragupta, 173
Carbon 14 dating, 17
Carey, William, 174–175
Caste system
classifications in, 11
as *varṇāśrama-dharma* in decay, 66
See also: Varṇāśrama-dharma
Cātur-varṇyaṁ mayā sṛṣṭaṁ
quoted, 65
Cause, ultimate
Brahman as, 21–22
Kṛṣṇa as, 48
puruṣa as, 31
Śaṅkara cited on, 49–50
Cause and effect
Vedic vs. Western conceptions of, 28
See also: Karma
Celibacy. *See: Brahmacarya; Sannyāsa*
Chāndogya Upaniṣad
cited on *Mahābhārata* & *Purāṇas*, 46
quoted on *guru* detecting *brāhmaṇa*, 11
quoted on *Purāṇas* & *Itihāsas*, 1
Chanting names of God, Caitanya cited on, 53
Chauvinism in European version of Indo-European origins, 18
Chavarria-Aguilar, O.L., quoted on Indians, 14
Cheating
of atheists by Śiva, 60
people prone to, 5
Child
brahmacārī training for, 68
purification at conception of, 69
Christ
cited in Müller's view of ancient religions, 178
Kṛṣṇa worship predates, 176
Vedic civilization predates, 14
Christianity
cited in Müller's view of India, 178
theology of, misapplied to Vedic literature, 33

READINGS INDEX